THE PERINATAL PATIENT

A Compassionate Approach to Treating Postpartum Depression, Anxiety, and Related Disorders

HILARY WALLER, LPC
with **KAREN KLEIMAN**, MSW, LCSW

THE PERINATAL PATIENT
Copyright © 2023 by Hilary Waller and Karen Kleiman
Published by
PESI Publishing, Inc.
3839 White Ave
Eau Claire, WI 54703

Cover and interior design by Amy Rubenzer
Editing by Jenessa Jackson, PhD

ISBN 9781683736561 (print)
ISBN 9781683736578 (ePDF)
ISBN 9781683736585 (ePUB)

All rights reserved.
Printed in the United States of America.

Table of Contents

Preface xi

Introduction xv

Section I: The Nuanced Perinatal Patient: What Every Perinatal Patient Asks Themselves 1

Chapter 1: "Is This Normal?" 3
   Defining the Terms 4
   Patient Handout: Perinatal Glossary of Terms 6
   What Is Normal for Women to Experience 7
   Newly Postpartum 7
   Patient Worksheet: Processing Your Birth Story 10
   Patient Handout: Baby Blues versus Perinatal Mood and Anxiety Disorders 12
   Patient Handout: Bodily Changes 15
   Patient Worksheet: How Do You Feel Postpartum? 17
   Normalizing Perinatal Difficulties 20

Chapter 2: "Is Something Wrong with Me?" 21
   Suffering in Secrecy 22
   Patient Worksheet: A Hopeful Letter to Myself 23
   Patient Worksheet: I Am Scared to Say How I Feel 26
   Overcoming Resistance 29
   Provider Handout: Resistance to Disclosure 30
   Patient Handout: Overcoming Resistance 31
   Normalize Seeking Help 33

Chapter 3: "What If I Feel Alone?" 35
   Types of Support Mothers Need 36
   Patient Worksheet: Reducing Isolation 37
   Patient Worksheet: Who Can Help? 40
   Patient Worksheet: What Do I Need? 42
   Barriers to Developing Perinatal Social Support Systems 44
   Patient Worksheet: Overcoming Logistical Barriers 46

Patient Worksheet: Overcoming Emotional Barriers 51
Parental Leave 55
Cultural Dynamics Relevant to Social Support 56
A Note on the Provider's Role 57
Underrepresented Groups and Social Support 58
Provider Handout: New Moms Groups 59

Section II: Perinatal Mood and Anxiety Disorders: When Perinatal Patients Suffer Too Much 61

Chapter 4: "What Are Perinatal Mood and Anxiety Disorders?" 63
Defining Perinatal Mood and Anxiety Disorders 63
Provider Handout: Perinatal Diagnostics 65
Provider Handout: Symptoms of Perinatal Mood and Anxiety Disorders 70
Perinatal Depression 72
Patient Handout: Perinatal Depression at a Glance 74
Perinatal Anxiety 76
Patient Handout: Perinatal Anxiety at a Glance 78
Perinatal Obsessive-Compulsive Disorder 79
Patient Handout: Perinatal Obsessive-Compulsive Disorder (OCD) at a Glance 81
Perinatal Panic Disorder 82
Patient Handout: Perinatal Panic Disorder at a Glance 83
Perinatal Posttraumatic Stress Disorder 84
Patient Handout: Perinatal Posttraumatic Stress Disorder (PTSD) at a Glance 86
Perinatal Bipolar Disorder 87
Provider Handout: Medication for Perinatal Women with Bipolar Disorders 88
Patient Handout: Perinatal Bipolar Disorder at a Glance 89
Postpartum Psychosis 91
Patient Handout: Postpartum Psychosis at a Glance 92
Increasing Level of Care in The Perinatal Period 93
Provider Handout: Discussing Escalations in Care with Patients 94
Provider Tool: Suicide Assessment 96

Chapter 5: "Do I Have a Perinatal Mood and Anxiety Disorder?" 99
Screening Tools 99
Provider Tool: Edinburgh Postnatal Depression Scale (EPDS) 101
The Importance of Follow-Up 103
Provider Handout: Tips for Talking About Perinatal Mood and Anxiety Disorder Screenings 104
Universal Screening 106

Overcoming Provider Challenges to Universal Screening 106
Provider Handout: Glossary of Maternal Mental Health Resources 109
Patient Worksheet: Maternal Mental Health Resources 110
Overcoming Patient Challenges to Universal Screening 113
Talking with Perinatal Moms and Understanding What They Need 114
Provider Handout: Counseling Skills: Open- and Closed-Ended Questions 116
Provider Handout: Counseling Skills: Active Listening 122
Self-Assessment for Mothers 124
Patient Handout: How Bad Are You Feeling? 125

Chapter 6: "How Do I Know if I'm at Risk?" 127
Know the Risk Factors 127
Patient Worksheet: Biological Risk Factors 129
Patient Worksheet: Perinatal Pain 135
Patient Worksheet: Social Risk Factors 140
Patient Worksheet: Cultural Expectations about Parenthood 148
Patient Worksheet: Psychological Risk Factors 152
Risk Reduction Via Self-Care 156
Patient Worksheet: Self-Care Checklist 158
Patient Worksheet: Caring for Yourself 160

Chapter 7: "What Can I Do for Relief?" 163
Patient Worksheet: Developing Expectations: How I Imagined Motherhood Would Feel 166
Patient Worksheet: Developing Expectations: The "Good Enough" Mother 168
Patient Worksheet: Developing Expectations: Feeding Decisions 170
Patient Worksheet: Developing Expectations: Baby Steps 172
Patient Worksheet: Identity Changes: Symptoms Experienced as Self 175
Patient Worksheet: Identity Changes: Imagining the Future 177
Patient Worksheet : Identity Changes: Becoming A Mother Changed Me 179
Patient Worksheet: Identity Changes: What I Have Gained, What I Have Lost 181
Patient Worksheet: Identity Changes: Planning Another Pregnancy 184
Patient Worksheet: Finding a New Normal: Daily Routine 189
Patient Worksheet: Finding a New Normal: How Will I Know When I Have
    Found a New Normal? 194
Patient Worksheet: Finding a New Normal: Your Relationship with Change 197
Patient Worksheet: Finding a New Normal: Understanding Changes 200
Patient Worksheet: Finding A New Normal: Are My Symptoms Back? 202
Patient Worksheet: Symptom Relief: Negative Self-Talk 205
Patient Handout: Symptom Relief: Strategies for Self-Soothing 207

Patient Worksheet: Symptom Relief: Talking with Providers and
   Support People about Scary Thoughts 209
Patient Worksheet: Symptom Relief: Thought Patterns of Perinatal Mood and Anxiety Disorders   211
Patient Worksheet: Symptom Relief: Breaking Down Hyperbole 215
Patient Worksheet: Symptom Relief: Rage 217
Patient Handout: Symptom Relief: Insomnia 220
Patient Worksheet: Symptom Relief: Coping with Perinatal Panic 223
Patient Handout: Symptom Relief: Making Sense of Birth Trauma 226
Patient Worksheet: Symptom Relief: Risk Management for Perinatal Bipolar Disorders 228
Patient Handout: Symptom Relief: Signs of Recovery 234

Chapter 8: "What If I Am Navigating Infertility, Loss, or Other Pregnancy or Postpartum Complications?" 237

Disenfranchised Parenting 238
Fertility and Infertility 238
Patient Worksheet: Learning and Sharing About Infertility Journeys.. 242
Non-Gestational Parents 246
Patient Worksheet: Supporting All Parents Experiencing Perinatal Mood
   and Anxiety Disorders 249
Bereavement: Pregnancy Loss and Stillbirth 253
Provider Handout: Talking About Miscarriage.. 255
Patient Handout: Supporting Parents After Stillbirth and Neonatal Death..................................... 259
Provider Handout: Helping Parents Process Stillbirth and Neonatal Death 261
Neonatal Intensive Care Unit (NICU) 262
Patient Worksheet: A NICU Parent's Losses 264
A Final Note to Providers.. 266
Provider Handout: Infertility Cheat Sheet... 267
Provider Handout: Non-Gestational Parents Cheat Sheet 269
Provider Handout: Perinatal Loss Cheat Sheet... 271
Provider Handout: NICU Experiences Cheat Sheet... 273

Section III: Therapy with Perinatal Patients: How to Support and Care for Perinatal Patients 275

Chapter 9: The Art of Holding Perinatal Women in Distress 277

The Holding Environment and The Good Enough Mother... 278
The Holding Environment for Perinatal Distress.. 279
The Holding Points 280
Engaged Empathy and the Holding Points 284

 Hard to Hold 285
 Provider Handout: Hard to Hold: Provider Personal History 286
 Provider Handout: Self-Care in Session and After Session 292
 Provider Handout: Self-Disclosure in Perinatal Work 293
 Cultural Humility: A Prerequisite for Holding 294

A Final Word from Karen Kleiman 295
References 297
About the Authors 305

Preface

Almost forty years ago, after the birth of my second child, I sat on my living room floor surrounded by baby paraphernalia, contemplating the future of my career as I navigated new motherhood. I pondered the possibilities that lay ahead of me: *How could I combine my education and interest in psychology with my new role as a mother?* I started wondering how the mothering experience impacts other women and whether there was, in fact, suffering associated with this major life transition. I did not experience postpartum depression myself, so I knew my early quest for information and answers would need to come from the women themselves.

So I put a small ad in the local newspaper asking anyone who experienced feelings of depression or stress after the birth of their baby to contact me for an interview. I received three responses. What surprised me was that two of the respondents were women over 70 years old. All three women met with me separately and related their stories of unexpected and life-altering depressions. The two older women shared similar stories of secret suffering, despairing thoughts, and paralyzing shame. They described the agony of isolation, the unrelenting feelings of grief and loss. They expressed self-loathing and the shock of not recognizing who they had become, along with the fear of letting anyone know what they were thinking or feeling. Both of these women said they eventually found a way out of the darkness and that I was the first person they had talked to about how bad they felt. I remember the unique pang of purpose in those brief yet meaningful exchanges, which paved the way for (and later would shape the course of) my professional journey.

I was struck by these women's profound and unwavering ability to suppress and deny such incredibly strong and scary emotions. I continued the crusade by creating a simple questionnaire on stressors related to pregnancy and the postpartum period, and I asked baby stores and doctor's offices to kindly display a box filled with a pile of stapled surveys, complete with self-addressed stamped envelopes, and a cardboard sign with the handwritten note: *Are You Pregnant? Had a Baby? Are You Anxious or Worried About How You Are Feeling?* Soon thereafter, I poured through the unexpected pile of anonymous responses. The majority stated how bad they felt and, most interesting to me, how no one else knew or understood how bad they felt. It became glaringly clear that the needs of postpartum women were falling through the cracks of the medical community.

No one was talking about it.

While loved ones were doting over the baby and focusing on this being the "best time of your life"—and physicians were concentrating on physical and medical recovery—moms were largely left to fend for themselves when it came to their emotional health. Due to the paucity of literature on the subject, I literally began knocking on doors, writing letters, and, ultimately, learning what I needed to know from the women who trusted me to listen to their stories.

I have never considered myself a pioneer in this field. Since I did not experience postpartum depression or anxiety, in some ways I felt like an outsider—someone who was peeking in and learning from afar. In other ways I felt uniquely situated with clarity and perspective on a subject that was not well understood. I wondered early on why it was so hard for women to admit that being a new mother sometimes did not feel so good. Why did new mothers feel compelled to say that everything was fine when they were struggling to get through the day? What dynamics were at play that reinforced their desire to sustain this pretense?

In 1994, Valerie Raskin, MD, and I wrote our groundbreaking book on the topic, *This Isn't What I Expected: Overcoming Postpartum Depression*. Considered by many as the "Bible" of postpartum mood and anxiety disorders, this book enabled women to put words to some of their hushed thoughts and feelings, and it brought to light the longstanding misinformation surrounding a woman's transformation into motherhood.

As I continued to study this major life transition, I learned more about the impressive and largely misunderstood silence that shrouded a majority of postpartum women—with and without depression—and the strong impulse to put forth a façade with a face that belied their suffering. When women began to reveal the depth of their unexpressed grief and anguish, a paradox quickly manifested. Why were moms not telling us how bad they felt?

We have since learned a great deal. We have grown to understand that our society makes it challenging to disclose vulnerabilities and that extreme feelings of loss, anger, and guilt associated with new motherhood induce shame that quiets any urge to seek help. Experts in perinatal mental health now view this ubiquitous silence as a hallmark feature of postpartum depression when describing and treating it.

When I provide professional trainings to enthusiastic perinatal therapists who are thirsty for knowledge and specific clinical skills, I now include Hilary Waller by my side, who has joined my enduring pursuit of a deeper appreciation of this unique population. While I have been studying, teaching, and experiencing the privilege of sitting with perinatal women in distress for decades, Hilary resides on the precipice of huge academic and clinical accomplishments with endless and impressive implications for our field. Together, we teach each other.

Hilary is a diligent, if not meticulous, worker, writer, and thinker, as well as a spectacular therapist. Throughout the years, her intrinsic capacity to process and understand nuanced information, coupled with her exceptional capacity to connect with colleagues and patients, have paved the way to her position of esteemed leadership within our community. Perhaps her most outstanding quality, one that aligns so perfectly with our theoretical foundation, is her unwavering belief and confidence in her professional self. She is literally becoming The Postpartum Stress Center right before my eyes. I couldn't be prouder. As a collaborative partnership, we are almost always in sync. Nonetheless, our differences are often quite conspicuous, both personally and professionally, something I attribute to the generational gap that unexpectedly rears its ugly head. I often find myself reminding her: *Our brains think differently, our clinical instincts impact our work differently, and we most certainly respond to the greater world differently. We process differently, we respond differently, and we regulate ourselves differently.* Which ultimately means, we sit with perinatal emotional distress differently.

For years, I have believed—and have imparted unto others—that my greatest therapeutic tool is the use of *myself*. I remain steadfast that this is a core principle of my work and teach this notion of the primary use of self to perinatal mental health trainees. I take pride in the effective use of my authentic self, my keen empathic perceptions, and my capacity to connect with those who resist connection—and I always rely on the irrefutable use of my magic that has yet to be put into words. I do not, however, claim to be a fan of the reliance on tools in therapy. This may simply reflect semantic ambiguity because what is a therapeutic tool, really? After all, I unquestionably use tools—such as morsels from cognitive behavioral therapy (CBT), dialectical behavior therapy (DBT), and eye movement desensitization and reprocessing (EMDR)—in my work. Still, I insist that the superpower of my work is defined by the organic exchange of human energy and the unequivocal, unspoken command of the turmoil piercing the heart of the woman sitting in front of me. I believe that our ability to tolerate and endure the chaos in her soul translates quickly into feelings of control and hope.

As all successful partnerships strive to balance strengths and vulnerabilities, I teach Hilary to find the power of her heart, and she teaches me to find the value in bringing structure and evidence-based strategies of intervention into the perinatal therapeutic space. We have both become stronger clinicians by integrating the wisdom of the other because we both know that this combination of heart and substance is how perinatal women in distress begin to heal. They need to feel heard, they need to feel cared for, and they need to know what to do.

The Perinatal Patient is the perfect blend of our two hearts and our two minds. Inspired by The Art of Holding Perinatal Women in Distress™, a supportive psychotherapeutic model of intervention, Hilary has gently and decidedly taken my years of work and turned it into a masterful collection of essential perinatal basics and treatment strategies. Unlike other resources that are currently available, this book provides this information through the lens of a Holding therapist, so the information is never just information. Every word in this book is written to increase the likelihood that providers are informed and that moms feel cared for.

The enduring force that drives our mission is the same as it was decades ago when I began knocking on doors: to ensure that perinatal women feel valued and that every clinician, medical provider, and perinatal professional is prepared with up-to-date, accurate information. Because, despite increased public awareness, legislation, research, advocacy, trainings, and momentum on behalf of perinatal women in distress, the reality is:

- Women are still not telling us how bad they feel.
- Providers are still not asking the right questions.
- Women are still saying they are "fine" while believing their children would be better off without them.
- Suicide is still a leading cause of maternal mortality.
- Mothers and babies are still dying.

If we do not do a better job understanding the extent to which perinatal women are suffering, they will continue to suffer in silence and continue to think about ways to kill themselves. This is why we have written *The Perinatal Patient*, which is a comprehensive collection of what providers need to better understand and treat perinatal women. The information presented here is essential for all providers who treat or support this population, and it also includes handouts and worksheets that provide invaluable and practical ways for women to feel heard and properly attended to. Our goal is to reduce the stigma of perinatal mental health, help women address strong emotions and symptoms head-on, and normalize asking for (and accepting) help.

This book is the compilation of almost four decades of clinical work focusing on the heart of a perinatal woman in distress. It is not enough to read the literature and lean on the academic material that is central to this work. We need to listen. We need to address the hole in women's souls. We need to pay attention to what they cannot say. This is how we treat perinatal mood and anxiety disorders. This is how we create a safe and healing space. This is how we restore hope. This is how we save women's lives.

Karen Kleiman, founding director, The Postpartum Stress Center, CEO, The Karen Kleiman Training Center, author of *The Art of Holding in Therapy* and numerous other books on perinatal depression and anxiety

Introduction

The idea of becoming a mother is often one of hope and fantasy. Images of snuggly, sweet-smelling babies, adoring and doting partners, and proud and beaming grandparents come to mind. Excitement, hope, and great anticipation of an unmatched love overwhelm the social narrative, while the recognition that babies are very hard work grows dim. Television shows, movies, books, and imagery across social media platforms reinforce this fantasy of blissful motherhood and instant attachment to a perfect new being.

But, in reality, motherhood is lonely. It is isolating. It is sitting alone in a crowd. There is no lonesomeness like that of a new mother, still bleeding, lactating spontaneously, belly deflated and sore, exhausted in ways that were previously unimaginable, rocking her sleepless baby at 2:00 a.m. *I am the only one awake in the entire world*, she thinks. While it is true that parenthood ushers our hearts into a world of emotions unknown to us before becoming parents, much of the time we find ourselves stuck at the gate wondering, *Do I feel so in love already?* When a budding perinatal mood and anxiety disorder is in the mix, that question is hauntingly answered: *No, I don't feel in love. This is not what love feels like. What kind of person doesn't love their child? A terrible mother doesn't love their child. I wish I had never become a parent. This baby would be better off with a different mother, and I would be better off alone. I'm not sure I even deserve to live.*

The fantasy of motherhood is shattered, and mothers are left feeling betrayed.

Reprinted with permission from *Good Moms Have Scary Thoughts* (Kleiman, 2019)

It was unsurprising, then, that when this comic, written by Karen and illustrated by artist Molly McIntyre, was posted to The Postpartum Stress Center social media in 2017, it quickly went viral. Since the posting, countless mothers have shared that this image exactly depicts their postpartum experience—feeling disappointed, overwhelmed, and urgently in need, but equally unable to speak their needs. When providers and patients alike asked us how we knew what mothers were thinking, we told them that we knew from listening, not only to what mothers were saying, but also to what they were *not* saying.

Karen has long stated that her patients have been her most important teachers. She has spent decades listening to her patients' stories and learning to interpret and understand the hushed language of perinatal mood and anxiety disorders. This book is written with their voices in our minds and hearts. It is our hope that this book will introduce all therapists, providers, and families to the secret world of the perinatal patient in the hopes of arming them with insight and tools so we can better understand, support, and intervene on behalf of women in distress.

What Is in This Book

This book is organized into three parts. In Section I, we provide insight into the typical experience during the perinatal period. The information in this section is applicable to all mothers experiencing pregnancy and early parenthood. Section II focuses on perinatal mood and anxiety disorders, providing general information and insight into how issues like depression and anxiety can differ during the perinatal period. Section III explores Karen Kleiman's theoretical approach to therapy for perinatal women, The Art of Holding Perinatal Women in Distress.

Recognizing that this book will be read by both mothers and providers, we include handouts and worksheets in each chapter that can be used by mothers doing their own self-help work or by providers in the context of a professional setting. Mothers, here and throughout the book, we encourage you to use these worksheets as a starting point. Although these worksheets include space for you to write your answers, know that writing is always optional and that you can think about or talk through the worksheet prompts instead. If you do not like how you are feeling before, during, or after reading this book, seek the support of a maternal mental health professional or talk with a trusted health care provider.

Providers, you will notice that many of the handouts and worksheets included here are designed to help you gather information, start conversations, and encourage patients to explore their thoughts and emotions. The goal of these tools is to equip you with phrasing and verbiage that will increase the likelihood that your patients will disclose their suffering—a difficult feat for perinatal women in distress. The content of this book and the included tools are wonderful resources to start learning about perinatal distress or to augment what you already know.

Keep in mind that mothers with higher levels of distress will benefit from more intensive therapeutic interventions than those included in this book. This is where we encourage you to rely on your current clinical expertise and seek further training in your own theoretical orientation. For example, training in cognitive behavior therapy (CBT) for perinatal distress is offered at The Beck Institute, courses in interpersonal therapy (IPT) for perinatal distress are available through the IPT Institute, and the EMDR International Association (EMDRIA) has approved trainings in eye movement desensitization and reprocessing (EMDR) for perinatal trauma. Our training center, The Karen Kleiman Training Center, LLC, also provides training in The Art of Holding Perinatal Women in Distress, a psychodynamically oriented approach to perinatal therapy.

However you proceed in practice and training, make no mistake, your work can only be as impactful as your patient will allow. We implore you to take seriously the unique needs of perinatal mothers, to read ahead, to listen, to learn. We are absolutely sure that your increased fluency in the language of perinatal distress will be lifesaving.

Section I

The Nuanced Perinatal Patient

What Every Perinatal Patient Asks Themselves

CHAPTER 1

"Is This Normal?"

Giving birth transforms the world of a woman. The process of labor and delivery takes her through varying states of incomparable physical and emotional sensation. Women writhe in physical discomfort as they leave the relative certainty of life before baby and enter the vulnerability of the postpartum state. When her newborn finally arrives, waves of hormones and emotions surge. Soon enough, mothers become preoccupied with their newborns, counting fingers and toes, learning when and how to change diapers and feed, and obsessing over early decisions like whether to endorse the use of a pacifier in hopes of a few more minutes of sleep.

Before long, mothers find themselves sitting alone in the middle of the night, rocking their babies, and wishing for rest. The distraction of novelty has lifted, and they realize, *Nothing feels the same anymore.* Some mothers can ignore this for a while, keeping busy with their new babies. Eventually, however, all mothers begin to search for themselves again, longing to reconnect with parts of their lives that were paused when their babies were born. Sometimes this search is energizing and rewarding. Falling back into old routines happens with ease, and before long, life feels similar to how it felt before—just with a baby in tow. For others, the past is distant. The search for familiarity feels hopeless and dejecting; integrating what *was* with what *is* feels like an insurmountable task. Whether "finding herself" happens over a period of several weeks, months, or in some cases, years, the pain of feeling lost and disoriented at this pivotal stage of life triggers a yearning for comfort and reassurance.

Nothing feels normal during this exquisite and precarious transition, which is why the pressure mothers feel to thrive during this phase seems inherently contradictory. We would argue that this paradox is attributable to both the prevalence of and secrecy around perinatal mood and anxiety disorders in mothers today. This is what Karen Kleiman and Valerie Raskin brought to attention in *This Isn't What I Expected* (1994), where they described the complex presentation of a perinatal woman in distress: simultaneously dressing the part of a mother who is keeping things together and sitting alone with incapacitating self-doubt.

Therefore, one of the core tenets of this book is that all mental health professionals, as well as all individuals who participate in maternal care, must be sensitive to the urgency of the questions new mothers are asking themselves: *Is this normal? Am I okay? Am I doing this right?* Further, we believe strongly that anyone involved in the caretaking of adults, providing either professional or social support, should be aware of these points:

- **All pregnant and postpartum patients are vulnerable and deserve specialized attention.** Parenthood is one of life's most significant transitions. It is normal for parents to experience feelings of self-doubt, insecurity, and grief related to losing the life they had before. It is also common for them to be confused about where to go to understand and cope with these feelings. Despite the high prevalence of anxiety and depression among new parents, mental health care is not routine prenatal care. It only benefits patients when providers understand the unique vulnerability of perinatal patients so they can facilitate an initial conversation about the importance of mental health care during this period.

- **Many mothers and providers misunderstand the overlap of "normal" perinatal experiences and presenting symptoms.** Patients may initiate therapy during the perinatal period but may not recognize that their symptoms are related to their pregnancy or baby. When the nuances of the perinatal state seem unrelated to the presenting problem, symptoms of a perinatal mood and anxiety disorder can easily go unnoticed and therefore untreated.

- **You cannot afford to miss a perinatal mood and anxiety diagnosis.** The prevalence of perinatal mood and anxiety disorders emerging in pregnancy or early parenthood, or *the perinatal period*, is extremely high. During pregnancy and/or the 12-month period postpartum, one in seven cisgender female patients experiences distress severe enough to meet clinical criteria for a diagnosable mood and anxiety disorder (Torres, 2020). Additionally, fathers, birthing people, and non-gestational parents also experience the emergence of mood and anxiety disorders during the period of adjustment to parenthood. So whether you (or they) recognize it, all new parents are navigating changes that significantly impact their experience in the world. Furthermore, many of these parents are navigating these changes with a highly disruptive mood and anxiety disorder.

Defining the Terms

For a long time, mood and anxiety symptoms that emerged during pregnancy and the postpartum period were described as "postpartum" issues, with the term *postpartum depression* used as a catch-all phrase to describe mental health symptoms related to childbirth. As attention to maternal mental health has increased, our understanding of mood- and anxiety-related issues during motherhood has expanded, along with access to the language we use to describe mental health issues during this period. We now recognize that symptoms can occur outside the window of the first few postpartum weeks and that *postpartum* is too limiting a term. Here we provide definitions for terms used in maternal mental health care:

- **Perinatal:** This term describes the period during which a patient is pregnant and postpartum. In the medical field, a patient is typically recognized as perinatal from the 20th to 28th weeks of pregnancy up until the first four weeks postpartum. In the field of reproductive psychology, however, most agree that patients should be recognized as perinatal throughout the entire period of pregnancy and the first postpartum year.

It is important to consider that in a mental health care setting, these windows of time describe the *onset* of pregnancy- or postpartum-related symptoms, but the specific *duration* of these symptoms has no set timeframe. This means that when assessing any parent who presents for therapy, questions about their current distress (and how this distress reflects the same symptoms they experienced during the perinatal window) can reveal an untreated or undertreated perinatal mood and anxiety disorder—even years after giving birth. When the perinatal experience is identified as a root cause for symptoms later in life, you can still use perinatal-specific interventions to help patients address unresolved trauma, negative cognitions, or incomplete identity transformation that stem from this time, augmenting and enhancing their recovery.

- **Postpartum:** The term postpartum refers to the period of time from birth through one full year, or 12 months after giving birth. While this term typically applies to birthing parents, it is important to note that this term can apply psychologically to non-birthing parents as well.

- **Perinatal Mood and Anxiety Disorder, or PMAD:** PMAD (sometimes pronounced as "P.M.A.D." or "p-mad") is a non-specific term used to describe the full range of mood and anxiety disorders that can occur during the perinatal period. These include perinatal depression, anxiety, obsessive-compulsive disorder, posttraumatic stress disorder, panic disorder, bipolar disorder, and psychosis.

- **Baby Blues:** Most mothers can expect to experience the baby blues sometime in the first few weeks postpartum. This time is characterized by tearfulness, worry, difficulty sleeping or resting, self-doubt, and sadness (Torres, 2020). The key to understanding baby blues is to know that these feelings are completely normal, provided that they are fleeting and do not persist past those first few weeks. When patients experience symptoms beyond this time frame, you should take a closer look at how they are feeling to rule out something more clinically serious. While the mother may not have a full-blown mood and anxiety disorder, you want to carefully assess symptoms to ensure that you, along with the mother, have a clear understanding of her experience and what she might need to feel better.

Providers can give parents the following *Perinatal Glossary of Terms* to help explain the differences between these common terms.

Patient Handout

PERINATAL GLOSSARY OF TERMS

Many parents are unaware that the postpartum period is longer than just a few days or weeks. It is important for you to understand the parameters of *your* perinatal period so you can be on the lookout for symptoms that might benefit from the care of a reproductive health specialist, like an OB/GYN, a maternal mental health specialist, or a midwife.

Perinatal: This term encompasses the entire period that you are pregnant and postpartum.

Postpartum: The postpartum period refers to any time in the first year after giving birth. Patients often believe that the postpartum period lasts only a few days or weeks and are unsure how to seek help after their obstetric care is finished at around six weeks postpartum. However, issues related to being pregnant or giving birth can still impact a person's physical, emotional, and mental health long after that six-week milestone. In fact, most maternal mental health care providers agree that patients are postpartum for *at least* the first year after giving birth—recognizing that postpartum-related issues can also emerge after a baby's first birthday. If you are experiencing any discomfort that you think might be related to your pregnancy, birth, or experience of new parenthood, please reach out to your OB/GYN or midwife, a maternal mental health care provider, or any other specializing practitioner, even if you're unsure whether you are still considered postpartum.

Perinatal Mood and Anxiety Disorder, or PMAD: PMAD (sometimes pronounced as "P.M.A.D." or "p-mad") is a non-specific term used to describe a full range of mood and anxiety disorders that can develop during the perinatal period, including perinatal depression and anxiety.

Baby Blues: The baby blues is not a perinatal mood and anxiety disorder. Rather, it is a feeling of sadness, emotional discomfort, or nervousness—likely due to a significant drop in pregnancy hormones—that can occur in the first few weeks after giving birth. The baby blues can feel like clinical depression or anxiety, but it only happens within the first three weeks postpartum and only lasts a few hours or days. If you are having symptoms of depression or anxiety that are persisting past these first three weeks, that do not improve with self-care (e.g., eating well and resting), or that are scaring you, please seek further evaluation from your OB/GYN, your midwife, or a maternal mental health professional.

What Is Normal for Women to Experience

One interesting way to think about the typical struggles of early motherhood is through the lens of human development. Reproductive psychiatrists Drs. Alexandra Sacks and Catherine Birndorf brought new life to the anthropological concept of "matrescence" in their 2019 book, *What No One Tells You: A Guide to Your Emotions from Pregnancy to Motherhood*, where they compare the transition to motherhood with another formative and pivotal phase of human transition: adolescence. Adolescence is a period that most people remember as emotionally fraught, even though most people do not develop a full-blown anxiety, depressive, or mood disorder during this period. Some will, most will not. But all will experience the physical changes, emotional lability, and identity searching that are hallmarks of adolescence—these are all normative experiences.

Similarly, Sacks and Birndorf advocate for normalizing the hormonal, social, and psychological upheaval of matresence. They suggest that recognizing matresence as a normal part of human development will increase understanding that perinatal women should anticipate a period of discomfort that improves with time, social support, and—often—professional support. In a similar vein, Karen Kleiman, renowned maternal mental health expert and coauthor of this book, coined the term *postpartum stress syndrome* to define mild symptoms of adjustment disorders that are often experienced in the postpartum period (Kleiman & Raskin, 1994).

According to the fifth edition of the *Diagnostic and Statistical Manual of Mental Disorders* (DSM-5; APA, 2013), adjustment disorders should be diagnosed when individuals experience symptoms, both emotional and behavioral, that cause distress and functional impairment within three months of a stressful event. While adjustment disorders do not cause the same level of impairment as their severe counterparts, they also do not generate as much attention. This can leave mothers suffering with intense feelings of self-doubt, role confusion, and identity searching that makes it hard to restore a confident sense of self.

The concepts of matrescence and postpartum stress syndrome serve to normalize that this period in life is emotionally difficult and overwhelming. They are reminders that therapists, providers, family members, and other forms of social support should encourage mothers to be open and honest about their emotional well-being. At the same time, perinatal women need to know that having *some* emotional discomfort is normal but that having too much is not—and that treatment is available when their symptoms fall outside the normal range.

Newly Postpartum

Women start wondering whether what they are experiencing is normal from the first moments of their baby's life. During these first weeks, mothers tend to have more social support and contact with professionals. Visits from family and friends and attendance at postpartum checkups offer many opportunities to ask questions and receive reassurance. As this newly postpartum period comes to an end, however, support becomes more difficult to access and these opportunities for education and reassurance become sparse. In turn, women receive the message that it is only these first few weeks of a baby's life that comprise the postpartum period.

While it is true that the first six weeks are ones of enormous change, the newly postpartum stage is just beginning. In fact, the majority of women who are diagnosed with a perinatal mood and anxiety disorder will experience either a continuation or an onset of symptoms *after* reaching the six-week milestone. In the following section, we review some of the events that take place during these first six weeks. This information clarifies some of the thoughts and emotions that women experience in these early days and the origins of some of their darkest fears and anxieties.

Birth

Emmy remembered birth this way:

> When I was 37 weeks pregnant, I started to hear "any day now!" I remember feeling nervous about having an early baby, but excited for the baby I had been imagining all this time to arrive. At 39 weeks pregnant, I heard "you're almost there!" which did little to soothe my aching body but provided mild encouragement. At 40 weeks pregnant, I felt dejected and impatient as we started to discuss whether an induction would be necessary. My husband asked the doctor why they bother with due dates at all. Wouldn't it just be better to assign a this-is-definitely-the-very-last-day-of-waiting date? When my baby was born at 41 weeks exactly, all I felt was relief, relief that the waiting was over. After that, things were a blur, until one day I woke up and felt a little more like myself. I just don't really remember when exactly that was.

Toward the end of pregnancy, women experience many biological, psychological, and hormonal changes that can impact how they feel physically and emotionally. Discomfort such as fatigue, heartburn, and poor concentration often reach their peak during this stage. In addition, many mothers expect that sleep will be disrupted after they give birth, but in the last few months of pregnancy, sleep is often disrupted by vivid dreams, the constant need to urinate, and restless legs—an often an unwelcome third-trimester surprise (Schaffir, 2014).

Psychologically, as birth approaches, mothers become aware that the baby they have been imagining is about to be born. Suddenly, the notion that birth is an uncertain and unpredictable event becomes a focus and a reality. Mothers begin to think about what birth will be like: *Will the doctor I hope for be present? Will my mother be intrusive? When should I start my maternity leave? Are these real contractions or not? What if my water breaks in my car or my baby is born in the bathtub?* When the moment of birth finally arrives, for a moment, those questions fly out of their minds. Mothers become distracted by the birthing experience itself and how they are feeling in that moment. As Sam described it:

> I heard her cry for the first time and, after a second, I realized, *That's her. That's my baby's voice. This is the sound that will rule my life forever now.* I forgot my worries about how birth would go, and I wasn't thinking about the fact that I wasn't pregnant anymore or that my doctor

was sewing up my belly at that exact moment. I was totally swept up in the sound of her cry. It wasn't a happy feeling or a panicked feeling; it was a unique feeling. It felt like the world stopped and started spinning in a different direction. But that only seemed to last a moment before I was on to new worries about her and also about myself.

Another mother, Mollie, described her experience with this shift:

> After I gave birth, I was awestruck. I didn't really know how I felt in those first moments. I was excited, confused, happy, overwhelmed; it was a mixture of complicated feelings. After an hour or two, I was taken from labor and delivery to my postpartum room. I felt good, I had a good delivery, and my baby was born healthy. I sent my partner to get something to eat and it was just me and the baby. I was in the bed and the baby was in the bassinette. I realized that my pain meds were wearing off and I was uncomfortable. My stomach ached—I wasn't sure why at the time—but eventually I realized that it must be from pushing, and my stitches started to hurt. I was looking for the button to call the nurse for some more medicine when the baby started to cry. I wasn't sure what to do and I realized in that moment, *Oh my gosh, this is motherhood.* Ten years have gone by since then and I'm still not sure if I felt accepting, motivated, excited, sad, or defeated in that moment. It was just this lightbulb moment and a mixed feeling that lasted for a while after that.

Some mothers, like Sam, feel pleasantly surprised when they first recognize themselves as a mother. Others, like Mollie, feel shocked. Some mothers can tolerate the discomfort and eventually accept this shift, while others struggle more. But all mothers, either consciously or unconsciously, recognize that everything is different now, and they are likely to *feel* and *believe* that they should intuitively know how to guide this change. When they perceive their intuition as lacking or wrong, thoughts like, *Maybe I'm not cut out for this* take hold. The next worksheet can help patients process the feelings behind their birth story.

Patient Worksheet

PROCESSING YOUR BIRTH STORY

Whether you have just given birth for the first time or the fifth time, delivering a baby is always a life-altering event. For many women, their own bodily needs and the needs of their babies take center stage. It is important in those first few weeks to be mindful of your emotional state as well. While it is never too late to talk about your birth with your provider or to record the details of your birth for your own purposes, taking some time to do this in the early postpartum days can be helpful for your emotional healing and adjustment. Consider writing down your birth story in the space below or in a journal. If it feels overwhelming to write it down right now, you may also consider typing your story or recounting it into a recording device.

_____

_____

_____

_____

_____

_____

_____

After you are finished, notice any parts of your story that make you feel unsettled or uncomfortable. You may decide that the level of discomfort you feel is tolerable for you right now. However, if you feel overwhelmed by your emotions, or if they feel overwhelming in a few weeks or months, consider reaching out to your provider or a maternal mental health provider for more support.

Weeks One and Two

The first two postpartum weeks are a whirlwind for the newly growing family, and a critical point of assessment for maternal care providers. For the family, when birth goes smoothly, mom and baby will return home from the hospital or birthing center, often feeling a mix of excitement and trepidation. Siblings and pets will meet the new baby, and everyone will be confronted with the challenge of welcoming this pooping, spitting up, screaming little creature into the house. The family will also need to adjust to the new logistics of having a baby in the home. *Where is the best place to keep the diapers? Where will baby nap and sleep? What do we do with the baby when we shower? Who wakes up for feedings? Do we take shifts at night? What do we do with the baby at mealtimes? They say babies shouldn't watch TV—does that mean we can't watch TV either?*

Medically, obstetric providers are likely to step back a bit during this time. Mothers will receive instructions from providers for self-care and may need to schedule a visit to have incisions or birth injuries checked. Ideally, moms are instructed to use this time to rest and recover. (A tall order if you consider the previous description of these two weeks!) Providers caring for the baby during this time are also monitoring for normal growth and development. Feeding is a major focus during these early weeks, as feeding can be a determinant of how well the baby is thriving. Some mothers are unaware that feeding support is available outside the hospital, so we strongly recommended that providers give mothers resources tailored to coping with the many stressors associated with feeding.

Physiologically, the body undergoes normal, but major, hormonal changes that help the body transition from a pregnant state to a postpartum state. These changes can lead to two very different mood-related issues. The first is the baby blues, which as we discussed earlier, is a nearly universal human experience. The second is postpartum psychosis, which is a rare but serious condition that affects approximately one to two out of every 1,000 mothers (Torres, 2020). Detailed information on postpartum psychosis, including risk factors, assessment tools, and interventions, can be found further on in this book. For now, it is important to know that while postpartum psychosis occurs infrequently, it always requires urgent medical intervention and follow-up psychotherapy with a well-trained provider.

In sum, while motherhood is a time of many emotional changes, you should always assess patients for symptoms of depression or anxiety instead of responding to concerns with dismissive statements like "Oh, it's just the baby blues." To help you remember this, and to help you convey this to others, consider posting the following *Baby Blues versus Perinatal Mood and Anxiety Disorders* handout in a place that is visible to you and the mothers with whom you interact.

Patient Handout

BABY BLUES VERSUS PERINATAL MOOD AND ANXIETY DISORDERS

It can be hard to tell the difference between the baby blues and a perinatal mood and anxiety disorder. Symptoms of the baby blues and postpartum depression and anxiety look and feel the same, but they are different in a few important ways. Review the following list of symptoms, then consider the points below to determine if what you are experiencing is the baby blues (which is normal and will resolve on its own) or if you should talk to a professional about your symptoms.

Symptoms of baby blues may include:

- Feelings of anxiety, sadness, worry, and panic
- Changes in sleep and appetite
- Low energy
- Poor concentration
- Tearfulness
- Increased emotional sensitivity
- Feelings of disinterest

The baby blues is a hormonal event that occurs after giving birth. If you are experiencing these symptoms during pregnancy, you should be further evaluated.

The baby blues occurs within the first three postpartum weeks. If you experience these symptoms beyond three weeks postpartum, you should be further evaluated.

The baby blues comes and goes within a few hours or days. If your symptoms are persistent and unrelenting, you should be further evaluated.

The baby blues never includes delusional thinking, paranoia, or hallucinations. If you are experiencing symptoms like these, or any other symptoms of psychosis or mania (hallucinations, delusions, mood swings, confusion, restlessness, personality changes), you should receive a psychiatric evaluation urgently by contacting your health care provider, heading to your nearest emergency room, or calling 911.

If you are pregnant or postpartum, whether you think you have the baby blues or not, you are entitled and encouraged to reach out for help and support. We are here for you.

Weeks Three to Six

During this time, postpartum bodies are continuing to change, the baby is growing rapidly, and the baby's primary activities are still pooping, spitting up, and crying. Parents might start feeling more familiar with their babies, which can make taking care of them a little easier, but for many, the unachievable task of differentiating between the baby's cries is still as elusive as a full night of sleep. The good news is that during these weeks, some babies will start to string together more consecutive hours of sleep and require less frequent nighttime feedings—that is, until a growth spurt hits and babies become cranky, hungry, and constantly needy. Of course, growth spurts are temporary and sometimes just last a day or two, but try telling this to a new mom who is living according to her baby's hunger clock or a partner who hasn't slept for more than a couple of hours at a time in weeks and has returned to working full time.

As we discussed earlier, six weeks is also an important milestone for postpartum families, as this is when mothers are traditionally discharged from obstetric care. At this appointment, mothers who have had a C-section are often given clearance to drive a car and to lift something heavier than their babies, and most are cleared to resume exercise and sexual activity. Women are also encouraged to make an appointment for their annual exams and are offered birth control. The implicit message at this appointment is that the pregnancy and postpartum journey is over. *You are now back to normal.*

While there should certainly be a point of closure or discharge from obstetric-related care, each body is different and, as any parent who has experienced more than one pregnancy can attest, every pregnancy and subsequent birth is different. Different types of births and birth complications result in different recovery and healing experiences. Giving birth (and recovering from birth) with a child or children at home is different from giving birth for the very first time. Furthermore, the body is still undergoing significant changes for many months beyond the first six weeks. Therefore, it is critical that obstetricians and midwives convey the following information to patients when they reach the six-week mark:

- **Postpartum mood changes can emerge at any time during the first, or even second, year.** If a patient is experiencing any emotional discomfort, encourage them to talk to a mental health professional who can help them determine whether they would benefit from self-help and self-care strategies or if ongoing counseling would be helpful. Let them know that your office can help them find this support at any time moving forward. Remember to also educate your patients on the difference between the baby blues and perinatal depression and anxiety.

- **It is normal for mothers to feel different in their body after giving birth. It is also normal for these differences to impact them in various ways** (e.g., how they feel in their clothes, how they feel when they move their body, how they feel about intimacy). Encourage mothers to communicate openly to their support system about what they are experiencing. It takes time for the postpartum body to heal and for new mothers to feel more like themselves. Communication with peers and health care providers can be reassuring and normalizing. It is especially important to encourage communication between new mothers and their partners about any changes related to physical intimacy. These conversations can increase emotional intimacy and bring to light any feelings of guilt, shame, or resentment that the couple may benefit from working through together.

- **The body is still undergoing changes.** Healing does not stop after week six. Encourage the new mother to be patient with her body as it heals and to report any ongoing physical discomfort to you or another medical care provider. The following *Bodily Changes* handout can help you describe what is happening to a mother's body in the first days, weeks, and months after giving birth.

Weeks Six Through . . .

At six weeks postpartum, a few wonderful changes are happening that can lift the spirits of exhausted new parents:

- Postpartum bodies are internally more similar to how they were pre-pregnancy, even though most mothers could not care less given that their breasts are still acclimating to nursing, their stretch marks are still revealing themselves, and they may still be discovering unwelcome postpartum changes.
- For nursing mothers, milk supply is becoming established, and feedings may be feeling more routine.
- The baby might be consolidating more hours of sleep at night.
- Healing in the postpartum body increases opportunity for socialization and getting out of the house, which can break up the monotony of caring for an infant.
- The baby may begin to interact more or even smile, a milestone that can elicit a new parent's delight (even if that joy lasts only a moment before cries, and stress, begin again).

For example, Lea remembered the following about her six-week transition:

> I think it was around six weeks postpartum that I started to wake up from my daze. Not every day was a good day or a happy day, and I definitely felt irritable and impatient sometimes, but overall, I could start to see that I might be becoming a mom. I remember it was around this time that I took the baby to the grocery store, plopped the carrier in the big part of the shopping cart, got what I needed, and put her back in the car to go home. When I got home, it dawned on me—*I just did it!* And from that point on, I kind of just knew that it would take time, but I would figure it out as I went along. A lot of motherhood is like that—the first day of preschool felt like such a big deal, but after a few days, it was just routine, just what we did. Things really do get easier as you go along, and once I could see that, I started to feel a lot more like myself, but myself as a mom.

Like Lea, many mothers begin to adjust at six weeks postpartum. However, while the body is becoming stronger and healing from the event of giving birth, at six weeks postpartum nothing feels *normal*! How could it? Instead of thinking about the six-week milestone as the end of the journey, let's consider six weeks the start of the next stage. There is still a lot changing and a lot to get used to. Let's put aside the idea of a "new normal" (for now) and recognize six weeks as an important turning point. The *How Do You Feel Postpartum?* worksheet can help mothers explore how they are feeling at this stage.

Patient Handout

BODILY CHANGES*

While the period of pregnancy is clearly understood, many mothers misunderstand what it means to be postpartum and think that they are only considered postpartum for a short period. In fact, the postpartum period lasts the entire first year after giving birth, so it is important to know what is happening to your body during this time so you can appreciate how hard it is working. It is also important to seek additional medical care after your formal postpartum care has ended for any ongoing concerns you may have.

Week 1

What's Happening? Recovery from labor and delivery

You Might Know: Vaginal bleeding and discharge are normal, and it can be difficult to move around due to the circumstances of your delivery (e.g., vaginal tearing or C-section). You will probably feel sore and tired, but getting up and moving around a bit is important for your recovery. If you are breastfeeding, your nipples may be sore and in need of some soothing lanolin ointment.

You Might Not Know: Your uterus is starting to contract back to its usual size, which can feel like contractions even after you deliver. Your breasts are preparing to lactate, and you may feel pain and swelling as they adjust to producing milk during the first few days postpartum. (Yellowish colostrum comes in to feed baby first.) If you are not breastfeeding, your body will likely think it still needs to lactate. The process of stopping lactation can take a few days and cause breast discomfort.

Week 6

What's Happening? Postpartum follow-up care with your medical provider to determine if things are returning to normal

You Might Know: Most people will be able to reengage in physical activity, including sexual activity, and many might be considering what form of birth control to use moving forward.

---
* From Rasminsky (2018)

You Might Not Know: Your uterus is just now returning to pre-pregnancy size. While vaginal bleeding has probably stopped for the most part, sometimes brief periods of bleeding can restart. If you had a C-section, your scar might still feel tender, numb, or itchy. If you are breastfeeding, your baby will have a growth spurt around this time that will help your milk supply become better established and more reliable. Most people experience pain during intercourse at this stage. Using lube can help; if not, contact your medical provider.

6 Months

What's Happening? Getting into the groove post-maternity leave

You Might Know: Many moms find that some or even many parts of their bodies and aspects of their lives feel normal or at least more familiar.

You Might Not Know: If you are still having difficulty with incontinence, it will help to consult your OB/GYN, midwife, or a pelvic floor therapist. You might be having concerns about milk supply again. This can be related to the return of your regular periods, changes in your feeding schedule due to baby's needs, or spending more time away from baby (at work, for example). Lactation consultants can help with this or any other breastfeeding questions (including how to wean if you are interested in that). Many women still do not have their libido back or are worried that resuming certain physical activities will be physically (or emotionally) painful.

1 Year

What's Happening? Happy birthing day!

You Might Know: Your baby is about to celebrate a first birthday! You made it and you should prepare to celebrate both your baby and yourself.

You Might Not Know: Your body is *still* working to recover from pregnancy and birth. You may be carrying extra weight, getting used to stretch marks on any part(s) of your body, or navigating breastfeeding with your older baby. You are likely dealing with sleep deprivation that causes you to sometimes feel tired, sometimes downright desperate for a nap. If you had a C-section, your scar probably still feels numb or tingly, and no matter what type of delivery you had, your stomach muscles are probably still working to regain their strength.

Patient Worksheet

HOW DO YOU FEEL POSTPARTUM?

Many parents associate the postpartum period with the length of time they feel entitled to recover from the experience of giving birth. The length of time that is perceived as appropriate varies widely, based on cultural and social norms, as well as messaging from the medical community. This worksheet asks you to consider how your pregnancy and postpartum experiences are impacting you now, regardless of how many weeks or months postpartum you are. It is important to recognize how your current physical and emotional state may be related to your perinatal experiences so you can access the most appropriate medical or psychological treatment and social support resources.

Biologically

Did you experience any medical complications during pregnancy or birth? If so, are these medical complications interfering with your ability to feel "like yourself" at this time?

_____

_____

_____

_____

How has your body changed because of breastfeeding or your decision not to breastfeed?

_____

_____

_____

_____

Copyright © 2023 Hilary Waller and Karen Kleiman, *The Perinatal Patient*. All rights reserved.

How have you been sleeping, and how has your sleep been disrupted by your baby?

_____

_____

_____

_____

On a scale from 1 (*completely recovered*) to 10 (*not at all like myself*) I feel: _____

Noticing the connection between these issues and the birth of your baby, which of these perinatal specialists could be helpful for you at this time?

- ❒ **OB/GYN or midwife:** Medical providers who provide care for pregnant, birthing, and postpartum women

- ❒ **Reproductive psychiatrist or reproductive nurse practitioner:** Medical providers who specialize in prescribing psychiatric medications to pregnant and postpartum women

- ❒ **International board-certified lactation consultant:** Providers who specialize in maternal and infant issues related to breastfeeding and lactation

- ❒ **Childbirth educator:** Educators who teach classes to expectant parents on expectations for birth, the perinatal period, and infant care

- ❒ **Birthing or postpartum doula:** A provider who is trained to give physical and emotional support to mothers and partners during childbirth and the early postpartum stage

- ❒ **Pelvic floor physical therapist:** A physical therapist who treats problems in the muscles of the pelvic floor, as pelvic floor injuries are common during pregnancy and the postpartum period

Emotionally

Which statements capture how you are feeling about yourself, your baby, your family, and your lifestyle?

- ☐ Much of my worries are related to my pregnancy or my baby.
- ☐ I feel overwhelmed by the added responsibilities of parenting.
- ☐ I feel that decision-making is harder than usual for me right now.
- ☐ I dread bedtime because I never know if my baby will sleep.
- ☐ I dread bedtime because I never know if I will sleep.
- ☐ It's hard for me to leave the house because I never feel prepared.
- ☐ It's hard for me to leave the house because I am afraid.
- ☐ I don't feel comfortable feeding my baby in public, so it's hard to go out.
- ☐ I think about my pregnancy/baby's birth a lot and it causes me distress.
- ☐ It's hard for me to shake worry about my baby; I feel overprotective a lot.
- ☐ I think about who I was before my baby. I'm not sure about who I am now.
- ☐ I don't want anyone to know that I'm having a hard time right now.
- ☐ I have scary thoughts about my baby that are upsetting to me.
- ☐ My marriage/partnership/relationships feel less fulfilling to me now.
- ☐ I am not as good of a partner/friend as I was before I had my baby.

Noticing the connection between these issues and the birth of your baby, consider looking for a maternal mental health care provider or mother's support group to connect with.

Normalizing Perinatal Difficulties

It is important to recognize the journey into motherhood as an endurance challenge, not a sprint. Although many mothers experience a shift in how they are feeling around six weeks postpartum, they may still have periods of stress, exhaustion, and emotional overwhelm. We hope that drawing attention to these difficulties will normalize the need for all women to receive support and access to mental health care during the perinatal period. We further hope that naming and validating these difficulties will normalize women's ability to have open and honest discussions about their emotional well-being.

At the same time, we want to recognize that it is during the six-week period when symptoms of a mood and anxiety disorder may start to emerge or worsen. Women tend to be incredibly motivated by the demands of motherhood and want to portray the image of what a "good" mother looks like. These factors can motivate them to maintain a level of functioning that allows their suffering to fly under the radar of those around them. As you read ahead, try to remain sensitive to the nuanced differences between mothers who are experiencing the normal distress of new motherhood versus mothers who are suffering too much.

CHAPTER 2
"Is Something Wrong with Me?"

Sometimes mothers are brave—or desperate—enough to tell someone that they are worried about how bad they are feeling. In response, they might hear something like "Don't worry, it will get better!" But to many new parents in the trenches, the battle is just beginning. The days are long. They are interminable. New parents do not yet have the perspective of really understanding in an embodied way that it *will* get better. Seasoned parents have the benefit of time. Time that positions them to understand that while the days are long, the years feel short in retrospect. They recognize, and remember, that it *does* get better. Their memories of sleepless weeks and ear-shattering tantrums are mitigated by hugs, fascination, and adorable words like "oatbump pease" ("oatmeal please!") and "paper-toilet" (instead of toilet paper). After some time, veteran parents watching their tween, teen, and adult children find themselves wistfully advising new parents, "Don't blink—it goes by too fast."

When motherhood is new and just beginning, time seems to stand still, marked by signs of their baby's hunger and the recognition that the routine of feeding, burping, soothing, and playing is beginning again for the nth time today. Some parents may be resilient to these changes and adjustments. While they, too, are likely to experience exhaustion, irritability, worry, and frustration, these parents hear hopefulness reinforced in statements like "It will get better." These parents cling to the belief that things, in fact, *will* get better and that time *will* pass more quickly than each long moment currently feels. We see this in our work with mothers who go on to have another baby after recovering from a previous perinatal mood and anxiety disorder. While they still struggle and can experience a recurrence of symptoms, they are often able to articulate that no matter how bad it feels right now, their struggles are impermanent and this too shall pass. This shift in thinking is a marker of recovery, in fact. It offers them hope.

However, for other mothers, the worries of new motherhood and whether something is "wrong" with them can feel all-consuming. For these mothers, well-meaning comments like "It will get better" or "You're doing great" can paradoxically activate a pattern of negative thinking. Mothers with perinatal mood and anxiety disorders tell us that this feedback causes them to feel more isolated and misunderstood. They report having thoughts like, *You must have no idea how hard this is; If only you knew what was happening inside my head or behind my closed doors;* or *If you think that, then something must really be wrong with me.* When women begin to believe these thoughts—which have been distorted by the presence perinatal distress—hope can be hard to find. The reignition of hope is a critical goal for women in the throes of perinatal mood and anxiety disorders. The following worksheet provides a template mothers can use to write a hopeful letter to themselves—a letter they can read when things feel dark to remind themselves that there is light on the other side.

Suffering in Secrecy

Years after recovering from postpartum depression, Jessica reflected on her experience through the eyes of a parent:

> Now I watch my preteen daughter and her friends play together on the playground at the end of the school day. They giggle together, climb, swing, and run. I wonder if any of the girls talked about how their mornings started today. At my house, I held my daughter in my arms while she cried about how her hair is all wrong and she has a pimple. She seemed comforted by me at first but then stormed away and yelled, "Why am I the only one who has to deal with this? None of my friends have these problems!" Five minutes later, standing at the bus stop, she turned to me and said, "Mom, you can't tell I was crying right?" and hopped onto the bus. None of her peers were the wiser. My younger daughter watched the whole thing. I thought about how it might be easier for her when she confronts these feelings having watched her sister go through it. She is privy to her sister's private world. She will know that other people have felt this way. But my older girl's world is terrifying and lonely. I watch her pretend that she is okay so her peers do not see her vulnerability and insecurity, but as a mom, I know they are all feeling this way. And if they aren't yet, they will.

Just as Jessica hoped that the journey into adolescence would be easier for her younger daughter to navigate, she felt differently about motherhood after experiencing it once. After the pain and change of early motherhood were revealed, she found them less frightening and easier to tolerate the second time around. However, many perinatal patients feel isolated and othered by their experiences, often completely unaware that other mothers have similar feelings, so they conceal their symptoms of distress and suffer in secrecy.

As we've discussed, secrecy is a hallmark feature of perinatal mood and anxiety disorders. Mothers are driven by a wish to feel healthy and in control, along with beliefs about how a good mother should look and behave. While conversations regarding perinatal mood and anxiety disorders are becoming more commonplace—and the media is increasingly depicting examples of good mothers who struggle with these symptoms—admitting to having one remains as stigmatized as ever (Mule et al., 2022). There still remains the pervasive and false assumption that women with perinatal mood and anxiety disorders are failures who are unfit to be mothers.

Patient Worksheet

A HOPEFUL LETTER TO MYSELF

When symptoms feel overwhelming or when treatment isn't working fast enough, mothers can begin to feel hopeless. They think that things will never get better; that things will never change. Use this worksheet to write yourself a letter so that if this happens to you, you can read it in times of difficulty as a reminder of hope.

_____

_____

_____

_____

_____

_____

_____

_____

_____

Therefore, as a provider you must:

- Facilitate a clear, collaborative dialogue with mothers that reinforces the message that if they do not like how they are feeling, support is available. As part of this discussion, encourage them to ask you for resources.

- Educate patients on how normal postpartum mood changes differ from those that may be associated with higher levels of distress. You should also discuss how to spot signs and symptoms that are causes for concern.

- Communicate clearly about what constitutes symptoms of a perinatal mood and anxiety disorder and how this differs from a perinatal mental health emergency.

- Be explicit in asking perinatal mothers about their emotional and physical discomfort. Questions like "Are any parts of your body hurting in ways that are worrisome?" and "Are you worried about how you are feeling emotionally?" will yield more complete answers from patients than broad or vague questions like "How are you feeling?"

Although providers are becoming more aware of the uniqueness surrounding perinatal patients and are responding with an impressive desire for comprehensive guidance, the intensely private nature of this population makes it challenging to conduct a precise assessment of symptoms. Further, the reliability of your assessment tools matters very little if you fail to prioritize increased disclosure of a mother's deepest fears. **At the heart of your work, always remember the critical paradox that the perinatal patient faces: the simultaneous desire to protect herself and her baby at all costs, and her desperate plea for help.**

Therefore, if you are a provider, you may want to consider how frequently new parents disclose symptoms to you, as this can indicate your current level of attunement to symptoms of perinatal distress. Keep in mind that one in seven postpartum patients meets criteria for a mood and anxiety disorder, so if your parents are not disclosing symptoms to you, ask yourself why. Is it because you have not yet been trained to recognize and screen for perinatal mood and anxiety disorders? Because you are unsure how to respond if a mother discloses to you that she does, in fact, have symptoms of a perinatal mood and anxiety disorder? Because your patients are reluctant to disclose their symptoms to you?

To put yourself in a better position to help these patients, we encourage you to continue reading ahead to learn more and increase the likelihood that mothers will feel comfortable expressing their distress to you. And if your patients are already disclosing symptoms to you, you are on the right track—the chapters that follow will augment your work.

> ### 🌿 Unique Challenges for Diverse Women 🌿
>
> In some communities, distrust of health care providers, or of individuals outside of the community itself, hinders access to perinatal mental health care (Nidey et al., 2020). Especially within the Black, Indigenous, and People of Color (BIPOC) community, a history of mistreatment—from microaggressions to intentional and systemic abuse—has created and reinforced mistrust in the health care system (Anderson et al., 2017; Browne, 2020). Therefore, it is incumbent on all providers to seek extensive specialized training to gain insight into the unique dynamics that prevent diverse communities from seeking mental health care and to develop environments that offer inclusive, equitable, and culturally competent services.

If you are a mother, rest assured that your reluctance to talk about how you are feeling is understandable. And yet, a provider who recognizes your suffering can show you a path toward healing, so we encourage you to discuss your symptoms with a professional you trust. However, it is often up to *you* to find that person. That last sentence probably sounds awful and may even feel difficult to achieve when you are weary, weak from fatigue, and wish that someone could do this for you—or wish that it weren't happening at all. Try to be hopeful, and consider using the following worksheet to explore the reasons for your secrecy and to gain access to the support you need.

Patient Worksheet

I AM SCARED TO SAY HOW I FEEL

Telling someone that you are struggling with symptoms of a perinatal mood and anxiety disorder can be very scary, no matter how much you love or trust that person. However, telling someone how you are feeling is an important step toward finding the support that can help you feel better. Recognizing your fears and preparing for these tough conversations can help you take this leap of faith.

Some people I could ask for support might be:

- ☐ My partner
- ☐ My parents
- ☐ My sibling
- ☐ My best friend
- ☐ My provider
- ☐ Others: _____

When I think about talking with these people, I think and feel:

- ☐ My partner: _____
- ☐ My parents: _____
- ☐ My sibling: _____
- ☐ My best friend: _____
- ☐ My provider: _____
- ☐ Others: _____

The easiest person to talk to might be _____ because they:

_____

The hardest person to talk to might be _____ because they:

_____

The following is something that prevents me from telling others how I feel: _____

_____

I am most afraid that: _____

_____

But when I think about that actually happening, I realize: _____

_____

After reflecting on your answers, you might find that you do have someone you could talk to and that you feel ready for that conversation. If so, the following conversation starters and conversation card can help you prepare. If you still feel unsure about whom to talk with, or are fearful about disclosing how you are feeling, look for a maternal mental health care provider. It is their job to create brave and safe spaces for mothers who are struggling with these disclosures to find comfort and healing.

Conversation Starters

I have been **feeling** ___(e.g., anxious, sad, scared)___ since ___(e.g., our baby was born, I gave birth, my baby turned four months old)___. I know its normal to have some of these feelings after having a baby, but I think this has been going on for too long, and I am hoping you can help me get some professional support.

I have been **worrying** ___(e.g., about being a bad mother, that I am having too much anxiety, that I am failing our baby)___. Even though people tell me not to worry about this, or that I am a great mom, I still worry and am hoping you can help me get some professional support.

Since ___(e.g., our baby was born, I gave birth, my baby turned four months old)___, I have not been feeling like myself. **I am really scared to talk about how I feel**, and I think I should talk to a professional who can help me. I am hoping you can help me find some professional support.

Conversation Card

Use this template to write down a few notes on an index card that you can hand to the person with whom you would like to share. If you do not have all of these answers, that's okay. Answer the questions you can or simply use them as a guide.

I need to tell you something about how I have been thinking and feeling.

Thoughts I am having: _____
_____

Emotions I am experiencing: _____
_____

Anything else I need you to know: _____
_____

It is hard for me to tell you this because: _____
_____

Please help me by: _____
_____

Overcoming Resistance

The simultaneous longing for privacy and support from others is the perfect recipe for resistance. New parents commonly fear that they will be viewed as incapable, lazy, or bad if they require help or guidance. However, the reality is that all moms need help. From learning a new baby's preferred soothing style to learning how to juggle multiple children, there is so much new material to master during pregnancy and early parenthood—no matter how many children a mother has. Hilary still remembers trying to (unsuccessfully) figure out how to open her new stroller after the birth of her second child. In retrospect, she realizes how silly it was to insist that she could do it on her own, especially because she never truly mastered the art of opening it one-handed. With some help, she probably would have succeeded.

However, new parents notoriously resist asking for any kind of help for many, many reasons. Perhaps most painfully, they fear being viewed or treated as an unfit parent. They also worry that their internal monologue, already plagued by doubt and what-ifs, will be validated if they ask for help. They feel guilty for imposing their problems on others. They worry that they will not live up to expectations. For all these reasons and more, they avoid asking for help and even deny or refuse help that is offered, no matter how badly it is needed.

Given the fear and vulnerability that drives a mother's resistance, it is crucial for providers to remain affirmative but gentle when assessing mothers for mental health issues during the perinatal period. If you are a provider, the *Resistance to Disclosure* worksheet can help you in this effort. If you are a mother, the *Overcoming Resistance* worksheet can help you to recognize and overcome the reasons for your reluctance, increasing the possibility that you will receive the help you need to begin feeling better.

Provider Handout

RESISTANCE TO DISCLOSURE

Many perinatal patients have a strong resistance to disclosing their symptoms and may be unwilling to share their concerns. The following is a list of common reasons why women may avoid opening up to you about how they are feeling. Recognizing and understanding these reasons can serve to increase empathy, guide your assessment, and increase your clinical sensitivity.

Reasons may include:

- Hope of spontaneous remission
- Lack of recognition that their level of distress may exceed what is considered normal during the perinatal period
- Denial
- Belief that they shouldn't be having these symptoms
- Shame and self-blame
- Certain symptoms (e.g., low energy, motivation) that interfere with help-seeking behaviors
- Opposition to therapy
- Distrust in health care providers or the medical system
- Worry about failing to meet cultural, familial, or personal expectations
- Unsupportive partner or family members
- Fear of being labeled a bad or unfit mother
- Fear of having their baby taken away

Patient Handout

OVERCOMING RESISTANCE

"Resistance to therapy is as old as therapy itself . . . Too much resistance is counterproductive. Too little may be also. Either way, resistance is a well-known psychological phenomenon in therapy because, well, change is hard . . . Postpartum women in distress do not have the time, the energy, the interest, the wherewithal, the resources, the finances, or the motivation to go to even one more healthcare provider. Add a therapist in the mix? *You've got to be kidding me.*"

—Karen Kleiman, *The Art of Holding in Therapy*

It makes a lot of sense that confronting how bad you are feeling seems like a terrible idea right now. Still, after feeling better, many mothers recognize that telling someone how bad they were feeling was the exact thing they needed to do to feel like themselves again. Sometimes gaining awareness into the reasons behind your resistance can help you move through it so you can do what is necessary, even if it is scary.

Put a check mark by any common reasons for resistance that apply to you:

- ❒ You hope that things will get better on their own.
- ❒ You are uncertain about whether what you are experiencing is normal for pregnant and postpartum women.
- ❒ You wonder if what you are feeling is just what being a mother feels like.
- ❒ You worry that your provider will not be able to help.
- ❒ You're afraid to know if something is really wrong.
- ❒ You believe that you should not be having these feelings.
- ❒ You worry that your feelings are your own fault and that no one can help you.
- ❒ Low energy or motivation is making it hard to talk to someone about how you feel.
- ❒ You dislike or oppose therapy or mental health care.
- ❒ You don't trust health care providers or the medical system.
- ❒ You worry about failing to meet cultural, familial, or societal expectations.

- ☐ You fear that your partner or family members will be unsupportive.
- ☐ You fear that you will be labeled a bad or unfit mother.
- ☐ You fear that your baby could be taken away.
- ☐ Other: _____

Now that you are aware of the reasons for your resistance, consider these tips for overcoming it:

- Sometimes resistance can stem from negative beliefs you have about yourself or a situation. While you can often find lots of evidence to support the negative belief, you can also find evidence to challenge the belief, which can shift your perspective a bit. For example, the belief, "I should not be having these feelings" may stem from cultural, societal, or familial expectations. You can disprove this belief by reading about (or talking to) other mothers like you, who have experienced similar feelings after having a baby and who were able to feel like themselves again after seeking help.

- Consider disclosing your resistance *itself* (as opposed to the symptoms you are experiencing). For example, you might tell your provider, "I am really afraid that if I tell you about what I'm feeling, you will make me go to therapy or put me in a hospital—and I really am not open to doing that." By expressing your reluctance in words, your provider can address your fears by clarifying what is likely to happen if you talk about your symptoms and by answering any questions you might have about the possible consequences or interventions.

- Use positive self-talk to increase your courage and commitment to seeking help even though you are scared. For example, use affirmations such as "This is really, really hard for me and I am really scared. But I am going to take a risk and tell someone who cares about me. I know other moms have felt this way and have ended up feeling better. I am going to try to find help for myself too."

Normalize Seeking Help

One extremely powerful way to combat resistance is to normalize the act of help-seeking during the perinatal period. If you interact with and provide care for perinatal mothers in any capacity, you should normalize *all* mothers' need for support, whether or not something is actually wrong. You can do so by encouraging all new mothers to seek resources for their mental health and emotional well-being, just as you would encourage all expectant mothers to seek prenatal care.

In particular, you should convey to mothers that:

- Seeking help for emotional health in the perinatal period is as normal as seeking assessment for an infant's breastfeeding latch. We recommend initiating conversations about mental health as routinely as you would initiate conversation about the baby's name or the mother's expected due date.
- There are many options for support and levels of care, depending on whether a mother is mildly stressed or experiencing symptoms of a full-blown mood disorder.
- The perinatal period extends far beyond the first few days or weeks postpartum, and help is available to them at any time during the first year postpartum (or beyond).

You also want to normalize any discomfort or difficulties mothers are experiencing by conveying the message that feeling vulnerable is okay. Carefully communicate that similar to the discomfort of colic or sleep regression, the emotional discomfort of early parenthood is likely to ease with time. When you destigmatize the secrecy that exists around mental health issues in general, you increase women's ability to access professional treatment and to seek support from friends and family.

At the same time, you want to take care to send the correct message—normalizing the fact that new mothers can expect some degree of discomfort and overwhelm during the perinatal period, but not too much. You want to communicate is that there is a threshold for what is considered normal perinatal distress. Even the most vigilant parents can fail to recognize when they have reached this threshold and crossed the line from transient stress to symptoms of a perinatal mood and anxiety disorder. For this reason, you want to emphasize that they seek help from a trained professional who is skilled at recognizing these subtle symptoms. These providers can help parents explore their individual thresholds for distress and determine what level of support is needed.

CHAPTER 3

"What If I Feel Alone?"

In our offices, we often marvel at the profound incongruity of mother's pleas for support and her simultaneous rejection of offers to help. We notice this both in the context of therapy and in our patients' reports of their daily interactions. In fact, it was our privileged view of this discrepancy that inspired Karen's 2019 book, *Good Moms Have Scary Thoughts*. Even though mothers reported that they were desperate for support, they weren't sure what to ask for, how to ask, if they were even entitled to ask, or whom to ask for what. Paradoxically, some mothers even reported feeling anxious when asked, "How can I help?" which made them feel further isolated, distressed, and misunderstood.

Hilary remembers witnessing this when a patient with postpartum depression attended a session with her baby and husband. When the couple had a hard time soothing their colicky baby, the husband lovingly looked at his wife and said, "It's okay, let me take him outside so you can focus on your session." Hilary remembers feeling struck by the juxtaposition of the husband's gentleness and his wife's simultaneous change in body language. The wife sunk deeply into her chair and said quietly, "See? I can't ever soothe the baby. Someone is always taking him from me because I can never do it myself."

For many new mothers, the idea of asking for help, or accepting help when it is offered, is complicated by strong emotions, compromised hormones, and sleep deprivation—just to name a few variables. Even basic needs are often masked by confusion and fatigue and can be hard to uncover, leaving mothers feeling profoundly alone and unsure of what they actually need or want.

However, the importance of social support in perinatal mood and anxiety disorders cannot be overstated. Studies consistently show that pregnant and postpartum women with stronger and more robust social support systems experience fewer symptoms of perinatal depression than women with scarce options for social support (Aktas & Calik, 2015; Biaggi et al., 2016). Ideally, social supports are individualized, addressing each mother's unique needs for peer support, professional support, and role-modeling from more experienced mothers (Machado et al., 2020; Stern, 1995). In this chapter, we guide you in developing a support system that addresses many general and individualized needs. We include tools that can be used to anticipate needs in advance, as well as tools that help women recognize when a need has arisen and how to ask for help in these moments.

Types of Support Mothers Need

Given that most mothers experience some feelings of loneliness, particularly during the early days of motherhood, we find that brainstorming support options and collecting resources early on can proactively reduce feelings of overwhelm. This preparation can further equip mothers with specific responses to well-meaning questions like "What can I do to help?" and actually increase the likelihood that they will accept help.

Although there are various types of support available, some common types of non-professional perinatal support include:

- **Practical support:** Individuals who can provide help with transportation, access to food, financial resources, childcare, infant care, scheduling, errands, house maintenance

- **Educational support:** Individuals who can problem solve common parenting concerns, provide parenting resources, and give parenting advice

- **Social support:** Individuals whose presence feels supportive, which can require developing relationships with peers and other new mothers

- **Emotional support:** Trusted individuals who can help mothers cope with the range of emotions during the perinatal stage and to whom mothers feel safe disclosing their distress and personal experiences

For some women, coming up with a list of support people is a quick and easy task. For others, it is a struggle. They don't know what they need, who can help, or how to ask for support. Furthermore, while mothers are typically aware of the important role that their OB/GYN or midwife plays during pregnancy, many are unaware of other professionals that can be helpful and supportive during the perinatal period, including:

- Mental health care providers
- Board certified lactation consultants
- Doulas
- Physical therapists
- Yoga teachers, chiropractors, acupuncturists, and Pilates instructors who have specialized training in caring for new mothers

The worksheets on the next pages can guide mothers though the process of identifying their unique needs, interests, and preferences, as well as their vulnerabilities. Encourage women to consider friends and family members, including partners, who can fill these roles, along with what support systems are available in their existing communities.

Patient Worksheet

REDUCING ISOLATION

Feeling isolated and alone is common in the early days of motherhood. The fact is that mothers do often spend a lot of time alone caring for their babies. But even when mothers are surrounded by support people, they can experience thoughts and emotions that make them feel isolated—as if they are alone. When these feelings surface, it can help to remember the people in your life who help you feel more understood or less alone.

Who in your life:

Can help you by running an errand? _____

Can help with housework? _____

Likes to cook or bake and can drop off homemade food? _____

Loves to care for babies and can give you a break to shower or rest? _____

Has a little one and might have supplies you can borrow in a pinch? _____

Has breastfed and can help you navigate difficulties? _____

Feels like a safe person to come help you breastfeed in person? _____

Can help you learn to use a breast pump? _____

Has bottle-fed and can help you navigate difficulties? _____

Can come help you in an emergency situation? _____

Can give you parenting advice? _____

Knows where other moms gather to socialize? _____

Knows where to find groups and activities for new moms? _____

Has a baby the same age and can relate to what you are going through? _____

Makes you laugh or smile? _____

Is a good listener? _____

Always knows the right thing to say? _____

Will always answer if you reach out? _____

Feels safe to talk to when you don't like how you are feeling? _____

 Review your answers and think about making plans with some of the people on your list. It's okay to make plans and to give the disclaimer that with a baby, you might need to cancel or change plans at the last minute. But having a plan in place increases the likelihood that it will happen and gives you something to look forward to on your calendar, which can reduce feelings of isolation and hopelessness.

 If there were any questions you were unable to answer, see if there is someone on your list who can help you find the answers. For example, would the person you trust for parenting advice be knowledgeable or helpful in researching places where moms go to hang out? Finally, do some of your own research and fill in your answers below.

What online support groups are available for new moms in your area or region? Consider checking Postpartum Support International (www.postpartum.net) if you are unsure.

_____

_____

_____

What meetup groups for new moms are available in your area? Search for local perinatal mental health care providers, pediatricians, hospitals, lactation consultants, or doulas who might be hosting a group. These groups are also often held at religious institutions, community centers, and libraries.

_____

_____

_____

Where are playgroups for moms and babies offered? These groups might also be offered by health care providers, lactation consultants, and doulas, or they may be hosted at religious institutions, libraries, and community centers. Local preschools, daycares, and museums host these groups too.

_____

_____

_____

What local places attract moms and their babies? This might include indoor playgrounds, outdoor splash parks, outdoor playgrounds, libraries, malls, and museums. Even if your baby is too young for the space (for example, an infant may not find much to do at a playground), you might still enjoy taking your baby for a walk there and being in the company of other moms.

_____

_____

_____

Patient Worksheet

WHO CAN HELP?

The importance of having different kinds of support in place when you are expecting a baby or recovering from giving birth cannot be overstated. It can be hard to know exactly what types of support you need and whom to ask for help. Use this worksheet to brainstorm and gather these resources.

Who can provide *practical* support (e.g., people who can assist with transportation, access to food, financial resources, childcare, infant care, scheduling, errands, house maintenance)?

_____

_____

_____

_____

Who can provide *educational* support (e.g., people who can problem solve common parenting concerns, provide parenting resources, and give parenting advice)?

_____

_____

_____

_____

Who can provide *social* support (e.g., people whose presence feels supportive, including peers and other new mothers)?

_____

_____

_____

_____

Who can provide *emotional* support (e.g., people you trust to help you cope with the range of emotions during the perinatal stage and to whom you feel safe disclosing your distress and personal experiences)?

_____

_____

_____

_____

Patient Worksheet

WHAT DO I NEED?

It can be extremely difficult to know exactly what you need as a new or expectant mother—and even more frustrating if some of your needs are not accessible at this stage of your life. This worksheet will help you think about which of your needs are being met now, what needs you can work on meeting in the near future, and what needs may be hard to fulfill for a short while as you navigate this period.

Review the pyramid and highlight any needs that you feel are being met.

Level 3: Personal Fulfillment Needs
Free time; Access to enjoyable activities; Restored sense of intimacy with others

Level 2: Support Needs
Support from peers who are having similar experiences; Role models who can help you navigate challenges; Family and friends who help you feel loved; Visitors to offer socialization; People to help with chores, childcare, and housework; Feeling like a capable mother; Feeling respected by others

Level 1: Basic Needs
Nutritious food for you and your family; Ample formula and lactation support to feed your baby; Safe housing for you and your family; Safe sleep, rest, and play spaces for your baby; Transportation and car seats for your children and/or baby; Weather-appropriate clothing; Access to necessary medical care providers

Now, list your unmet needs in the space provided, along with any other needs that come to mind. Note what is getting in the way of these needs being met and what you can do to fulfill these needs now or in the future. For example, perhaps your need for alone time with your partner is not being met because you are exhausted from sleepless nights and don't have available childcare. To help fulfill this need, you might start looking for a childcare provider, family member, or close friend who can enable you to nap or take a walk alone with your partner.

_____

_____

_____

_____

If there are any challenges that you cannot overcome, think of a reassuring statement to remind yourself that change is always happening. For example, perhaps your need for physical intimacy is not being met because your body is still healing from pregnancy and giving birth. Since there is not much you can do to speed up your healing process, you can say to yourself something like "I have taken control of what I can. My body will heal over time. If I am feeling uncomfortable, nervous, or impatient with my healing, I can call my OB/GYN to find out what pain is normal and how long it should take to heal."

_____

_____

_____

_____

Barriers to Developing Perinatal Social Support Systems

If you are a mental health care provider, developing plans for increasing social support and providing resources is likely a familiar task to you. However, like most other aspects of motherhood, invisible barriers exist for new mothers that may go unrecognized if you don't know what to look for or how to ask about them. Barriers are multifaceted, but common themes are found in the form of logistical and emotional barriers.

Logistical Barriers

Logistical barriers can include, but are not limited to, financial stressors, lack of access to childcare, and limited availability of services. Some mothers might not even know where to access these resources, which is a logistical barrier in itself. Fortunately, some of these barriers can be addressed with thoughtful planning, research, and creative thinking. The following *Overcoming Logistical Barriers* worksheet can guide you and your patients through this process. If there are certain barriers that continue to interfere with a mother's ability to access support, we encourage you to consider other ways that your practice can help patients overcome issues related to accessibility, affordability, and other logistical barriers.

For example, you might consider creative solutions to help your patients afford services, such as offering pro bono services to a certain number of patients, giving patients the option to have shorter 30-minute sessions instead of 50-minute sessions, running therapy or support groups that are more inexpensive than individual services, or investing in the training of intern-level practitioners who see patients at a lower cost. Financial accessibility is a real concern, particularly among those lower in socioeconomic status. Many patients understandably prefer to use their insurance plans for services, but many specialized health care providers are out of network, and these patients are unable or unprepared to navigate out-of-pocket claims or reimbursement systems. Furthermore, some patients may find that their health care plan does not sufficiently cover their needs. Giving up can feel easier than navigating these issues, especially when wait times to speak to an insurance agent or to get an appointment with a therapist are long.

Bear in mind that household income may not be the only cost-related barrier. Women who are experiencing domestic violence or financial abuse, facing complexities related to immigration, struggling with language barriers or refugee status, or encountering strong anti-mental health messaging within their communities may only be able to utilize mental health care services offered at low or no cost (Ranjii et al., 2019). While you always want to keep your professional boundaries in mind, we encourage you to think creatively about developing opportunities for mothers to receive equitable mental health care support. Doing so is important to counteract the disappointment, grief, and frustration they are likely feeling. It is also crucial to lessen any feelings of hopelessness, which can exacerbate the very symptoms for which a mother is seeking help.

Another helpful avenue to overcome logistical barriers is telehealth services, which have become a lifeline for perinatal mothers. For many mothers, telehealth can ease logistical obstacles related to childcare, transportation, and ability to travel (Yang et al., 2019). It also increases privacy for women who may not be ready to disclose to loved ones that they are seeking professional help, and it provides specialized care options for women who live in geographically isolated or underserved locations (Marcin et al., 2016). For mothers with infants in the neonatal intensive care unit (NICU) or who are limited by their own physical needs, such as prenatal bedrest—both of which are risk factors for perinatal mood and anxiety disorders (Levinson et al., 2022; Sundaram et al., 2014)—telehealth provides them a means by which they can receive essential support. While there is little doubt that in-person therapy adds a dimension that is limited with teletherapy, we strongly feel that *any* opportunity to connect with a professional for support far outweighs the challenges of telehealth.

Finally, we want to acknowledge that perinatal mothers are not alone in their difficulty identifying potential resources for support. Doctors, midwives, and nurses who work within the reproductive mental health sphere are often unsure what resources are available to their patients, which becomes a disincentive to provide referrals. Therefore, it would behoove you to take the time to notify local OB/GYN and midwifery offices, doulas, lactation consultants, and other providers of the support services you offer. Make it easy for them to pass along your contact information to patients. Also consider how you can use digital resources to advertise your services directly to mothers.

Patient Worksheet

OVERCOMING LOGISTICAL BARRIERS

Sometimes there are logistical barriers that can get in the way of your ability to access the support you need. These barriers can include, but are not limited to, financial limitations, lack of childcare, and limited availability of services in your area. You might find that some of these barriers can be addressed with thoughtful planning, research, and creative thinking.

What logistical barriers are standing between you and potential social supports?

- ☐ Financial limitations
- ☐ Lack of access to childcare
- ☐ Limited availability of services in my area
- ☐ My child's needs (such as adherence to nap and feeding routines)
- ☐ Lack of local social supports
- ☐ Unsure of where to find support
- ☐ Other: _____
- ☐ Other: _____

To help you brainstorm potential solutions to these barriers, read through the following problem-solving tips and put a check mark by any you'd like to consider.

Tips for Problem-Solving Childcare

- ☐ Consider asking a neighbor or friend with children if they would like to share the cost of childcare by finding a childcare provider who would be willing to care for both of your children at the same time. This can reduce the cost of childcare, and your baby can benefit from increased social interaction.

- ☐ Instead of hiring a babysitter or nanny, think about looking for a teenage "mothers' helper" or a "parents' helper." Younger teens who might not be quite old enough to babysit alone but who enjoy playing with children are wonderful helpers when you need another set of hands in your home. (For example, younger teens can play with or watch your children while you

46 Copyright © 2023 Hilary Waller and Karen Kleiman, *The Perinatal Patient*. All rights reserved.

- attend a telehealth therapy session in another room of the house. Set boundaries for the helper and let them know when and how they can interrupt you for help if it is needed.)

- Explore the option of a babysitting cooperative with other parents in your community (one might exist already). In a babysitting co-op, parents exchange babysitting services with each other instead of exchanging payment for childcare.

Tips for Problem-Solving Financial Barriers

- Connect with the "Buy Nothing Project," which encourages participants to share various goods and services with neighbors. The sharing and giving of baby-related items is particularly popular. You can find a local group via social media or the Buy Nothing website (buynothingproject.org).

- Look into frugal parenting groups as well as secondhand shops and yard sales. These options allow parents to receive or purchase baby items at low or no cost, freeing finances in your budget to cover costs associated with receiving the support you need.

- Many professionals offer free or lower cost services to mothers or families with financial needs. Ask your providers if they offer any reduced rates, therapy groups, or support groups that may be less expensive than individual services, or services provided by an intern who is training in the perinatal specialty. While it can be difficult to ask for financial help, this is a commonly asked question that maternal care providers are used to answering.

- Some providers (especially those who specialize in perinatal health) accommodate the presence of young children in their practices, particularly babies. It is very common for new mothers to bring their babies along with them to appointments. Ask your provider questions, like whether their office is stroller-accessible, breast and bottle-feeding friendly, or equipped with a place to change diapers.

Tips for Problem-Solving Limited Access to Specialists

- Mental health care providers are licensed to work with patients located anywhere in the state (or states) in which they are licensed. Many clinicians are licensed in more than one state, and many provide telehealth services. When searching for a provider, consider searching your entire state rather than limiting your search to your geographical area. You can also search for specialized providers via centers that train clinicians to work with perinatal patients. The Postpartum Stress Center and Postpartum Support International are just two of the many perinatal training centers that allow specialists who train with them to advertise their services on their websites.

☐ Do not discount the power of word of mouth. As isolating as motherhood feels, remember that you are not alone in your community looking for support. Try asking neighbors or community members with older children how they found support when their children were small. Crowdsourcing via social media can be a very helpful way to discover lesser-known options. You can also crowdsource anonymously in many social media groups by asking a group administrator to post on your behalf.

After checking off potential solutions, choose a solution you'd like to try first. Then use the space here to create steps for following through with the solution and consider who may be able to help you take these steps.

_____
_____
_____
_____
_____
_____
_____
_____

Sometimes the hardest part of overcoming a barrier is asking for the help you need to follow through. How are you feeling about needing to ask for support?

_____

_____

_____

_____

_____

_____

Who or what can help you manage the feelings you are having so that you are able to ask for the support you need?

_____

_____

_____

_____

_____

_____

Emotional Barriers

A perinatal woman's strong desire to retreat when she is feeling out of control and exceedingly vulnerable is understandable. For mothers who try hard to preserve an image of perfection, or even almost perfection, disclosing how badly help is needed can feel humiliating or terrifying. There are several negative beliefs associated with help-seeking—such as the belief that mothers who seek help are weak, unfit, or inept—which can perpetuate the secrecy of emotional pain during the perinatal period and leave mothers to continue suffering in isolation. It should come as no surprise that emotional barriers are some of the most significant hindrances to women's ability to develop and utilize support during the perinatal period (De Sousa Machado et al., 2020).

Some of the most common themes that underlie these emotional barriers include:

- Guilt related to consuming resources like time and money
- Fear of discrimination, judgment, or competition from potential support people
- Fear of disappointing others due to failure to fulfill expectations for how mothers "should" feel, behave, and present
- Feeling misunderstood and further isolated by potential social supports, some of whom may not be struggling (or have no experience) with symptoms of a perinatal mood and anxiety disorder
- Fear that she could be perceived as incompetent or unfit as a mother and be separated from her baby

To help patients recognize and overcome these emotional barriers, you can use the following *Overcoming Emotional Barriers* worksheet, which is designed to help patients break through their resistance to seeking help and find the courage to ask for support during times of need. If you are not a mental health care provider, we encourage you to use this worksheet to help mothers problem solve in the present. If you are a mental health care provider, we encourage you to include both short- and long-term goals associated with overcoming emotional barriers into your treatment plans, regardless of your therapeutic modality.

For example, a short-term goal may focus on helping a patient ask her neighbor to drive her older children to school while she is recovering from birth. Long-term goals may involve addressing deeply held core beliefs and cognitive distortions that drive the underlying pain associated with help-seeking. Some of these beliefs may significantly predate parenthood, or even adulthood, and take some time to resolve. We encourage you to reinforce that motherhood can bring up feelings of guilt, shame, and fear associated with help-seeking and that a mental health care provider can help patients work through these emotions.

Above all, make sure to recognize and validate women's distress and perceived reluctance to ask for help. In the throes of a perinatal mood and anxiety disorder, finding the nerve to ask for help can feel exhausting. Nevertheless, social supports can provide a needed lifeline that makes it worth all the effort.

Patient Worksheet

OVERCOMING EMOTIONAL BARRIERS

Sometimes, mothers do not realize that they need help or that they are having a hard time. Other times, mothers are very aware that they are struggling, but their feelings of fear, guilt, and shame prevent them from reaching out to others. Just like all skills, asking for help takes practice. The first step is to become aware of warning signs that indicate you could use some support and to then explore where your resistance to help-seeking is coming from. Then you can explore potential tools for overcoming this resistance.

Signs That Help Is Needed

☐ You are having a hard time making decisions.

☐ You are not sure where to turn.

☐ You feel alone or isolated.

☐ You feel overwhelmed, drained, or depleted.

☐ You think things like, *I am a bad mother* or *I should know how to do this.*

☐ You are wondering things like, *Can I do this?* or *Am I doing this right?*

☐ You are feeling exhausted and sleep deprived.

Recognize Your Sources of Resistance

What beliefs do you have about mothers who need help?

_____

_____

_____

_____

What did your own caregivers or parents teach you about asking for help when you were growing up? How do these early life lessons impact your view of help-seeking today?

_____

_____

_____

_____

Have you had difficulty asking for help in the past? If so, with what sorts of things?

_____

_____

_____

_____

What are you afraid might happen if you ask for help? What emotions come up for you when you think of asking for help?

_____

_____

_____

_____

Tips for Overcoming Resistance

On a separate piece of paper, write down the advice you would give a friend in need of help. Now write down this advice again in the space below, but address the note to yourself. Read and reread it. Notice if you feel a shift in your belief system.

_____

_____

_____

Create a self-compassion statement to soothe any difficult emotions you may be experiencing in response to your need for help, such as guilt, shame, or disappointment. An example of this type of affirmation is, "May I accept that all mothers need help sometimes and that asking for the help I need is the right thing to do for myself and my baby."

_____

_____

_____

Identify a past situation when asking for help was beneficial, even if it was difficult. What enabled you to get the help you needed then? Alternatively, can you remember a time when you wish you had reached out for help but did not? What were the consequences of this choice?

_____

_____

_____

_____

Make a list of the different types of help you need and a second list of people who might be able to assist in each area. Next, sort these lists by difficulty level, starting with the easiest person to ask for help *or* the type of help that will be easiest to access. Finally, contact the most accessible person on your list or start taking the steps needed to complete the easiest item on your list.

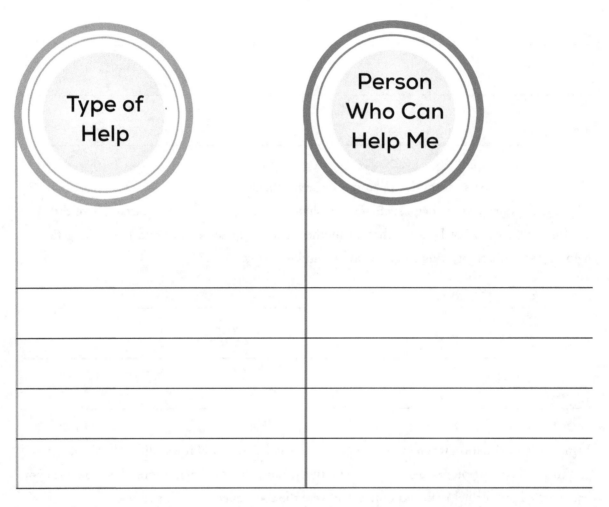

Create some sample help request templates. These templates can be useful when you can't find the words to use when asking for help. Try using one or a few phrases below as a guide:

- I am struggling with _____ right now. Can you find time to help me with that by _____?
- I need some advice about _____. Can we talk about that soon?
- I have a hard time asking for help, so this is tough for me, but are you able to help me with _____?
- I so appreciate everything you have done for me. One thing I am still figuring out is how to _____. Is that something you could help me with? If not, can you help me think of someone who can help out with that?

Parental Leave

Parental leave, or the lack thereof, is another factor relevant to social support that can weigh on the minds of new parents. Although parental leave benefits vary from country to country, the United States is the only developed nation without a paid leave requirement for families with newborns. Vulnerable populations—such as those with inadequate housing, limited educational opportunities, and lack of insurance—are even more unlikely to receive any parental leave (Weber et al., 2018), which further underscores the amplified challenges that disadvantaged communities face. For many new parents, this lack of guaranteed leave can be a burden, as research underscores the importance of ample parental leave in promoting infant and maternal health for *all* new parents—gestational and non-gestational parents alike (Arnautovic & Dammann, 2022; Weber et al., 2018).

Parents who present to our offices commonly describe intense pressure, anxiety, and worry about the amount of leave that is available to them. During pregnancy, they dread scheduling appointments, ruminate on unexpected complications, and pray that they (or their other children) do not fall ill during this time so they can save their paid time off for the postpartum period. If pregnancy or postpartum complications do arise, such as maternal bedrest or an infant admission to the NICU, mothers must revisit any maternity leave plans they have made as their paid hours off quickly tick by. In some cases, parents are only entitled to a few weeks of paid vacation or sick time, which forces them to take unpaid time off to adjust to new parenthood.

For many families, this type of extended leave is unaffordable, so mothers return to work after just a few weeks postpartum. This shortened leave time can lead to pervasive worries that the mother-baby bond will be negatively affected, which reinforces women's negative cognitions about themselves. Mothers wonder if their babies will forget them or think they are bad mothers for returning to work so early on. For mothers with perinatal mood and anxiety disorders, the situation becomes further complicated, as they must decide whether to return to work before their symptoms fully resolve or navigate taking a medical leave of absence (should that option be available to them)—a process that can be confusing and leave mothers feeling vulnerable and exposed.

In working with new parents, it is critically important for providers to understand what benefits are available to their patients and to gain awareness of what benefits are lacking. For example, in the United States, some companies grant new parents 16 or more weeks of paid parental time off. Other parents only receive benefits via the Family and Medical Leave Act (FMLA), which is a federal law that protects the job security of new parents and mandates that employers (meeting certain criteria) provide 12 weeks of unpaid family and medical leave to employees (who must also meet eligibility criteria). But for many new parents, taking unpaid leave is simply not an option financially, so they must use any available sick, personal, or other accrued paid time off to give birth and care for themselves and their newborns.

As a provider, we encourage you to empower your patients to advocate for themselves and to request that their needs be met, though we recognize that new parents may be significantly limited by company policy and human resources requirements and expectations. In companies with a lot of flexibility, you might encourage parents to have open conversations with supervisors about their schedules, routines, and benefits. In more highly regulated companies, you can help parents think creatively about maximizing benefits that are already offered. For example, some of our patients spread their paid time off out over a period of weeks by scheduling a weekly day or half day off to be with their children. Others have been able to negotiate a paced return to work at the end of their parental leave, returning for half days before full days. For parents whose workplaces are entirely inflexible or deny creative requests, your empathy, validation, and expressions of support can go a long way to soften the blow of these inequities and losses. **Sometimes, it can be one sentence, said the right way, by the right person, at the right time: "Returning to work before you are ready can really feel devastating and unfair. We can take as much time as you need to process this transition."**

Cultural Dynamics Relevant to Social Support

As we've been discussing, women often feel solely responsible for developing their own social support systems, particularly within the culture of American individualism, where prescribed social support is less common. Indeed, compared to other nations, the United States lags in its standards for supporting new mothers during this role transition. This disparity is especially true for mothers living in disadvantaged communities characterized by a lack of resources. Socioeconomic status is predictive of many physiological, psychological, and social outcomes, including maternal and infant mortality, food insecurity, substance use, chronic stress, and mental health diagnoses. Perhaps most salient is the association between socioeconomic status and hope, as individuals from lower socioeconomic backgrounds engage in less hopeful thinking (Lei et al., 2019). When access to financial resources, health care, basic necessities, and optimism are lacking, the pressure of parenthood is amplified tremendously, rendering the need for strong and secure social support systems even more imperative.

In contrast to the United States, many collectivistic cultures honor the transition to motherhood with practices that are intended to provide various types of social support to new mothers. For example, in many European countries, home visits are provided during the immediate postpartum period by health care providers who follow up on the mother and baby's physical and emotional well-being. In Eastern countries such as China, Japan, Taiwan, and Malaysia, prescribed confinement practices require new mothers to prioritize rest and physical recovery (Corrigan et al., 2015). Mothers are often cared for by family members, community elders, and professional maternity care givers and healers who provide emotional, logistical, and informational support.

While having these forms of support embedded within the culture can alleviate the pressure that mothers feel to seek out their own support system—normalizing the act of giving and receiving support—some mothers may feel obligated to participate in these rituals and may even feel stifled by community or family expectations. In these cases, rituals intended to support a mother's healing become a source of stress, family conflict, and isolation. Women experiencing these feelings can feel alienated from peers or unentitled to express their personal needs. In chapter 6, we explore some of these rituals in detail and discuss how they can inform women's expectations for motherhood.

A Note on the Provider's Role

Providers occupy a private and intimate space with perinatal women. In our work at The Postpartum Stress Center, women have told us that they are most inclined to disclose their distress to their providers, more so than their mothers, partners, or closest friends. That means that, as a provider, you are often a new mother's first point of contact, uniquely positioned to soften her resistance or hesitation and empower her to seek out additional help. However, there is often a lack of clarity around what role different providers should play in this domain (Leahy-Warren et al., 2018), which can lead to confusion about what constitutes best practice. We believe the most important thing providers can do is develop an empathic and collaborative relationship with their patients, as patients will be more likely to follow up with longer-term, enduring care if their early contacts with you endorse this process (Bauer et al., 2017). The impact of *perceived* support is powerful in this regard, as perinatal women who view their support systems as consistent, individualized, and available experience fewer depressive symptoms than those who feel more isolated (Leahy-Warren et al., 2018).

Providers should be especially mindful of their role in offering *appraisal* support, which involves giving mothers positive feedback on their parenting skills to boost their self-image and self-evaluation. As you keep in mind a new mother's longing for approval, think about how comforting and reassuring it might feel for her to hear you reflect that she is doing well. Interestingly, appraisal support during pregnancy can foster the development of self-confidence, ultimately increasing confidence in a mother's parenting skills (Renbarger et al., 2021).

Keep in mind, though, that mothers who receive this form of support through the lens of a perinatal mood and anxiety disorder can find that it triggers depressive emotions, intrusive thoughts, or distorted thinking. For example, if you tell a mother with a mood or anxiety disorder that she is a good parent, she is likely to question your authenticity. She might think you are lying, trying to make her feel better, or misunderstanding that she is absolutely convinced of her failure. When giving mothers appraisal support, try pointing out something specific that she is doing to bolster your feedback, such as "I notice that when you held your baby that way, she calmed down quickly. She seems to feel so comforted by you." You might help her process appraisal feedback by following up with a question, such as "What is it like for you to know that I think you are a good mother?"

Finally, we encourage you to consider facilitating support groups for families with babies and young children. It's worth noting that some mothers worry that attending such a group might reinforce their feelings of failure and inadvertently reinforce their tendency to compare themselves to others. They may also find group support more intimidating or anxiety-provoking than individual support. At The Postpartum Stress Center, we ask the therapist facilitating the group to contact each interested participant individually as part of the group registration process. This gives the facilitator a chance to provide insight about group dynamics, such as how long the group has been meeting, what it is like when a new participant joins, and how group members interact. Patients report feeling comforted and encouraged by this outreach and appreciate having a chance to ask their questions and to meet the group leader.

For providers interested in facilitating support groups for new mothers, the following handout provides recommendations for establishing groups that break down social expectations of perfection and create safety for genuine interactions between mothers.

Underrepresented Groups and Social Support

Although we have discussed many topics related to the issue of social support in this chapter, we want to recognize that there are unique circumstances faced by members of underrepresented communities. Today, babies are born into incredibly diverse environments that may include LGBTQIA+ parents, cohabitating parents, interracial parents, same-sex parents, single parents, trans parents, and more—our minds are opening widely to what a typical family looks like.

With so many different family presentations, each one deserving of resources that meet its unique needs, it becomes harder to ensure that appropriate social support programs will be available. Furthermore, although Americans as a whole are becoming increasingly supportive of multiculturalism and diversity, the reality is that judgment, stigma, and oppression remain prominent in many communities and groups (Thomas, 2020). The emotional burden and trauma of disenfranchisement, systemic bias, and a history of oppression can reinforce the isolation and marginalization of these underrepresented groups, further hindering access to much needed support.

While it is not our expectation that every provider reading this book will develop expertise in every type of family system presentation, we do implore providers to become aware of their own internal biases and to be knowledgeable about local resources for parents who do not comprise a "traditional" family structure. If no resources exist in your area, perhaps you might create some. Doing so is important to not only develop cultural competence, but also cultural humility. Chapter 9 explores internal bias, and its relevance specifically to perinatal work, in more depth.

Cultural Competence vs. Cultural Humility

Cultural competence and cultural humility are two related, albeit different, concepts. Cultural competence involves understanding the ways in which other cultures differ from your own, which enables you to better understand and connect with patients with diverse cultural backgrounds (DeAngelis, 2015). Cultural humility is a distinct concept that requires you to set aside your own expectations, preferences, and beliefs to gain a deep appreciation for each patient's perspective and worldview (Lee & Haskins, 2020). To do so, you must be curious and eager to learn about other cultures, which requires self-reflection and a willingness to explore your implicit and explicit biases. **We cannot overstate the importance of increasing your understanding of reproductive issues in diverse racial, national, and ethnic communities, as well as across the gender spectrum, when conducting reproductive mental health work.**

Provider Handout

NEW MOMS GROUPS

If you would like to offer support groups for new moms during the perinatal period, not only will you need to make decisions about what type of group you will offer, what you might ask people to pay, and when your group might meet, but you may also wish to consider the following questions as you plan for your group.

Logistical Questions

- How will you determine eligibility for the group? Are you a therapist who is equipped to hold a therapy group (perhaps meeting the needs of more severely symptomatic women) or would you prefer to offer a support group?
- If you offer a support group, how will you establish boundaries around what content is appropriate to share in the group? For example, it can be helpful to provide psychoeducation about intrusive thinking in motherhood and give mothers a chance to talk about their experiences, but, depending on your desired group dynamics and professional skillset, you may wish to limit discussions about the specific intrusive thoughts a mother is having.
- Will you accept the presence of babies in your group space? Until what age? Will babies who are crawling or walking be able to attend?
- Will your space be conducive for feeding babies via breast or bottle during meetings? What language will you use to encourage feeding? For example, saying, "Mothers are welcome to feed their babies" sends a different message than, "Breastfeeding is welcome!"
- Is your space stroller accessible?
- How can your group accommodate mothers who may not have childcare, transportation, or the financial means to attend?

Group Topics

If your group is topic driven, what topics might you incorporate? Groups conducted at The Postpartum Stress Center typically include:

- Psychoeducation on perinatal mood and anxiety disorders versus the baby blues

Copyright © 2023 Hilary Waller and Karen Kleiman, *The Perinatal Patient*. All rights reserved.

- Improving decision-making skills when feeling sleep deprived, overwhelmed, and uncertain
- Developing cooperation and communication skills so that partners can collaborate on decision-making
- Developing independence in the perinatal period
- Establishing priorities and boundaries
- Managing expectations
- Developing self-care routines
- Psychoeducation on infant emotional needs and infant play
- Cultural myths about motherhood
- Stress reduction techniques
- Strategies for increasing emotional intimacy with partners

Building a Safe Environment

- What ground rules can you establish to reinforce emotional safety in the therapeutic space?
- How will you respond to comparisons that may arise between group members?
- How will you respond to questions about parenting styles and strategies that may arise within your groups?
- What if your participants' parenting decisions differ from your own parenting decisions?
- What if parents in the group disagree on a parenting strategy?

Resources for Mothers in Need of More Support

- Do you have additional resources available for moms who may require referrals? For example, to:
    - Therapists who specialize in perinatal care
    - Lactation consultants
    - Pelvic floor physical therapists
    - Other maternal care providers

Section II

Perinatal Mood and Anxiety Disorders

When Perinatal Patients Suffer Too Much

CHAPTER 4

"What Are Perinatal Mood and Anxiety Disorders?"

When we talk with women about what they fantasized becoming a mother would feel like, most expected to feel overwhelmed in both wonderful and frightening ways. This expectation is reasonable. Becoming a mother does welcome women into a world of both extraordinary wonder and intense fear. However, few mothers expect to feel more disappointed, helpless, and hopeless that anyone else could possibly understand, let alone help. In turn, when the fear that something is wrong descends upon them, mothers frantically look for ways to help themselves—desperate to maintain the illusion that everything is okay. At first, this is not a bad thing. Mild perinatal distress responds well to self-help and social support. However, when the distress becomes too intense and prolonged, it can move into the realm of perinatal mood and anxiety disorders.

In this chapter, we explore perinatal mood and anxiety disorders in detail and provide insight into the unique symptom profile for each type of disorder. We also discuss how a patient's perinatal state adds complexity and urgency to diagnosis. For example, we discuss what constitutes a perinatal mental health emergency and how to handle these emergencies with sensitivity and care. If you are a provider, consider how you will convey the information in this chapter to your patients. You may provide them with relevant worksheets, develop talking points or a class from its content, or even decide to share this chapter in its entirety.

If you are a mother, you may begin to recognize yourself in these pages. If that is the case, know that the worksheets and handouts we have provided here can help you cope with any feelings you may be experiencing. You may also decide that now is the right time to seek further support. As a reminder, this book does not serve as a diagnostic tool, but it does aim to empower you to talk to someone who can help you sort out what you are experiencing.

Defining Perinatal Mood and Anxiety Disorders

Perinatal mood and anxiety disorders are defined by the presence of mood- and anxiety-related symptoms that meet the threshold for a diagnosis of a mood or anxiety disorder during the pregnancy or postpartum period. The term *mood disorder* specifically refers to an overall disruption to one's emotional state.

Depression and bipolar disorders are examples of mood disorders. While an *anxiety disorder* can certainly impact and disrupt mood as well, its defining feature is excessive fear or worry. Generalized anxiety disorder (GAD) and panic disorder are both examples of anxiety disorders.

Bear in mind that when we refer to perinatal mood and anxiety disorders, we are referring to:

- Perinatal depression
- Perinatal anxiety
- Perinatal obsessive-compulsive disorder (OCD)
- Perinatal panic disorder
- Perinatal posttraumatic stress disorder (PTSD)
- Perinatal bipolar disorder
- Postpartum psychosis

As a reminder, the baby blues do *not* reflect a perinatal mood and anxiety disorder. The baby blues are a normal occurrence in the immediate postpartum period in which women experience anxious feelings or overall emotionality. These symptoms are transient, lasting only a few hours or days during the first two weeks postpartum.

It is important to keep in mind that perinatal-specific diagnoses do not appear in diagnostic manuals, so practitioners must apply a general mood or anxiety disorder diagnosis while noting that the disorder's onset is in the perinatal period. It is therefore crucial that providers be aware of the more general diagnostic criteria *and* the nuances of presentation in the perinatal period. For example, patients with perinatal depression often present in a particularly agitated state, but since this disorder does not appear with its own unique diagnostic criteria in the DSM, patients may be misdiagnosed (perhaps with an anxiety disorder) or underdiagnosed, (perhaps with an adjustment disorder).

The *Perinatal Diagnostics* handout on the next page outlines some of the diagnostic features for each mood and anxiety disorder (versus the baby blues or postpartum stress syndrome) and is annotated with perinatal-specific detail. We have also included "at a glance" fact sheets throughout this chapter for each of the perinatal mood and anxiety disorders that will be helpful for both providers and for patients to review.

Provider Handout

PERINATAL DIAGNOSTICS

Baby Blues

Baby blues are considered a normal part of postpartum adjustment. The blues are understood to be related to hormonal shifts following delivery, affecting up to 85% of new mothers (Rai et al., 2015). Transient periods of sadness, alternating with joy, are typical. Other manifestations include frequent crying, anxiety, fatigue, and irritability. The blues are self-limiting and require no treatment. Symptoms generally appear within three to four days after delivery, peak on the seventh postpartum day, and remit spontaneously within two to three weeks. For most women, the blues are uneventful and fleeting. There is, however, some evidence suggesting that women who experience the blues are at risk for postpartum depression (Moyo & Djoda, 2020).

- **Differential diagnosis tip:** The blues do not interfere with maternal functioning. If emotional vulnerability lasts beyond two to three weeks postpartum, it is not the blues.

Postpartum Stress Syndrome

Postpartum stress syndrome is another term for an adjustment disorder, and it presents when a mother struggles to get through the day with persistent distress that does not resolve with reassurance or self-help measures. She may feel consumed by feelings of anxiety and self-doubt and feel pressure to be the perfect mother who is always in control during this life transition. If left unsupported, postpartum stress syndrome can lead to perinatal depression.

- **Differential diagnosis tip:** Symptoms of distress are pervasive but do not meet diagnostic criteria for a major depressive episode or anxiety disorder.

Perinatal Depression

Perinatal depression is an affective mood disorder presenting with symptoms similar to the baby blues. However, symptoms of depression are more disruptive and persist beyond the first two to three weeks following delivery. Onset is usually within the first three months postpartum. To an untrained eye, symptoms of perinatal depression can be difficult to distinguish from "normal" postpartum conditions associated with being a new mother. Symptoms, which can emerge any time during the first postpartum year, might include:

- Insomnia
- Significant changes in appetite
- Moderate to severe anxiety with scary and obsessive thoughts
- Weepiness
- Feelings of inadequacy
- Irritability or anger
- Hopelessness
- Suicidal thoughts
- Difficulty functioning
- Difficulty concentrating
- Loss of pleasure

It should be noted that a high number of women report feeling depressed during pregnancy, which is now believed to be a major risk factor for postpartum depression.

The release of the DSM-5 brought both good news and not-so-good news regarding perinatal depression. The good news is that perinatal depression, now referred to as peripartum depression, is officially recognized for the first time, expanding criteria to include the important fact that depression can begin during pregnancy. This diagnosis is made when someone meets criteria for major depressive disorder during the postpartum period, which is clarified with the specifier "with peripartum onset." This specifier is applied when the onset of mood symptoms occurs during pregnancy or within four weeks following delivery. Unfortunately, clinicians were hoping that this specifier would be extended to six months after delivery, but this did not happen. Furthermore, there are no *distinct* diagnostic criteria for perinatal depression. Patients are simply diagnosed with major depressive disorder and given the specifier "with perinatal onset" if their symptoms occurred during pregnancy or within four weeks after childbirth.

- **Differential diagnosis tip:** A feature of perinatal depression that distinguishes it from most other depressive disorders is that it is marked by prominent anxiety. It is not uncommon for women with perinatal depression to have comorbid symptoms such as panic attacks, obsessions, compulsions, or psychotic features.

Generalized Anxiety Disorder

Generalized anxiety disorder (GAD) is marked by excessive worry. During the postpartum period, women report feeling tense and irritable, nervous in social situations, and preoccupied with uncontrollable worries related to the physical well-being of themselves and others, particularly the baby. They also commonly report a sense of impending doom. Frequently, there is an increase in physical symptoms as well, such as nausea, shakiness, blurry vision, insomnia, fatigue, restlessness, racing heart, and shortness of breath.

- **Differential diagnosis tip:** While worry is normal, women with generalized anxiety experience excessive, uncontrollable worries more of the time than not. These worries are pervasive and associated with significant emotional distress.

Obsessive-Compulsive Disorder

Obsessive-compulsive disorder (OCD) is characterized by obsessive and intrusive thoughts, images, or urges that may or may not be accompanied by compulsive behaviors. These unwanted thoughts seem to appear out of nowhere and are highly distressing. While women understand that any actions taken in response to these thoughts would be wrong, they are extremely agitated by the thoughts and worry that they may actually act on them. A diagnosis of OCD requires the presence of significant distress and impairment of a woman's ability to function.

- **Differential diagnosis tip:** Sometimes the boundary between excessive worry and obsessive thinking is indistinct. Often, a diagnosis of OCD is made when a woman's preoccupation with the intrusive thoughts becomes unequivocally disruptive.

Posttraumatic Stress Disorder

Posttraumatic stress disorder (PTSD) used to be classified as an anxiety disorder in previous editions of the DSM, though it is now listed as a trauma- and stressor-related disorder. Perinatal PTSD can arise when a mother experiences actual or threatened death, violence, or serious injury to herself or her infant. Witnessing such an event and reacting with horror, or feelings of helplessness, contribute to the definition of trauma. Women who experience trauma related to childbirth might experience nightmares, flashbacks, hypervigilance, irritability, and anxiety (Shuman et al., 2022).

- **Differential diagnosis tip:** The criteria for a diagnosis of PTSD includes direct or indirect exposure to a traumatic event, followed by symptoms in these four clusters: (1) intrusive thoughts, (2) avoidance of reminders associated with the trauma, (3) negative changes in thoughts and mood, (4) changes in arousal or reactivity.

Panic Disorder

Panic disorder manifests as distinct periods of intense fear and typically involves palpitations, sweating, chest pain, shortness of breath, dizziness, lightheadedness, numbness, and fear of dying or losing control (Beck, 2006). Most of the time, panic involves catastrophic misinterpretations of normal bodily sensations.

- **Differential diagnosis tip:** In contrast to GAD, in which women focus on the object of their worry, women with panic disorder become preoccupied with the panic *itself*. They fear having a panic attack and often change their behavior in an attempt to avoid having a future attack. Mothers with primary panic disorder or OCD do not describe a depressed mood and are able to enjoy their usual activities. On the other hand, women with perinatal depression may also present with symptoms of panic disorder or OCD (Sit & Wisner, 2009).

Bipolar Disorder

Bipolar disorder is a mood disorder characterized by periods of extreme highs (mania) and lows (depression). During pregnancy and the postpartum period, it can be difficult to diagnose bipolar depression unless a careful history of mood, sleep, and activity levels is collected. Bipolar I disorder is primarily distinguished by the presence of manic episodes (persistent elevated mood and energy), while bipolar II disorder is characterized by hypomanic episodes (a less severe form of mania). Although hypomania may not be associated with major impairment in functioning, it is not uncommon for it to be linked with a subsequent, significant depression.

Signs of perinatal bipolar disorder include hypomania, onset of depression immediately after delivery, uncommon symptoms (e.g., hypersomnia or an increase in appetite), racing thoughts, and an irregular response to antidepressant treatment (e.g., emergent mania, hypomania, or an unusually rapid or poor response; Sharma & Corpse, 2011). Women with a personal history or family history of bipolar disorder are at an increased risk of experiencing an episode during pregnancy and postpartum and should be carefully monitored. They are also at risk for postpartum psychosis.

- **Differential diagnosis tip:** Bipolar II disorder is often misdiagnosed as perinatal depression because its symptoms are often subtler than bipolar I disorder. Understandably, it may be difficult to differentiate normal postpartum elation from abnormal mood elevation. This is why screening is so important. Women should be asked if they feel as if their mind is racing, or if they have an unusual increase in energy despite a lack of sleep. They should be asked if they feel a decreased need for sleep, have experienced an abnormal surge of goal-directed energy (e.g., cleaning in the middle of the night), are spending more money than usual, or are feeling hypersexual. Due to the high prevalence of hypomania in the postpartum period, routine screening for symptoms of mania or hypomania should be considered (Freeman & Goldberg, 2022).

Postpartum Psychosis

Postpartum psychosis is the least common, but most serious, of the perinatal illnesses. It affects 1 to 2 per 1,000 women after childbirth and typically appears within the first month after delivery. It involves the presence of psychotic symptoms, such as:

- Delusions
- Hallucinations (often involving the infant)
- Loss of touch with reality
- Extreme agitation
- Confusion
- Inability to sleep for several nights
- Significant irritability
- Racing thoughts
- Rapid speech
- Mood swings
- Paranoia
- Suicidal and/or infanticidal thoughts

These symptoms necessitate aggressive medical treatment and, most likely, hospitalization.

Since psychosis is strongly associated with bipolar disorder, women with a personal or family history of bipolar disorder should be carefully assessed. Contrary to women with OCD, those suffering from psychosis rarely experience distress over their symptoms and *are* at risk to act on their delusions. Despite its severity, research indicates a good prognosis for most women who experience psychosis during the postpartum period (Arampatzi et al., 2022).

- **Differential diagnosis tip:** The clinical presentation of postpartum psychosis is severe, abrupt, and usually immediately following childbirth. Anxiety disorders and severe OCD should be considered as differential diagnoses, but typically you can obtain a history of OCD or OCD-like tendencies without a delusional component, making the differentiation clearer.

Provider Handout

SYMPTOMS OF PERINATAL MOOD AND ANXIETY DISORDERS

While each perinatal mood and anxiety disorder has unique features, there are common symptoms that can occur across the full spectrum of these disorders. The following list includes some emotional, physical, and cognitive symptoms that should stand out to providers, which can be used to educate mothers on perinatal mood and anxiety disorders and can also be used as part of routine screening.

Common Emotional, Physical, and Cognitive Symptoms

- Feelings of sadness, anxiety, overwhelm, fear, or frustration
- Feelings of regret, including regret about having a baby
- Feelings of hopelessness or helplessness
- Feelings of guilt, shame, or self-doubt
- Feelings of rage, anger, or irritability
- Feelings of dependence
- Worry or fear that disrupts sleep or makes it difficult to leave the house or be alone with the baby
- Intrusive anxious thoughts about herself or her baby (e.g., "What if I drop the baby down the stairs?")
- Difficulty with decision-making, concentration, memory, or maintaining daily routines
- Upset stomach
- Changes in appetite or eating habits
- More caffeine than usual in her diet
- More alcohol than usual in her diet
- Shortness of breath or tightness in chest
- Heart palpitations
- Racing heart
- Dizziness
- Feeling shaky or nervous
- Headaches
- Urges to isolate from family, friends, and social environments
- Loss of interest or enjoyment in previously pleasurable activities
- Thoughts that her family and/or baby would be better off without her
- Thoughts of harming herself
- The urge to run away
- Thoughts or fantasies of suicide

Common Statements Mothers Might Make

- "I am supposed to be happy and enjoying this time."
- "I am always worried now."
- "I am worried about how I am feeling."
- "Other people are worried about me."
- "Something really doesn't feel right."
- "I feel so out of control."
- "I feel so powerless over how I am feeling and thinking."
- "I'm so afraid everyone who loves me will abandon me."
- "I think I am a bad mother."
- "This must be how motherhood feels. I will always feel this way now."
- "I'm not sure if I love my baby."
- "I don't think my baby loves me."
- "I am afraid to leave my baby."
- "I am having scary thoughts about myself or my baby."
- "I am having scary thoughts about harming my baby."
- "I am scared to talk about how bad I am feeling."
- "I don't recognize who I am anymore."
- "I'm afraid I might not ever feel better."
- "I have never felt this bad before."
- "I wish I didn't have to be here anymore."

Perinatal Depression

Perinatal depression is one of the most common perinatal mood and anxiety disorders, yet it is arguably the most difficult for mothers and providers to recognize. It is commonly accepted that new mothers experience some degree of heightened emotionality that may feel, at times, like depression. What remains unclear to many is at what point these symptoms are indicative of a major depressive disorder and not a byproduct of the early postpartum baby blues or overall adjustment to motherhood.

Perinatal depression requires the presence of symptoms that fit DSM criteria for major depressive disorder. Patients must experience low mood and/or a loss of interest or pleasure in activities they used to enjoy (or feel they should enjoy). They must also experience a combination of other symptoms like changes in weight, sleeping patterns, and energy; difficulty concentrating; and frequent negative thoughts about themselves or their lives. When comparing these symptoms to the normal experience of a new mother, the similarities are strikingly obvious. The provider's role is to help a mother recognize when these symptoms are too intense, too frequent, and too long lasting, resulting in disruptions to her overall well-being and interfering with her ability to function throughout the day.

Paradoxically, mothers with perinatal depression tend to work hard to actively engage with tasks related to the baby or motherhood, and they also tend to report high interest in and love for their babies (though this is, of course, not *always* the case). Mothers tend to feel highly motivated to care for their infants, often driven by the fear of judgment by others or themselves, leading them to direct all of their available energy to infant care. Therefore, what may appear normal from the outside may, in fact, be a result of over-functioning or overcompensating in response to the depressive symptoms. One of the main challenges in recognizing perinatal depression is subjectivity around what it means to be *functioning* at this stage. Clinically, it is important to assess the degree to which a mother is meeting her basic needs, including:

- Accessing and ingesting an adequate amount of nutrition for herself and her baby
- Using infant safety equipment, like a car seat, properly
- Maintaining weather-appropriate dress for herself and her baby
- Sleeping an amount that is appropriate considering her baby's needs
- Engaging in basic hygienic routines, including self-care related to the physical impact of pregnancy, labor, and birth

A mother's subjective perspective provides important data for clinicians and should be explored when assessing the severity of symptoms. It is necessary to consider each mother's individual experience of "functioning," as this can vary from person to person. This can be addressed by simply asking how she feels she is functioning now compared to how she typically functions. The *Finding a New Normal: Daily Routine* worksheet in chapter 7 can help each mother determine what functioning means to her. This worksheet can also clarify for clinicians how wide the gap is between their patient's current state and how she would like to feel.

Keep in mind how the presence of a newborn baby, with whom the mother is developing a new relationship, adds complexity when assessing a mother's mood and interest level. While some mothers with perinatal depression show classic signs of depression, like disinterest in, poor attachment to, or lack of desire to care for their babies, many others report loving their babies and the experience of motherhood. Interestingly, in both circumstances, we observe that mothers tend to prioritize caring for their infants because of their strong desire to fill the role of the "good mother," leading them to divert all their available energy to ensuring that the baby's needs are met. Therefore, a mother with perinatal depression who has the energy to expertly change diapers, wash bottles, and play with her infant may not seem to be lacking in pleasure or interest. In many cases, mothers actually do find joy in their mothering experience and report that their relationship with their new baby is the one factor in their lives that is keeping them going.

Ultimately, we strongly believe that the key to accurate treatment and diagnosis lies at the intersection of a mother's ability to identify that she is in distress, her willingness to share this experience with someone who can help, and the expertise of the person to whom she is disclosing. And while we must caution that self-diagnosis without professional assessment and monitoring is not recommended, we do believe that women should trust their instincts if they think something doesn't feel right and follow up with professional guidance. We advocate for empowering mothers by teaching them to recognize what is normal and what is not. In fact, one of the main reasons we wrote this book was to provide necessary resources to guide mothers and increase their access to help.

Patient Handout

PERINATAL DEPRESSION AT A GLANCE

Prevalence: Approximately 10% of pregnant and 15% of postpartum women experience symptoms of clinical depression, with rates increasing for teenage mothers, women living in poverty, and BIPOC communities (Postpartum Support Virginia, 2023).

Onset: Any time during pregnancy or the first postpartum year

Symptoms:

- Anger, irritability, crying, sadness, guilt, shame, hopelessness
- Loss of interest or pleasure in previously enjoyable activities
- Loss of interest in or feelings of disconnection from baby
- Thoughts of harming self or baby
- Over-functioning to care for baby or under-functioning and inadequate ability to care for baby.

These symptoms must occur consistently and persistently over a period of two weeks.

A mother with perinatal depression might say, "I feel like I am living in a cave. I am up all night, it's always dark. When the sun comes up, somehow it still feels dark. But there I am—with a smile on my face, trying to zip up my jeans and get ready for story time. Nothing feels right, I don't feel like myself. I don't want the other moms to know I cried all the way here."

Risk factors:

- Personal or family history of depression, anxiety, or postpartum mood disorder
- History of premenstrual dysphoric disorder (PMDD) or premenstrual syndrome (PMS)
- Environmental stressors or other life adjustments, both positive and negative (new house, marital stress, financial changes, job changes)
- Pregnancy or birth complications
- History of fertility treatments
- Inadequate access to social and logistical support
- History of thyroid dysfunction
- Symptoms of depression during pregnancy

Unique perinatal features: Depression in the perinatal period often includes the presence of significant anxiety and can also feature panic attacks, obsessive thinking, compulsive behaviors, and a higher-than-expected level of functioning for someone with depression (often due to high motivation to care for one's baby).

These symptoms can further conceal some of the typical symptoms of depression, so depression in perinatal women may not look like depression at all. This underscores the importance of correct differential diagnosis and relevance of the clinical interview to gain understanding of cognitive symptoms of depression, like low self-esteem, negative intrusive thoughts, and suicidal ideation.

Perinatal Anxiety

All parents experience some degree of anxiety related to parenthood. The recognition that this vulnerable and precious infant is theirs to protect and raise is quite compelling. As a result, many parents lose sleep or feel stressed due to the anxiety about their children or their parenting from time to time. This worry is natural when navigating new parenthood. Like symptoms of depression, symptoms of worry, muscle tension, edginess, or sleep disturbance are all normal parts of this adjustment. However, also like depression, anxiety can quickly spiral out of control.

For example, a mother who worries about falling down the stairs while carrying her baby is likely to walk carefully as she descends each step. In this instance, the mother's anxiety is adaptive because it warns her of the danger of falling and causes her to react appropriately. However, for a mother with postpartum anxiety, this same worry is so intense that she may have difficulty bringing herself to take her baby up and down the stairs. She may experience freezing, panic, or intrusive thoughts that we refer to as *scary thoughts*, a term that Karen Kleiman and Amy Wenzel (2010) first coined in their book, *Dropping the Baby and Other Scary Thoughts*. In a paragraph that so precisely captures the inner world of an anxious mother's thoughts, they write:

> Scary thoughts refer to negative, repetitive, unwanted, and/or intrusive thoughts or images that can bombard you at any time. We gave the use of this term considerable thought after initial reservation from esteemed colleagues who wondered whether the phrase might minimize the gravity of the subject matter. There was concern that scary thoughts might conjure up cartoon-like images of a child's nightmare that would be unsuitable for the clinical seriousness of the experience, such as monsters under the bed. But monsters are indeed terrifying. They are gigantic, nasty beasts who are ugly and gross and scary. And yet, there is no real danger. There is only perceived peril. And this is precisely the point. (p. 8)

Importantly, research shows *no* correlation between the presence of anxiety-driven, scary thoughts (or, in clinical jargon, "ego-dystonic thoughts") and a mother's risk of harming her baby, even when the thoughts feature the mother herself intentionally inflicting harm on her baby (Collardeau et al., 2019). In fact, the prevalence of infant abuse among perinatal women who have unwanted intrusive thoughts of harming their infants is lower compared to levels of child abuse in the general population (Fairbrother et al, 2022). Therefore, the problem with unwanted intrusive thoughts is not the thoughts themselves, but the distress that the presence of these thoughts provokes within the mother. Our focus is to treat the distress she feels and to help her develop adaptive responses to these thoughts.

While perinatal anxiety can be debilitating, mothers with these symptoms are often experts at concealing the depths of their distress. This complicates a provider's ability to obtain accurate assessment and diagnosis, as does the fact that depression and anxiety often go hand in hand. It can be very difficult to discern the primary issue since perinatal depression typically presents with agitation and a high level of anxiety, while perinatal anxiety typically presents with negative thoughts about the self, suicidal ideation, and feelings of guilt and shame. Providing women with psychoeducation and building patient-provider trust are keys to helping mothers express how they are feeling so appropriate treatment can begin.

Patient Handout

PERINATAL ANXIETY AT A GLANCE

Prevalence: Approximately 1 in 5 pregnant and postpartum mothers develop perinatal anxiety (Fawcett et al., 2019), though it is believed that this number is largely underreported (Misri et al., 2015).

Onset: Any time during pregnancy or the first postpartum year

Symptoms:

- Persistent worry
- Racing thoughts
- Scary, unwanted intrusive thoughts
- Restlessness
- Sleep and appetite changes
- Feelings of dread
- Somatic or physical symptoms, like stomach upset, racing heart, and dizziness
- Social anxiety, including fear of going out

A mother with perinatal anxiety might say, "My head is spinning all the time, I can't stop it. I can't eat normally, and I dread going to sleep because no matter how tired I am, I keep getting up to check on the baby. My thoughts don't slow down, and half the time I can't figure out what I need. I lose track of when I have to eat, when I am tired, and even when I have to pee. I can't think of anything but the baby. I worry constantly."

Risk factors:

- Personal or family history of anxiety, depression, or postpartum mood disorder
- History of thyroid dysfunction
- Symptoms of anxiety during pregnancy that may not reach the level of severity associated with a diagnosis of a perinatal anxiety disorder

Unique perinatal features: In the perinatal period, anxiety often occurs alongside depressive symptoms, requiring careful assessment. The content of anxious thinking often centers on the physical well-being of the mother, baby, or other immediate family members. Health-related anxiety is common and can often impact a mother's willingness to access social support in the form of childcare or nurturing friendships for herself and her baby.

Perinatal Obsessive-Compulsive Disorder

Obsessive-compulsive disorder (OCD) is marked by recurrent and persistent distressing thoughts, known as obsessions, which a person seeks to relieve or avoid by engaging in a certain behavioral or mental activity. These acts, known as compulsions, are repetitive in nature and may take a long time to perform, sometimes to the point of functional impairment. For example, a person with OCD may experience repetitive, intrusive, anxiety-producing thoughts about contracting the common cold (obsession), leading them to behave in ways that they believe will mitigate their chances of contracting the cold virus (compulsion). The compulsive system they develop may be logically connected to the obsession (like repeated handwashing) or may be unrelated (needing to recite the lyrics to a specific song in their minds). It is important to note that individuals with OCD tend to be insightful about their obsessive thoughts and compulsive behaviors. They recognize their thoughts and behaviors as disruptive and in response only to excessive worry rooted in their own minds.

The perinatal stage is recognized as a period of increased vulnerability for the onset and exacerbation of OCD symptoms. Though more research is needed to fully understand the mechanisms underlying this increase in susceptibility, it is believed that the overwhelming and substantial increase in responsibilities associated with motherhood is an important part of the psychosocial picture (Fairbrother & Abramowitz, 2007). Like mothers with postpartum depression or anxiety, mothers with postpartum OCD have a strong tendency to worry about their babies, along with a fierce desire to protect them. It makes sense that most of the time, perinatal obsessions focus on the baby and on parenting. Obsessions about violence, injury, and harm befalling the baby are particularly common.

Some examples are:

- Fear for the baby's well-being ("What if the detergent I used poisons the baby?")
- Thoughts or images of accidentally harming the baby ("What if I drop this knife and it cuts the baby?")
- Thoughts or images of intentionally harming the baby ("What if I use this diaper to smother my baby when he's screaming during a diaper change?")
- Self-focused intrusive thoughts ("I don't think my baby loves me.")

The upsetting nature of these thoughts, and any accompanying visuals a mother might imagine, often cause extreme distress, as well as feelings of guilt and shame. Although these thoughts are not associated with any increased risk of harm coming to the infant, no matter how graphic or disturbing the thoughts are, they can still cause a mother to quickly spiral to the depths of low self-esteem. They not only disrupt a mother's thinking process, but they also interfere with her chance to experience any joy with her baby.

In response to these scary thoughts, women with perinatal OCD engage in compulsions that are intended to protect the baby from harm. Given that the imagined threat often includes the mother herself, compulsions may result in maternal avoidance, which reinforces her false belief that she is a bad, unworthy, or unfit mother. For instance, consider a mother who experiences obsessions related to infant feeding.

She may obsess over the formula or breastmilk being warmed to the correct temperature, resulting in compulsive behaviors like repeated temperature taking, throwing away and remaking the bottle, or even insisting that another person feed the baby so she can avoid feeding the baby herself.

Mothers with perinatal OCD have an exceptionally difficult time breaking the cycle of intrusive thinking and can feel tortured by the particularly graphic, gory, or frightening nature of these thoughts. Although symptoms of perinatal OCD are highly distressing for mothers, it is worth noting that it can be distressing for providers to encounter women with these symptoms as well. If you ever feel unsure or distressed by a patient's symptoms—OCD or otherwise—we encourage you to seek out additional supervision and training. The importance of provider self-care and professional development, particularly when working within the field of reproductive mental health, is discussed further in chapter 9.

Patient Handout

PERINATAL OBSESSIVE-COMPULSIVE DISORDER (OCD) AT A GLANCE

Prevalence: Approximately 2.9% of pregnant and 7% of postpartum mothers develop perinatal OCD (Fairbrother et al., 2021), a disorder that is largely misunderstood, misdiagnosed, and mistreated.

Onset: Any time during pregnancy or the first postpartum year

Symptoms:

- Intrusive thoughts that occur as images or ideas and often involve harm coming to the baby
- Repetitive actions or thoughts intended to neutralize the obsessive thoughts and alleviate anxiety
- Feelings of horror, guilt, or shame about having the obsessive thoughts
- Hypervigilance

A mother with perinatal OCD might say, "The thoughts I have are just too much. It started at bath time when I thought, *Oh my god, what if I push his head under the water?* But instead of just shaking that thought off, because I know I would never do that, I could suddenly see myself doing it—on purpose. I could hear what it would sound like if I drowned him and it's too much. I can't say it out loud. It was horrible, and now every time I see the bath, I panic. I can't even hold him if I'm in the bathroom without getting scared. I haven't been able to bathe him myself since."

Risk factors: Personal or family history of OCD.

Unique perinatal features: Perinatal OCD typically appears rapidly and soon after giving birth. It is characterized by highly distressing obsessions related to harming the infant, while non-perinatal OCD typically involves obsessions about contamination, cleanliness, or order, for example. Thoughts of harming the baby can reflect accidental or intentional harm and can significantly interfere with a mother's ability to comfortably interact with her baby. It's important to note that these thoughts of harm, whether accidental or intentional in nature, are not associated with any increase in risk to the baby among mothers with perinatal OCD (Fairbrother et al., 2022).

Perinatal Panic Disorder

Many people report having panic or even a panic attack at some time in their life. Though panic feels intense and paralyzing, panic symptoms usually only last a few minutes before they subside. Panic symptoms are associated with intense fear and discomfort, and they involve physical symptoms like shortness of breath, dizziness, heart palpitations, shaking, numbness, and chest pain. Often, people also experience racing thoughts and a fear that something terrible is happening to them, or that they are having a heart attack or dying.

People with panic disorder experience recurrent and sudden panic attacks, as well as intense worry about having another attack. In fact, the worry about having a future attack can become so disruptive that people are inclined to modify their lifestyles to avoid any panic-related triggers. For example, a mother who experienced a panic attack during story time at the library may avoid attending in the future out of fear that she will experience panic again in that setting. It is important to note that panic attacks can co-occur with any anxiety or related disorder, so it is important for people who report the presence of panic to be fully assessed for additional symptoms.

In addition, there is one glaring difference that distinguishes the experience of panic in the average person from the experience of panic in the perinatal woman: the presence of her baby. Symptoms of panic involve the entire body and can be very difficult to override. Imagine experiencing shakiness, dizziness, shortness of breath, and fear of death while trying to care for a dependent and vulnerable infant. Therefore, while any accompanying anxiety or depressive symptoms need to be addressed in women who are experiencing panic, helping them develop skills to cope with panic and increase self-regulation should be a priority. The *Coping with Perinatal Panic* worksheet in chapter 7 provides some recommendations to help mothers feel more capable in the face of panic while also considering their child's presence and needs.

Patient Handout

PERINATAL PANIC DISORDER AT A GLANCE

Prevalence: 9.9% of perinatal mothers experience perinatal panic (Misri et al., 2015).

Onset: Any time during pregnancy or the first postpartum year

Symptoms:

- Intense fear, dread, or nervousness
- Trembling
- Heart palpitation, numbness, and chest tightness

Symptoms may start gradually or suddenly and tend to increase in intensity for some time until they subside.

A mother with perinatal panic disorder might say, "When the panic happens, I feel like my world is collapsing or something terrible is happening to me. I don't know whether to hold the baby tighter or put the baby down in her crib so I can breathe more deeply. I don't know if I should call an ambulance or my partner or if I'm just going crazy. All I do know is that it is terrifying, and I am petrified it will happen when I am taking care of the baby alone."

Risk factors:

- Personal or family history of panic or anxiety
- Tendency to catastrophize uncomfortable physical sensations
- History of health-related anxiety
- Major stressful life event

Unique perinatal features: A panic attack is a very uncomfortable, vulnerable, and often scary experience. Having an attack while trying to care for a baby can be terrifying and reinforce depressive thoughts such as *My baby would be better off with a mother who didn't have panic attacks*. Therefore, it is important that mothers with perinatal panic disorder also be assessed for depressive thinking associated with the presence of panic.

Perinatal Posttraumatic Stress Disorder

Posttraumatic stress disorder (PTSD) occurs when a person has been impacted by real or threatened death, serious injury, or violence and experiences symptoms like flashbacks, intrusive memories, or nightmares related to the traumatic event for longer than a month. PTSD is also marked by avoidance of people, places, and things that serve as reminders of the trauma, as well as changes in mood and overall reactivity. People with PTSD may describe feeling frozen, petrified, hyperaroused, or panicky. It is important to note that to diagnose PTSD, a patient must experience a combination of these symptoms, but women who do not fit all diagnostic criteria may still experience symptoms of PTSD in the perinatal period. When this happens, it can still be valuable to consider use of treatment modalities that are indicated for PTSD, such as EMDR. It is also interesting to note that specifically during pregnancy, symptoms of PTSD can diminish or worsen (Muzik et al., 2016).

> ### EMDR for Perinatal Mood and Anxiety Disorders
>
> Eye movement desensitization and reprocessing (EMDR) is a therapeutic intervention developed for the treatment of PTSD in the 1980s by Francine Shapiro. As researchers and providers are becoming more aware of the need for empirically supported interventions for perinatal women, EMDR is receiving increased attention. It is becoming a recognized treatment not only for pregnancy, birth, and postpartum-related PTSD, but also for perinatal distress. In fact, the EMDR International Association (EMDRIA) now endorses trainings and workshops for providers who wish to learn more about perinatal patients and to adapt EMDR practices for this population. We recommended that providers visit www.emdria.org for more information on EMDR and perinatal patients.

In our experience, patients who present to our offices exhibit two pathways to PTSD in the perinatal period: (1) via a triggering of a historical traumatic experience, or (2) via a trauma related to the pregnancy, birth, or infant. Historical traumas can include previous sexual trauma, adverse childhood events, domestic violence, or other events associated with grief and loss. Many women we work with express surprise that their historical traumas are impacting them during the perinatal period and feel unprepared to revisit these events. Some report having received therapy in the past for the trauma and consider it resolved.

However, as clinicians, we are not surprised when a woman's earlier life trauma gets reactivated. The transition to motherhood typically involves physical pain, intrusion, and bodily discomfort, as well as emotional upheaval. We anticipate that women will revisit past experiences at this time of transformation. During this transition, women also have a proclivity to confront their self-worth and sense of responsibility. They may question their grit, perception of control, and feelings of safety. Indeed, the intensity and intimacy of the perinatal period can leave women feeling uniquely exposed. Our task is to help women fortify their social support systems and encourage them to engage in ongoing self-monitoring for any worsening symptoms so they can seek help when needed.

For many women with perinatal PTSD, the traumatic event can also occur during the pregnancy, birth, or postpartum period itself. While maternal and infant morbidity and mortality rates have decreased significantly with the advent of modern science and medicine (Loudon, 1992), many women still experience medical crises during pregnancy or the birthing process that are—or can be perceived as—life threatening. In the urgent and overstimulating atmosphere of labor and delivery, it can be hard for mothers to discern what is happening around them and to what extent they or their babies may be in danger. Therefore, a woman may register her birth as traumatic and develop symptoms of PTSD regardless of whether her birth is considered medically traumatic.

Indeed, a common misunderstanding, including among different types of providers, is that when a mother and baby leave the hospital in good physical health, the birth outcome is unquestionably a success. From a medical standpoint, this is the definition of success, but from a mental health perspective, if a woman perceived herself or her baby as being in danger *during the journey* to that outcome, she may be at risk for developing PTSD. Keep in mind that some women who experience medical trauma or life-threatening events during pregnancy or birth may not develop symptoms of PTSD. This does not mean that the experience itself was not traumatic; it simply means that their need for clinical intervention may be less urgent.

Finally, in the world of maternal mental health, we notice that women use the term *trauma* to describe a wide variety of experiences. When working with postpartum women, remember that births always involve physical or emotional pain, discomfort, and unfamiliar sensations that can be deeply impactful. For this reason, we believe that all mothers can benefit from having an opportunity to process their birth experiences by debriefing with a medical provider or simply sharing their birth stories. The *Making Sense of Birth Trauma* handout in chapter 7 can be helpful for mothers who are seeking outlets to share. It is very important to honor the experience of a new mother who perceives her birth as a traumatic event, regardless of if her birth included an event that her family, friends, or care providers perceive as traumatic, or if it meets diagnostic criteria for PTSD.

Patient Handout

PERINATAL POSTTRAUMATIC STRESS DISORDER (PTSD) AT A GLANCE

Prevalence: The prevalence of perinatal PTSD varies widely based on many variables and can range anywhere from 0 to 35% (Yildiz et al., 2017). Women who experienced their birth as traumatic may present with symptoms of posttraumatic stress but may not fit full criteria for PTSD.

Onset: During or after pregnancy (in response to triggers for a previous traumatic event) or during pregnancy, birth, or the postpartum phase

Symptoms:

- Intrusive re-experiencing symptoms (e.g., nightmares, flashbacks)
- Avoidance of places, people, or things that serve as reminders of the traumatic event
- Increased emotional or physical arousal
- Feelings of disconnection or detachment from reality

A mother with perinatal PTSD might say, "On the one hand, I am so grateful for my baby and am so thrilled to be her mother. But every time I look at her beautiful and perfect face, all I can see is the cord around her neck and her blue lips, and suddenly I'm back in the delivery room. She is dying, I'm begging for someone to tell me what's going on, and no one can hear me because they're rushing me into surgery. When I talk about it now, it feels like I'm in that room again."

Risk factors:

- Perinatal emergencies
- Unexpected events or outcomes in pregnancy or the labor and delivery process
- History of past trauma (e.g., sexual abuse, prior traumatic birth, adverse childhood experiences)

Unique perinatal features: Many perinatal women experience feelings of guilt in response to the feelings of horror, as well as the avoidant urges, that are common for people with PTSD. When a mother experiences or perceives her birth experience as disappointing or traumatic, it can reinforce the negative thoughts she has about herself or her role as a mother. It can also make her worry that she does not love her child. Even in the absence of other depression or anxiety symptoms, clinicians should carefully assess and provide treatment for these cognitive distortions.

Perinatal Bipolar Disorder

Although it is beyond the scope of this book to delve into the specific criteria for bipolar disorder, here we provide some overall guidance to help simplify a complex diagnosis. Generally, individuals with bipolar disorder experience a period of persistent, abnormally elevated mood (mania or hypomania) that is typically followed by a period of depressive symptoms. Individuals can be diagnosed with either bipolar I or bipolar II disorder, depending on the severity of the (hypo)manic symptoms. In bipolar I disorder, manic symptoms tend to cause more severe impairments in functioning (sometimes requiring hospitalization), whereas bipolar II disorders involve less intense hypomanic episodes that cause less disruption.

While bipolar disorder is a serious diagnosis that requires treatment in all populations, it is especially important to correctly diagnose and treat bipolar symptoms in the perinatal period. Mothers with bipolar disorder are at a higher risk for developing severe perinatal depression and other complications, such as suicidality or psychosis. We will discuss postpartum psychosis in further detail later in this chapter, but it is worth underscoring here that a personal or family history of bipolar disorder is a leading risk factor for postpartum psychosis. Due to the urgent and severe nature of postpartum psychosis, every effort should be made to mitigate risk factors with appropriate prevention and treatment. Some strategies to consider are outlined in the *Risk Management for Perinatal Bipolar Disorders* handout in chapter 7.

If you are a mother with a personal or family history of bipolar disorder, try not to feel disheartened by your medical history or by any discouraging messaging you receive about your treatment options during pregnancy or the postpartum period. It may take some extra effort on your part to ensure that you have the right care in place, but we encourage you to be hopeful and continue advocating for yourself.

Provider Handout

MEDICATION FOR PERINATAL WOMEN WITH BIPOLAR DISORDERS

Helping mothers prioritize mental health during pregnancy and the postpartum period is of the utmost importance. However, many medications that are often needed for the successful treatment of bipolar disorder have long been considered incompatible with pregnant and breastfeeding states. Understandably, pregnant women and their providers are wary of introducing anything into a mother's body that could potentially harm a developing and growing baby. In the past few years, however, a growing body of literature has explored the impact of various psychotropic medications on fetuses and infants. The field of reproductive psychiatry is expanding as well, and perinatal women now have access to prescribers who specialize in caring for women with psychiatric needs during pregnancy and breastfeeding.

While every individual case must be carefully and uniquely managed by perinatal specialists, Dr. Lee Cohen, the Director of the Ammon-Pinizzotto Center for Women's Mental Health at Massachusetts General Hospital, provides excellent guidance for providers. Dr. Cohen (2019) writes:

> "If there is a single critical guiding principle for the clinician when it comes to managing bipolar women during pregnancy and the postpartum period, it is sustaining euthymia. With the recent focus of the U.S. Preventive Services Task Force on prevention of postpartum depression, nothing is more helpful perhaps than keeping women with bipolar disorder well, both proximate to pregnancy and during an actual pregnancy. Keeping those patients well maximizes the likelihood that they will proceed across the peripartum and into the postpartum period with a level of emotional well-being that optimizes and maximizes positive long-term outcomes for both patients and families."

In other words, maintaining the mental wellness of people with bipolar disorder during the perinatal period is of critical and central importance. All providers should be mindful of this and aware of their scope of clinical expertise. We recommend that providers, both mental health providers and prescribers, who may be new or less experienced in the treatment of perinatal bipolar disorder and postpartum psychosis, receive clinical consultation, guidance, and supervision to ensure that their patients are receiving optimal care. Postpartum Support International's Perinatal Psychiatric Consult Line offers medical providers the opportunity to have a consultation with a reproductive psychiatrist at no cost. Call 1-877-449-4773 to schedule a consultation appointment and to learn more about this service.

Patient Handout

PERINATAL BIPOLAR DISORDER AT A GLANCE

Prevalence: Perinatal bipolar disorder occurs more rarely than postpartum depression or anxiety, affecting 2% to 8% of pregnant and postpartum women (Masters et al., 2019). Interestingly, studies show it, too, is commonly misdiagnosed. In fact, one study found that of the 14% of new mothers who were diagnosed with depression, 26% were actually experiencing symptoms of bipolar disorder (Gorrell, 2021).

Onset: The onset of bipolar disorder in women typically occurs between the ages of 12 and 36 years—the height of the reproductive stage. When bipolar disorder emerges during the perinatal period, symptoms tend to begin within the first two months of giving birth. Although some women experience their first bipolar event during the perinatal period, women with preexisting bipolar disorder are six times more likely to experience an episode, particularly during the first four weeks postpartum (Gilden et al., 2021). For this reason, each perinatal patient who presents for treatment at The Postpartum Stress Center is assessed for a history or symptoms of bipolar disorders using the Mood Disorders Questionnaire (Hirschfeld et al., 2000).

Symptoms:

- Bipolar I disorder involves a period of unusually high mood, agitation, impulsivity, grandiosity, rapid speech, and low need for sleep (mania) that is typically followed by an episode of severe depression.

- Bipolar II disorder includes all of these symptoms but also involves symptoms of hypomania that are less pronounced and disruptive.

A mother with perinatal bipolar disorder might say, "I am feeling great! Really! I hardly even need to sleep." Later, that same mother might report, "I haven't been able to get out of bed. I am exhausted. It takes every bit of energy to follow through with the simplest things. Everything is so hard."

Risk factors: Personal or family history of bipolar disorder or psychosis.

Unique perinatal features: It may be difficult to distinguish normal perinatal mood swings, which feature elation, irritability, agitation, and depressive symptoms, from symptoms of bipolar disorder. We believe it is best practice to screen all women for symptoms of bipolar disorder

Copyright © 2023 Hilary Waller and Karen Kleiman, *The Perinatal Patient*. All rights reserved.

whether or not they have a recognizable history of bipolar symptoms. Women with a history of bipolar disorder are extremely vulnerable, as between 50 and 70% will experience symptoms of their disorder during the postpartum period (Gorrell, 2021). These women are also *significantly* more likely to experience postpartum psychosis compared to women who have never been diagnosed with bipolar disorder (Clark & Wisner, 2018).

Postpartum Psychosis

Although postpartum psychosis is rare, it is the most severe and medically urgent of the perinatal mood and anxiety disorders. While symptoms of non-postpartum psychosis may not become immediately disruptive or obvious, the onset of postpartum psychosis occurs rapidly, typically within the first four weeks postpartum, during the period of the most dramatic hormonal change. Postpartum psychosis is an emergency that requires immediate medical intervention. While the consequences of having a psychotic episode during the perinatal period can be dire, the prognosis for this disorder is excellent when women receive adequate and skilled treatment.

The symptoms of postpartum psychosis are the same as psychosis experienced at any other time in life, including delusions; hallucinations; disorganized ideas, speech, and/or thought; sleep disruption; rapid speech and mood swings; and paranoia. However, psychosis in the postpartum period can also feature feelings of love toward the baby that wax and wane more so than in the general population, which complicates accurate diagnosis (Barnes & Brown, 2016).

Aside from the devastating impact an episode of psychosis can have on a new mother's confidence and sense of self, the most concerning feature of postpartum psychosis is the way a mother's instinct to protect and care for her baby can manifest in delusional thinking (O'Hara & Wisner, 2014). For example, a woman with postpartum psychosis may believe that her baby has been possessed by evil and that to save her baby, she must do something to relieve the baby of this evil. In the mind of the psychotic mother, whatever method she uses to save her baby from evil is an act of love and altruism, even if it is one that harms her baby. It is important to note that while only mothers with postpartum psychosis are at risk for harming their infants, the rates of infanticide during an episode of postpartum psychosis are shocking; left untreated, it can result in a 4 percent risk of infanticide (Hatters Freidman, 2009) and a 5 percent risk of suicide (Spinelli, 2021). Bear in mind that not all mothers with psychosis have fantasies that involve harming themselves or their baby. Mothers who have lost touch with reality can experience a wide range of delusions. Whether or not the content of delusional thinking or hallucinations is harmful, the symptom itself is reason for concern and requires immediate medical attention.

Two important ways to mitigate the risk of developing postpartum psychosis are to (1) carefully screen mothers for a history of psychosis or bipolar disorder, and (2) proactively develop a specific plan for postpartum intervention and care. This plan should specifically involve guidelines for protecting a new mother's sleep, starting from the very first night of motherhood. Sleeplessness is strongly associated with symptoms of psychosis, both as a symptom and a risk factor.

Patient Handout

POSTPARTUM PSYCHOSIS AT A GLANCE

Prevalence: Postpartum psychosis is rare, affecting 0.1–0.2% of new mothers, or 1 to 2 in every 1,000 deliveries (Sharma et al., 2022).

Onset: Within the first 4 weeks postpartum

Symptoms:

- Paranoid delusions and hallucinations that often focus on aspects of parenthood or the mother's baby or children
- Changes in speech patterns
- Disruption to sleep
- Abrupt changes in mood

A mother with postpartum psychosis might say, "The other day, the strangest things happened. I was changing the baby, and I suddenly saw this centipede on his shoulder. Then there were two—then three! I tried to brush them off, but they kept coming back, so I thought about pouring hot water or bleach on him because I couldn't bear the idea that there could be such a gross bug on him."

Risk factors:

- Personal or family history of psychosis
- Personal or family history of bipolar disorder

Unique perinatal features: Diagnosing psychosis in the perinatal period can be complicated by the waxing and waning of symptoms, meaning that symptoms may or may not be obvious to the assessing clinician or even to the patient's family members.

Increasing Level of Care in The Perinatal Period

For the majority of mothers we treat, a treatment plan that includes a combination of outpatient therapy, support groups, self-care, self-help, family support, and sometimes medication is sufficient. Many mothers can recover in the comfort of their homes, and certainly in the presence of their babies. As providers, it is a relief when mothers do not require inpatient hospitalization, particularly given that this often involves being separated from their babies.

Sometimes, though, the symptoms of a perinatal mood or anxiety disorder so severely impact a mother's functioning that her level of care must be escalated beyond the offices of a therapist or psychiatrist in an outpatient setting. In these cases, the benefits of temporarily being separated from her baby can outweigh the costs. When this occurs, a referral to an inpatient, partial hospitalization, or intensive outpatient program is warranted.

The presentations that benefit the most from these interventions typically include:

- **Profound functional impairment:** While many women with perinatal mood and anxiety disorders are high functioning, some experience symptoms that cause profound impairment, such as significant difficulty with decision-making, low or no motivation to participate in infant and childcare, inability to sleep, and very poor cognitive focus. For women who are unable to follow through with routine activities, consideration for a higher level of care may be warranted.

- **Suicidal ideation:** Mothers are extremely vulnerable to suicidal ideation and also to follow through on suicidal thoughts and urges during the perinatal period. Suicide is a leading cause of perinatal death, so any active or passive suicidal ideations should be taken seriously, including thoughts of disappearing or "just getting away for a while." The *Perinatal Suicide Assessment* at the end of this chapter provides more information on suicide assessment and suicidality in the perinatal period.

- **Postpartum psychosis:** As we've discussed, postpartum psychosis always requires urgent psychiatric evaluation and immediate medical attention that extends beyond typical outpatient treatment.

- **Substance use and domestic violence:** If a mother is struggling with severe substance abuse or domestic violence, it is important that therapists work as a team with case managers or other providers so any factors that could be threatening the mother or baby can be addressed.

In addition, it is important to consider how to talk to perinatal patients if their circumstances require an escalation of care. As providers, we clearly recognize that perinatal mood and anxiety disorders are not an indication of a mother's failure or incapacity, but many mothers *do* view these symptoms as evidence of their personal failings. This puts providers in the delicate position of reminding perinatal patients that they are, in fact, good mothers, while also juggling the responsibility of escalating their care and support—all while protecting the precarious balance of the therapeutic alliance. Providers can use the following *Talking with Patients about Escalations in Care* handout to maintain a strong therapeutic alliance when having these conversations, potentially softening a mother's resistance to necessary interventions that may leave her feeling exposed and punished.

Provider Handout

DISCUSSING ESCALATIONS IN CARE WITH PATIENTS

Few things strike terror in the heart of a perinatal mother like the recommendation that she seek a higher level of care for the symptoms she is experiencing. Although many patients respond to this news with uncertainty, resistance, or fear, for new mothers, these feelings are intensified by a singular factor: her baby. Ensuring that perinatal patients receive the appropriate level of care is lifesaving, but delivering this news can be hard for a provider and even harder on the therapeutic relationship.

To facilitate these difficult conversations more effectively while preserving the therapeutic alliance, follow these guidelines:

- Be prepared to offer specific referrals for programs or providers that offer the level of care you are recommending. Given the unique presentation, concerns, and vulnerability associated with mood and anxiety disorders during pregnancy and the early days of parenthood, do your best to provide a referral to a treatment facility specializing in perinatal mental health. Options for these programs are increasing across North America, and Postpartum Support International maintains a list of these programs on their website: https://www.postpartum.net/get-help/intensive-perinatal-psych-treatment-in-the-us/

- Prepare to answer questions she may have about the program or provider you are recommending.

- Consider reviewing the website or brochure for the recommended program or provider with your patient. Your patient may also request that you call for an initial intake or evaluation together in a session.

- Encourage your patient to call a support person, such as a partner or family member, if she has not brought someone for support to her session. This way, you can convey important information about your reasons for referral, and the referral itself, to your patient's support team.

- Encourage your patient to sign a release of information and explain that you would like to maintain contact with any new members of her treatment team so that you are in the best possible position to help her once she is ready to return to your care.

- Let your patient know that you can provide resources for her partner, who may also be in need of social, logistical, or emotional support, and follow through by offering referrals to other therapists, support groups, or parental support resources.
- Above all, reinforce that you are making this referral in service of her healing. Make sure that your patient knows this referral is being given in response to her *symptoms*, not because you think she is a bad or unfit mother. Remind her that you will be available to her when she completes her higher level of care program and that you look forward to reconnecting and working with her. It is imperative to convey that you care.

Provider Tool

SUICIDE ASSESSMENT

These questions are in no particular order and have not been validated in any way. It is recommended that these or similar questions be part of the initial clinical interview when triaging a woman with postpartum depression.

Note: All clinicians administering the Edinburgh Postnatal Depression Scale should ask the following questions of every patient who answers question #10 ("The thought of harming myself has occurred to me") with a score of 1, 2, or 3.

1. How often are you having thoughts of hurting yourself?

   _____

2. Are you able to describe them to me?

   _____

3. Have you ever had thoughts like this before?

   _____

4. When have you had thoughts like this before?

   _____

5. What happened the last time you had these thoughts?

   _____

6. Does your partner know how bad you are feeling? If not, why not?

   _____

7. Who do you consider your most primary connection for emotional support?

   _____

8. Does this person know how you are feeling? If not, why not?

   _____

9. Does anyone in your family know how you are feeling?

   _____

10. Have you ever acted on suicidal thoughts before?

    _____

11. How do you feel about the thoughts you are having?

    _____

12. Do you have specific thoughts about what you would do to harm yourself?

    _____

13. If you do have a plan, do you know what is keeping you from acting on it?

    _____

14. Are there weapons in your home? If so, do you have access to them? Can these weapons be removed from your access?

    _____

15. Do you have access to medications that could be harmful to you? If so, can these medications be removed from your access?
   _____

16. Is there anything else you can think of that I can do right now to help you protect yourself from these thoughts?
   _____

17. Have you thought about the impact that acting on these thoughts would have on your baby?
   _____

18. Do you feel able to contact me if you feel you cannot stop yourself from acting on these thoughts?
   _____

Important Points to Keep in Mind

- Be clear about your ability to help her.
- Determine whether hospitalization is required.
- Contact family members, if indicated, in her presence.
- Initiate psychiatric contact.
- Follow up with any and all requests (e.g., weapons out of the house).
- Determine level of follow-up (e.g., "Report in" phone calls to and from the patient to ensure safety).
- Do not avoid questions that make you uncomfortable.

CHAPTER 5

"Do I Have a Perinatal Mood and Anxiety Disorder?"

We are frequently asked how working with perinatal women is different from working with individuals at other times in life or through other life transitions. One example lies in the complexity of screening. Perinatal women, who are especially inclined to withhold the extent of their suffering, are best served by providers who present screening tools in a manner that increases feelings of emotional safety. Providers often wonder why their screening tools fail to identify so many new mothers who are struggling. While validated and easy-to-administer tools for assessment and diagnosis exist, if providers are screening, but their patients aren't disclosing, these tools aren't enough.

To help you overcome these obstacles, this chapter provides insight into some of the drawbacks of available screening tools, as well as some ideas for improving their utility. Since many mothers do not even realize that what they are experiencing may be outside the range of what is considered normal in the perinatal period, this chapter also discusses how providers can administer screenings to perinatal patients in ways that target specific symptoms and increase patients' understanding of what they are experiencing.

Keep in mind, there is no tool to reliably gain access to a mother's inner pain—pain that she fiercely keeps hidden from others. Therefore, in the pages that follow, we also hope to provide mothers with insight into the screening process so they can more clearly understand the questions they are being asked and understand that disclosing their symptoms will bring healing instead of continued suffering.

Screening Tools

Mental health care providers who do not specialize in perinatal mental health often wonder whether they can use their practice's routine anxiety and depression screening tools to identify symptoms of perinatal mood disorders. While screening tools for depression and anxiety may not be contraindicated in the perinatal period, at the time of this writing, only a few screening tools are validated for pregnant and postpartum populations.

These tools include:

- Edinburgh Postnatal Depression Scale (EPDS)
- Postpartum Depression Screening Scale (PDSS)
- Perinatal Anxiety Screening Scale (PASS)
- Patient Health Questionnaire (PHQ-9)

Of these tools, the EPDS is most widely preferred for its perinatal-specific sensitivity, brevity, ease of administration and scoring, and free accessibility. You can review the EPDS and its scoring information on the following page. If you are a mother and decide to take the assessment while reading this book, we encourage you to let your health care provider know your results.

Provider Tool

EDINBURGH POSTNATAL DEPRESSION SCALE (EPDS)*

Name: _____ Date: _____

☐ Pregnancy   ☐ Pregnancy loss   ☐ Postpartum _____ days/weeks/months

Please circle the answer that comes closest to how you have felt in the **past 7 days**:

1. I have been able to laugh and see the funny side of things.
    - 0 As much as I always could
    - 1 Not quite so much now
    - 2 Not so much now
    - 3 Not at all

2. I have looked forward with enjoyment to things.
    - 0 As much as I ever did
    - 1 Somewhat less than I used to
    - 2 A lot less than I used to
    - 3 Hardly at all

3. I have blamed myself unnecessarily when things went wrong.
    - 0 No, not at all
    - 1 Hardly ever
    - 2 Yes, sometimes
    - 3 Yes, very often

4. I have been anxious or worried for no good reason.
    - 0 No, not at all
    - 1 Hardly ever
    - 2 Yes, sometimes
    - 3 Yes, very often

5. I have felt scared or panicky for no good reason.
    - 0 No, not at all
    - 1 Hardly ever
    - 2 Yes, sometimes
    - 3 Yes, very often

6. Things have been too much for me.
    - 0 No, I have been coping as well as ever
    - 1 No, most of the time I have coped well
    - 2 Yes, sometimes I haven't been coping as well as usual
    - 3 Yes, most of the time I haven't been able to cope at all

---

* Cox, J. L., Holden, J. M., & Sagovsky, R. (1987). Detection of postnatal depression: Development of the 10-item Edinburgh Postnatal Depression Scale. *British Journal of Psychiatry, 150*, 782–786.

7. I have been so unhappy that I have had difficulty sleeping.

    | 0 | No, not at all | 2 | Yes, sometimes |
    | 1 | Hardly ever | 3 | Yes, very often |

8. I have felt sad or miserable.

    | 0 | No, not at all | 2 | Yes, sometimes |
    | 1 | Hardly ever | 3 | Yes, very often |

9. I have been so unhappy that I have been crying.

    | 0 | No, never | 2 | Yes, quite often |
    | 1 | Only occasionally | 3 | Yes, most of the time |

10. The thought of harming myself has occurred to me.

    | 0 | Never | 2 | Sometimes |
    | 1 | Hardly ever | 3 | Yes, quite often |

Total Score: _____

Scoring Information:*

0–6: No or minimal depression

7–13: Mild depression

14–19: Moderate depression

19–30: Severe depression

---

* McCabe-Beane et al., 2016

The Importance of Follow-Up

Routine screening for perinatal mood and anxiety disorders has the potential to increase awareness, reduce stigma, and create an opportunity for psychoeducation surrounding these conditions. When mothers recognize their symptoms on a screening form, it helps them feel less alone and validates that someone understands what they are experiencing and that other women may be feeling similarly. However, we have found that many women are given these screenings without any explanation or follow-up discussion, which can lead them to misunderstand the questions being asked and to experience uncertainty about what their score means. This combination of confusion and fear can reinforce the secrecy and shame surrounding the perinatal period, alienating women from providers who could offer guidance and support.

For this reason, it is critical that providers who conduct these screenings receive specialized training to learn to administer these tools with attention to the mother's experience. When administered this way, the use of validated screening tools is an excellent way to differentiate normal levels of distress from a perinatal mood and anxiety disorder. Best practices include a collaborative dialogue to ensure accurate interpretation of the questions, and a safe, non-judgmental environment to promote disclosure. Of course, we recognize that in non-mental health settings, such as OB/GYN offices, there are other important things to discuss. It is not our expectation that every provider will include a full psychological interview in each of their appointments with perinatal women.

For this reason, the following handout includes some tips to help you clearly convey the following to your patients:

- You are informed about perinatal mood and anxiety disorders and are available to discuss any concerns they have about their mood now or in the future.

- You will take their feelings and symptoms seriously.

- You will work with them to get the help they need.

- You are motivated to identify women with perinatal mood and anxiety disorders because these disorders are extremely treatable and there are helpful resources available.

- Women may receive screenings many times during pregnancy and the first postpartum year, as well as by various providers, including the lactation consultant, the visiting nurse, and the pediatrician.

- Screenings are repeated many times because symptoms of a perinatal mood and anxiety disorder can emerge in pregnancy and beyond the first few postpartum weeks.

- Each time a screening is given, it is best for women to answer the questions according to how they have experienced symptoms in the weeks leading up to the screening—not since giving birth.

Provider Handout

TIPS FOR TALKING ABOUT PERINATAL MOOD AND ANXIETY DISORDER SCREENINGS

While practices for perinatal mental health screening are increasingly common, the accuracy of these screenings depends on the patient's willingness to disclose how they are feeling. You can increase the likelihood of disclosure by building trust. From a supportive psychotherapeutic point of view, it is recommended that you follow the steps below.

Before the Screening

- Clarify that your patient should answer questions based on how she has been feeling over the past two weeks, regardless of what her answers might have been on previous screenings.

- Invite your patient to ask for clarification on any questions that they find confusing and to review the questions with you before they begin the screening. This is especially important when administering a screening using a translator or when providing the English version of the screening to a patient whose first language is not English.

After the Screening

- Sit facing your patient and make eye contact with her.
- Thank your patient for completing her screening.
- Ask your patient whether she has questions about the screening or her results.
- Ask your patient how it felt to answer the questions.

Explain the Results

- For women scoring lower than 10 on the EPDS:
    "I see that your score is lower than 10, which tells me that you might not be experiencing symptoms of postpartum depression or anxiety. Even though your score is low today, women can experience symptoms of perinatal depression or anxiety anytime during the first year postpartum. If you start to worry about how you are feeling at any time, please contact our office and we can talk more about it. In the meantime, I will give you resources for support just in case it would be

helpful for you to have them. I would also like to ask you to talk a little about how you have been feeling."

- For women scoring higher than 10 on the EPDS:

    "I see that your score is higher than 10, which tells me that you might be experiencing symptoms of postpartum depression or anxiety. Your score tells me that you might be having a hard time right now. This is very common among my pregnant and postpartum patients, so let's talk a little more about how you are feeling. Then we can make a plan to help you start feeling better."

Ask Follow-Up Questions, Regardless of Scoring

- Tell me how you are taking care of yourself. How is sleep going for you? For your baby?
- Who are your main supports? A partner, friends, family members?
- How is feeding going? Are you having any difficulties feeding your baby?
- Are you having thoughts that are scaring you?

Assess Question #10 Further

- "Question 10 about self-harm and suicidality can be very difficult to answer. I see you chose ____. Can you tell me a little bit more about that choice?"
- Conduct a suicide assessment for any patient who answers this question with a 1, 2, or 3.

Closing

- Validate your patient's willingness to talk with you about her symptoms and provide resources for follow-up, including a fact sheet about perinatal mood and anxiety disorders, as well as contact information for emergency hotlines, local maternal mental health care providers, and support groups.
- Ask your patient if she has any additional questions. If your staffing allows, you might offer to help her make an initial contact to a mental health care provider before she leaves your office.
- For patients with symptoms of suicidality or psychosis who require emergency intervention, provide them with additional support to ensure a smooth transition to an emergency care provider.

Universal Screening

In 2021, the American College of Obstetricians and Gynecologists reinforced a recommendation that every perinatal patient be universally screened for symptoms of depression and anxiety. They directed OB/GYNs to use standardized and validated tools, with a preference for the EPDS, at least once during the postpartum period, often at the time of the patient's six-week postpartum visit. They further recommended that providers closely monitor women with suicidal thoughts, a current mood disorder or a history of mood disorders, and specific risk factors for perinatal mood disorders (including lack of social support, lower socioeconomic status, and the presence of other stressful adjustments during the perinatal period). They also pointed out that while screening alone is beneficial, providers should be prepared to refer patients to appropriate resources for behavioral health support.

> ### Screening Recommendations
>
> Developing standard best practices for screening frequency requires additional and ongoing empirical research (Bhat et al., 2022), but we recommend following the guidelines provided by the Massachusetts Child Psychiatry Access Project for Moms (MCPAP; Byatt et al., 2014):
>
> - Screening in obstetric settings should occur at the first prenatal visit, at the beginning of the third trimester, and at six weeks postpartum, with an additional screening at two weeks postpartum for women who are at an exceptionally high risk for perinatal mood and anxiety disorders.
>
> - Screenings should also occur in pediatric settings within the first month postpartum; at the two-, four-, and six-month visits; and then additionally during the first year, if possible.
>
> - Bear in mind that screening *all* new parents (regardless of gender) for mental health symptoms multiple times during the first year of parenthood is an important and recommended practice (Kennedy & Munyan, 2021).

Overcoming Provider Challenges to Universal Screening

OB/GYNs, midwives, doulas, lactation consultants, and other maternal health care providers recognize the importance of screening for perinatal mood and anxiety disorders and embrace recommendations like those from the American College of Obstetricians and Gynecologists. As mental health care providers, we also applaud these recommendations enthusiastically, but in our work, we have noticed a few challenges that providers and patients commonly encounter—especially for providers in non-mental health settings.

In this section, we hope to answer some of these concerns and to provide tools that will increase your comfort when screening for perinatal mood and anxiety disorders in your office:

There is not enough time. In mental health settings, where a clinical interview is part and parcel of the process, discussions about a patient's answers on the screening tool should be a routine aspect of postpartum visits. However, for other health care providers, particularly those in non-mental health settings, there is barely enough time for the physical examination, let alone a thorough mental health assessment. For these providers, it is acceptable to omit a full clinical interview, provided that you ask if there is anything else they would like you to know and further assess women for thoughts of self-harm (question 10 on the EPDS), as suicide is a leading cause of death for perinatal women. Given women's inclination toward secrecy regarding these thoughts postpartum, reviewing this question in detail can be lifesaving. You may also consider using an abbreviated three-item version of the EPDS to augment your understanding of the written answers given on the standard EPDS. **Whichever screening tool you choose, remember that your attitude toward screening can make the difference between a woman feeling safe to disclose or not.**

EPDS-3

For providers who may not have time to administer and review the full EPDS with their patients, using a three-item version of the EPDS can suffice (Kabir et al., 2008). One such example is the EPDS-3A (Marshall, 2013), which specifically examines the presence of postpartum anxiety using questions 3, 4, and 5 of the EPDS: "I have blamed myself unnecessarily when things went wrong," "I have been anxious or worried for no good reason," and "I have felt scared or panicky for no very good reason."

Research also suggests that questions 2, 5, and 7 can provide an accurate assessment for symptoms of perinatal depression (Martinez et al., 2022)—specifically anhedonia ("I have looked forward to the future"), anxiety ("I have felt frightened or panicky for no very good reason"), and difficulty sleeping ("I have felt so bad that I have had difficulty sleeping").

There is still need for further research on abbreviated versions of the EPDS to explore specific cutoff scores and best practices for administration. However, from a relational perspective, the use of any screening tool can serve to build patient-provider trust by introducing the possibility of communication about mental health symptoms, treatment, and supports.

Many women do not follow through with postpartum follow-up appointments. Use of the EPDS is not limited to obstetric or mental health care practices, which is why we advocate that *all* maternal care providers learn how to use this tool. This way, women who do not attend their postpartum obstetric follow-up appointments can be screened in pediatrics offices, at lactation appointments, or in community mental health settings. While compliance with postpartum medical care tends to be low (Pluym et al., 2021), postpartum women are often highly motivated to engage in behaviors that protect the health of their babies (Polk et al., 2021). By recommending that all postpartum medical providers screen for perinatal mood and anxiety disorders, we hope this will decrease the likelihood that women who are suffering will continue to fall through the cracks.

Providers are not always aware of local resources. For many providers, it may not be clear which resources are best for perinatal patients. While we strongly recommend that you have a list of trusted *local* resources and referrals available, the resources listed on the following provider handout apply to patients anywhere in the United States, Canada, and Australia (and in some other countries as well). These will be excellent starting places for patients to search themselves. Patients who want to take the extra step can use the *Maternal Mental Health Resources* worksheet to identify useful resources in their area.

Many providers also have questions when it comes to following up with patients and determining if they followed through on referrals. If your offices are well-staffed and a staff member is available to check in to see if patients pursued your recommendations, please do so. If this is not possible, remember that administering screenings with compassionate attention while providing access to resources for support may be sufficient. By letting your patients know that you understand what they are feeling, that help is available, and that you care about their well-being, you increase the likelihood that they will follow through with your recommendations.

Provider Handout

GLOSSARY OF MATERNAL MENTAL HEALTH RESOURCES

The fields of reproductive psychiatry and maternal mental health are growing with well-trained providers around the world. Still, given the sea of health care physicians and professionals, it can be difficult to identify which individuals are appropriate referrals for your patients. Below is an overview to help you better understand the roles of various providers who work with new mothers.

Providers trained to provide psychotherapy have masters or doctoral level degrees in psychology. This includes **psychologists**, **social workers**, and **licensed counselors** with credentials such as LPC, LMFT, or LCPC. Some **psychiatrists**, who are medical doctors that prescribe medications, also provide psychotherapeutic services. Please note that **psychotherapists** who specialize in maternal mental health have often received specialized training in perinatal mental health from organizations like The Postpartum Stress Center, Postpartum Support International, The Seleni Institute, or The Centre of Perinatal Excellence.

Keep in mind that people using the credential **"PMH-C"** (perinatal mental health certification through Postpartum Support International) are trained to provide specialized mental health-informed care to patients but may not be trained to provide psychotherapy. This includes **doulas**, **international board-certified lactation consultants**, **peer counselors**, and **life coaches**. Sometimes people with these credentials are also licensed in one of the above-mentioned fields that do provide psychotherapy.

You might consider searching for resources in your state or geographical area via the extensive resource lists available at The Postpartum Stress Center (www.postpartumstress.com) and Postpartum Support International (www.postpartum.net). Non-specializing physicians who would like a patient consultation with a **reproductive psychiatrist** can also schedule one free of charge via Postpartum Support International.

Patient Worksheet

MATERNAL MENTAL HEALTH RESOURCES

If you are pregnant or postpartum, or you recently had a baby and are worried about the way you feel, talking with a maternal mental health professional can help. Perinatal depression and anxiety affect one in seven women, with symptoms ranging from very mild to very severe. While the symptoms can fill you with self-doubt, shame, or terror, they are extremely treatable and respond well to support. Use this guide to identify resources in your area and to keep track of how to access them.

Search for Providers

Look for local resources on your own by searching the internet for "maternal mental health care providers" or "therapists who treat perinatal mood and anxiety disorders." Then list three resources you found:

1. Name of resource: _____

    Phone number: _____ Email: _____

    Website: _____

    I reached out for an initial appointment: Yes   No

2. Name of resource: _____

    Phone number: _____ Email: _____

    Website: _____

    I reached out for an initial appointment: Yes   No

3. Name of resource: _____

    Phone number: _____ Email: _____

    Website: _____

    I reached out for an initial appointment: Yes   No

Ask for Referrals

Ask your obstetric provider (OB/GYN), doula, pediatrician, lactation consultant, or other health care professional for referrals to a therapist who specializes in maternal mental health. Then list three resources you received:

1. Name of resource: _____

    Phone number: _____ Email: _____

    Website: _____

    I reached out for an initial appointment: Yes   No

2. Name of resource: _____

    Phone number: _____ Email: _____

    Website: _____

    I reached out for an initial appointment: Yes   No

3. Name of resource: _____

    Phone number: _____ Email: _____

    Website: _____

    I reached out for an initial appointment: Yes   No

Visit Postpartum Support International

Postpartum Support International is an organization that helps mothers around the world find perinatal mental health care support. Visit www.postpartum.net to search for your local support coordinator.

Name of the coordinator closest to me: _____

Phone number: _____ Email: _____

Additional U.S. Resources for Moms

The following are some national resources if you need support. Be aware that some states offer state-specific hotlines for perinatal mothers. Please explore your own public health resources to find out what might be available to you.

1. **Postpartum Support International HelpLine:** Call 1-800-944-4773. This is not an emergency line. Callers leave a voice message that will be returned by a HelpLine volunteer.

2. **988 Suicide and Crisis Lifeline:** Call 988 (www.988lifeline.org)

3. **National Crisis Text Line:** Text HOME to 741741

Overcoming Patient Challenges to Universal Screening

In our practice, every patient who is pregnant, has a child under the age of two, or who has experienced a perinatal loss is screened using the EPDS. Over time, we have observed an interesting trend: There is often a discrepancy between what patients disclose on the EPDS and in other parts of our intake procedure. For example, a woman may check off "No, not at all" on EPDS question #4 ("I have been anxious or worried for no good reason")—but then endorse answers associated with anxiety and intrusive thoughts on The Postpartum Stress Center's own symptom list. Clinicians at our practice are trained to notice these differences and to explore them in the clinical intake interview. Patient feedback when confronted with these discrepancies includes:

- "I've seen the EPDS a hundred times already, so I didn't pay much attention to it this time."

- "But I am anxious for *very* good reasons—I have a new baby! I *should* be worried about my baby! So, no, I'm *not* worried for 'no good reason'!"

- "I answered these questions honestly before and ended up here in your office, so I don't really want to answer them again and get the wrong score. There's nothing wrong with me, is there?"

- "I'm not really able to focus. I didn't understand what the question meant."

To all providers who administer screenings, this feedback should reinforce how important it is to make sure patients understand the reason they are administered repeat screenings throughout the perinatal period. If you have time available in your appointments, we also encourage you to discuss the answers to each question with your patients. Sometimes patients will misinterpret normal perinatal symptoms, which can influence the answers they choose. By taking the time to sit down and discuss their answers, not only will both of you gain clarity on the questions being asked, but you will gain an opportunity to strengthen patient-provider trust, opening the door for women to disclose additional information about how they are feeling. Just consider how it feels for a new mother to realize that she is experiencing symptoms of depression and anxiety at this time in her life. As one mother powerfully stated, "Oh, great. So I have a baby, and now I have mental health problems. What a good mother I am, right?" Do all you can to convey that your role is to support her and to help her find (and receive) the best treatment. And perhaps most importantly, remind her that good mothers experience symptoms, and with your help, she will feel like herself again.

Finally, a note to mothers: It is understandable that repeat screenings can be irritating, especially if you have felt unheard before. While it is our sincere hope that providers will conduct screenings with the sensitivity that we recommend, we want to remind you that your voice is a powerful tool. If your provider does not understand what you are telling them, clearly repeat your concerns again. And if this doesn't work, or you do not feel safe disclosing your symptoms or fears to them, do not hesitate to ask for a different provider or to seek help on your own.

Talking with Perinatal Moms and Understanding What They Need

With so many barriers in the way, how can providers help mothers feel safe talking about how bad they feel? When resistance and fear are so strong, how can providers build trust? In her decades of practice, Karen has developed an approach to therapy referred to as The Art of Holding Perinatal Women in Distress. Although holding is discussed in more detail in section III, for now we suggest using two basic counseling skills that are central to therapeutic holding—the use of questions and active listening—to augment your assessments of perinatal women.

First, we encourage using both open- and closed-ended questions to gather information during the clinical interview and foster open communication and trust. Karen's work relies on carefully worded questions that address the nuances of the perinatal experience with traditional interview questions. She starts by opening the interview with a closed-ended question that authentically captures an aspect of the patient's lived experience. This normalizes the patient's experience and conveys that Karen has the expertise to understand what the patient is going through. She then continues with an open-ended follow-up question, where she invites the patient to share further.

To illustrate how this can work in practice, consider what happens when providers ask mothers, "How are you and your baby sleeping?" Oftentimes, mothers will respond by describing how their babies' behaviors and needs are impacting their own sleep patterns. While the provider's question is well-meaning and certainly relevant, it does not convey an understanding that a mother's sleep can be disrupted by her own mood and anxiety symptoms. A better question to ask is, "Are you sleeping at night when your baby is asleep?" This question communicates the understanding that moms may not want to sleep during the day (daytime sleep can be discussed separately) and that moms typically experience disrupted sleep at night due to the baby's behaviors and needs.

Regardless of how a mother responds, the provider must then ask open-ended follow-up questions. A mother who states that she is "exhausted and getting no sleep" may not be sleeping due to her infant's frequent waking (a typical experience) or due to intense anxiety that is keeping her awake (a symptom of a perinatal mood and anxiety disorder). In this case, the disclosure "I am not sleeping" is only as helpful as the answers to follow-up questions reveal. It is easy to assume that the disclosure of poor sleep is par for the course in motherhood. An ear attuned to the symptoms of perinatal mood and anxiety disorders recognizes that *not sleeping* requires further probing. Therefore, if a mother answers yes to the previous closed-ended question, a provider may respond with, "Can you tell me what is helping you fall asleep right now?" If she answers no, they may ask, "What gets in the way of your sleep at night?" Moving back and forth between open- and closed-ended questions helps build trust and gain a clear understanding of what your patient is experiencing.

The second basic counseling skill that is helpful for all providers to master is active listening, which involves carefully listening to what the patient is saying and then thoughtfully responding in a way that helps the patient feel understood. Active listeners will often ask clarification questions and make sounds such as *mm-hmm* to encourage the speaker to continue sharing. It is important to keep in mind that no matter how sensitively you communicate with your patients, they may still be reluctant to tell you how bad they feel. Therefore, we encourage providers to let patients know that even if they feel okay now, it's possible that reaching out for support will still be beneficial to them. Furthermore, all patients should still be given instructions for how to access support during the perinatal period regardless of what their screening suggests. Sometimes mothers just need to take advantage of these resources in their own time.

Provider Handout

COUNSELING SKILLS: OPEN- AND CLOSED-ENDED QUESTIONS

The most effective interviews and assessments will include a combination of closed- and open-ended questions. Closed-ended questions are those that can be answered using a single word or short phrase (e.g., "What is your baby's name?"), while open-ended questions invite the interviewee to provide longer, more thoughtful, and complex answers (e.g., "Can you please tell me about your baby's name?"). Strategic use of both types of questions can keep conversation between two people flowing, providing opportunities to build rapport and, eventually, trust.

Since women tend to be fiercely private in the perinatal period, it is important that every question you ask convey a deep understanding and empathy for what patients may be experiencing. One question asked the wrong way can rupture trust entirely.

The questions below are worded in a way to encourage openness and convey your expertise in the perinatal experience.

Reproductive History

Goals:

- To learn about the patient's reproductive history, including any difficulty becoming pregnant or pregnancy losses
- To express your recognition that a patient's most recent pregnancy (or number of children) does not tell their whole reproductive story
- To invite the patient to share her fertility journey/experience

Closed-ended questions:

- "Is this your first pregnancy or baby?"
- "Have you experienced any pregnancy or infant losses?"
- "Have you experienced treatment for fertility challenges?"

Open-ended questions:

- "Can you tell me about your reproductive history and any difficulties you may have experienced reaching this point?"

Pregnancy and Birth Experience

Goals:

- To learn about the patient's pregnancy and birth experience(s)
- To validate the relevance of her expectations for pregnancy, birth, and transition to motherhood

Closed-ended questions:

- "Did you have any pregnancy complications?"
- "Did you experience any complications during labor and delivery?"
- "Did you or your baby experience any complications after delivery?"

Open-ended questions:

- "Can you describe some of the ups and downs of your pregnancy experience?"
- "Can you describe some of the ups and downs of your labor/delivery/postpartum experience so far?"

Infant Feeding

Goals:

- To identify any difficulties or feelings the patient may be having related to infant feeding
- To convey an interest that the infant's physical needs are being met via any means
- To increase the patient's comfort talking with you about feeding choices
- To express nonjudgmental acceptance of breastmilk and formula-feeding practices
- To convey recognition that breastfeeding may not work out for a wide variety of reasons that may or may not have anything to do with a mother's preferences

Closed-ended questions:

- "Are you breastfeeding, bottle feeding with breast milk or formula, or combination feeding (using both breast and bottle to feed baby)?"
- "Are you using a breast pump?"
- "Have you had any challenges with feeding?"

Open-ended questions:

- "Can you tell me about feeding your baby? How is it going for you?"
- "How does feeding seem to be going for your baby?"
- "What has your experience been with any feeding guidance you have received from a lactation consultant, pediatrician, or other support person?"

Sleep

Goals:

- To identify difficulties the patient may be having with sleep that are unrelated to infant sleep
- To convey the understanding that mothers often experience sleep disruption due to anxiety and mood-related symptoms
- To express the understanding that nighttime sleep is different from daytime sleep, especially among mothers who prefer not (or are unable) to sleep during their baby's nap times

Closed-ended questions:

- "Are you sleeping at night when your baby is sleeping?"
- "Are you able to fall back to sleep after your baby returns to sleep at night?"

Open-ended questions:

- "What kinds of things disrupt your sleep at night?"
- "Can you describe a typical night of sleep for you and also a typical night of sleep for your baby?"
- "How have you and your support people/partner/husband been navigating sleep routines?"
- "What kinds of systems do you have in place to ensure that you are getting enough sleep?"

Self-Care

Goals:

- To identify any self-care routines a mother may be engaged in
- To express understanding that mothers can experience guilt related to self-care, especially during the perinatal period

Closed-ended questions:

- "Are you practicing self-care activities?"
- "Are you eating/sleeping/staying hydrated/spending time alone/exercising/connecting with your partner?"
- "Do you have time for self-care?"

Open-ended questions:

- "How are you finding time to take care of yourself?"
- "Can you talk to me about some of your self-care routines?"
- "It can be hard for mothers to find time to take care of themselves when they are so busy taking care of their babies. How have you been doing in this area?"

Perinatal Mood and Anxiety Symptoms

Goals:

- To identify the onset of symptoms
- To validate and educate that symptoms can begin in pregnancy, or even predate pregnancy, and still be relevant in the postpartum period

Closed-ended question:

- "Did your symptoms start during pregnancy or after you gave birth?"

Open-ended question:

- "When did you first notice that you were not feeling like yourself?"

Intrusive or Scary Thoughts

Goals:

- To assess for scary thoughts
- To convey insight that perinatal women often experience unwanted intrusive thoughts
- To normalize the fact that uncomfortable thoughts are a common symptom in your practice
- To normalize talking about these thoughts and symptoms

Closed-ended question:

- "Are you having any thoughts that are scaring you?"

Open-ended question:

- "Lots of parents tell me that they have thoughts about themselves or their babies that scare them or make them feel uncomfortable. Can you tell me about any thoughts like that you may be having?"

Support System

Goals:

- To identify the presence or lack of social supports
- To convey recognition that the perinatal period can feel extremely isolating while stressing the importance of social support in this period

Closed-ended questions:

- "Does anyone know how bad you are feeling?"
- "Who in your life is supporting you?"

Open-ended questions:

- "What have you shared with other people in your life about how bad you have been feeling?"
- "Are there barriers to sharing with others how you have been feeling?"

Medication

Goals:

- To determine the patient's openness to using medication during the perinatal period
- To normalize conversations about using medication
- To convey your openness to talking about resistance to and opportunities for using medication

Closed-ended questions:

- "Are you willing to take medication while you are pregnant or breastfeeding?"
- "I would like to share some information about how we use medication to help mothers who come to our practice, is that okay?"

Open-ended questions:

- "What are your thoughts and feelings about using medication during pregnancy and while breastfeeding?"
- "How might you know if you needed to revisit the option of medication?"

Provider Handout

COUNSELING SKILLS: ACTIVE LISTENING

Active listening is a key counseling skill that conveys to the speaker that you are paying attention to them, that you are undistracted, and that you care about what they are trying to communicate. Some aspects of active listening include attending to verbal and non-verbal communication, as well as using questions and reflective feedback to demonstrate that you have really heard what the other person is saying.

Verbal communication: Involves using words and sounds to encourage the speaker to continue sharing. Examples include:

- *Mm-hmm . . .*
- *Go on . . .*
- *Tell me more about that . . .*
- Using the speaker's words in a follow-up comment or question, such as "You said Dr. Smith was your OB/GYN. Was Dr. Smith also the person who delivered your baby?"

Non-verbal communication: Involves using body language to encourage the speaker to continue sharing. Examples include:

- Making eye contact.
- Putting down your phone or electronic device. If you are a provider who takes notes electronically or on paper, tell your patient, "I am going to be using this computer/device/notepad to jot down some of the things you are telling me." Then make it a point to maintain eye contact while speaking with your patient.
- Sitting face to face with your patient while you are talking instead of completing other parts of their exam or doing other activities.
- Avoiding any interruptions.
- Sitting up straight.

Asking Questions

- Use both open- and closed-ended questions.

Giving Feedback

- Summarize and paraphrase what your patient has said to confirm your understanding while also giving opportunities for them to add additional information.

- Use clarifying phrases like "I want to make sure I understand correctly" and "Can you tell me more about that?" to ensure your full understanding of the patient's report.

- Reflect observations of your patient with statements like "When you said that, I noticed your eyes welled up with tears. What emotions were you having just then?"

Steps to Practice Active Listening

- Find a family member, friend, or colleague and ask them to tell you about their day.

- Notice what it feels like to put your phone aside, shut down your computer, or (if connecting by phone or computer) turn off your alerts.

- As the other person speaks, pay attention whenever your mind wanders, which it will from time to time. You might feel an urge to check your notifications, think about whether you need to run to the store, or wonder what the weather is like outside.

- Whenever your mind wanders, try to bring your focus back to the conversation by using a mindfulness strategy. For example, you might shift your body to feel your feet planted on the floor, reengage eye contact with the speaker, or focus on the speaker's voice.

- Write down some of the things you found distracting or that took your attention away from the speaker.

You may find it helpful to give this worksheet to loved ones in your patients' lives to help build communication between your patient and their social supports.

Self-Assessment for Mothers

It is understandable that many mothers feel confused by the symptoms they are experiencing during the perinatal period. In the blurry exhaustion of pregnancy and the early days of caring for a baby, their feelings change from moment to moment. Moreover, a person's tolerance for each postpartum symptom is unique. For example, crying during the postpartum period is normal, as the combination of hormonal changes, exhaustion, and new emotions during this period typically results in tearfulness. However, crying *too much* is not expected in the perinatal period, but how do you know how much is too much? Each mother needs to make this assessment for herself by considering the frequency, duration, and intensity of the symptoms she is experiencing, as well as the extent to which this symptom is disrupting her daily activities.

- **Frequency:** How often is the symptom occurring each day or week?
- **Duration:** How long has this been going on?
- **Intensity:** How strong is the symptom, and what effect does it have when it occurs?
- **Disruption:** How often does the symptom interrupt regular activities? Is it disruptive due to its frequency, duration, intensity, or a combination of those three factors?

The following *How Bad Are You Feeling?* handout can help mothers recognize when the *expected* features of the perinatal period may be symptoms of a perinatal mood and anxiety disorder—in other words, when the distress the symptom is causing exceeds the amount of distress she can tolerate. If you are a mother, keep in mind that your symptoms may change. If so, we encourage you to bring your updated assessment to a provider you trust or a maternal mental health specialist.

Patient Handout

HOW BAD ARE YOU FEELING?

It is true that most parents experience some increased emotionality after having a baby. As the hormones, exhaustion, stress, anxiety, overwhelm, and joy flood your system, it can feel like you're hitting start on an emotional roller-coaster ride. But it can sometimes be difficult to know when that roller-coaster ride has become too rough, as the symptoms of perinatal mood and anxiety disorders are very similar to the normal emotional ups and downs of early motherhood.

For example, it is common for new moms to experience some or all of the symptoms described below:

- Sadness, anxiety, overwhelm, panic, anger, and irritability
- Frequent guilt, shame, or self-doubt
- Worry that disrupts sleep or makes it difficult to leave the house or be alone with the baby
- Difficulty with decision-making, concentration, memory, or maintaining daily routines
- Intrusive scary or anxious thoughts about themselves or their babies (e.g., "What if I drop the baby down the stairs?")

What differentiates a perinatal mood and anxiety disorder from normal postpartum symptoms is the **frequency**, **intensity**, and **duration** of these symptoms. In other words, is your symptom happening so frequently, with enough intensity, and or lasting long enough to disrupt your quality of life or functioning? If so, talking with a maternal mental health professional may be beneficial for you. You might not have a mood and anxiety disorder, but you may still find it helpful to have a better understanding of how to cope with your symptoms when they occur.

If you are experiencing any of the following mood-related symptoms, it is important to talk with a health care provider:

- Feeling hopeless
- Thinking that your family would be better off without you
- Thinking your baby would be better off without you
- Thinking you might harm yourself
- Feeling an urge to run away
- Experiencing any of the symptoms mentioned in the first list every day for two weeks or more

Copyright © 2023 Hilary Waller and Karen Kleiman, *The Perinatal Patient*. All rights reserved.

When you are stressed and sleep deprived, it can be difficult to recognize whether your symptoms are becoming more or less disruptive. Note the date, your symptom, and the severity of the symptom on a scale from 0 (*not disruptive at all*) to 5 (*most severely disruptive I have experienced so far*) to notice any important trends. You can track this information in a journal, on your phone or tablet, or using a chart like the one here:

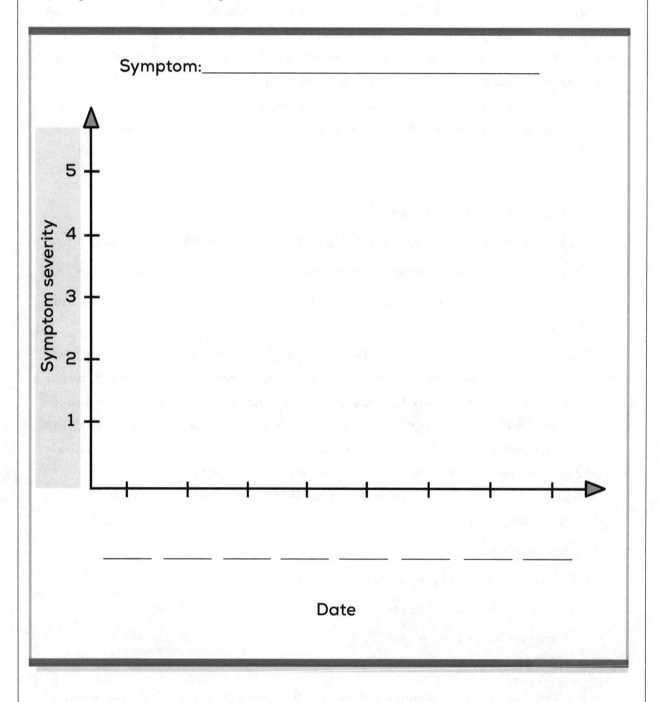

CHAPTER 6

"How Do I Know If I'm at Risk?"

Modern science, research, and medicine now enable medical providers to identify and reduce a mother's risk for many pregnancy and postpartum complications, which has increased the likelihood that they (and their babies) will experience healthy and positive outcomes. We hope that one day we will also be able to predict when a woman's transition to motherhood will be marred by the pain of a perinatal mood and anxiety disorder, so we can significantly reduce that likelihood too. For now, mothers are best served by identifying and reducing some common risk factors for these disorders. Among the most notable are any personal or family history of anxiety, depression, or other mood disorder; thyroid changes; painful or traumatic labor or birth; history of trauma or abuse; racism; and social isolation.

In this chapter, we will discuss these risk factors in depth and also provide resources on the topics of risk prevention and risk reduction. The tools in this chapter are designed for mothers to use independently or in conjunction with a trusted provider to identify their unique risk profile and develop plans for prevention. Since no mother is immune to developing a perinatal mood and anxiety disorder, we recommend that these tools be given to *all* mothers.

Know the Risk Factors

Historically, it was believed that perinatal mood and anxiety disorders developed in response to the rise and fall of hormones involved in the reproductive and stress systems. More recently, researchers are recognizing that reproductive hormones are only one part of a complex whole, and that myriad factors contribute to the development of perinatal mood and anxiety disorders, including biological, psychological, social, and environmental factors. In this section, we dive into these risk factors in detail and provide recommendations for risk reduction.

Biological Risk Factors

Many biological variables can impact mood, including our genetics and epigenetics, immune system functioning, hormones created by the endocrine system, and the state of our nervous systems. Although it is beyond the scope of this book to dive deeply into every biological risk factor, we strongly recommended that those specializing in the care of perinatal women inform themselves about breakthroughs in this field.

For our purposes, a few key biological risk factors are important to keep in mind:

- Changes in the *thyroid* are common during the perinatal period (Rad & Deluxe, 2022), and these changes can mimic symptoms of perinatal mood and anxiety disorders. Women with a personal or family history of thyroid changes or problems should talk with their obstetric care provider, primary care physician, or endocrinologist (if they already have one) to ensure that thyroid evaluation is prioritized during their perinatal care.

- Many of our patients report becoming complacent about their *general health* during their reproductive life stage and consider their obstetric provider their primary doctor. Indeed, general preventative medical services are often underused by women (Phipps et al., 2019), so mothers may need to be reminded that routine primary care visits are as important for them as pediatrician appointments are for their babies. Checking for adequate levels of iron (Hameed et al., 2021) and vitamin D (Trujillo et al., 2018) in particular, as well as maintaining proper nutrition and hydration, are all important parts of the whole picture.

- During the perinatal period, the body undergoes changes that not only feel foreign, but that also cause *physical discomfort and pain*. While results are mixed regarding the experience of pain during labor and delivery and its impact on postpartum mood, a link between general pain and depressive symptoms is well-documented (Chimbo et al., 2021; Kimura et al., 2021). While many people believe that the postpartum body will (or should) feel back to normal a matter of weeks or months following delivery, mothers often experience ongoing pain and discomfort (Daly et al., 2022). This pain ranges from "this part of me doesn't feel like it used to" to pain that is severe and debilitating. This pain feels different from that experienced at other times in life and occurs in intimate, private parts of the body that women are often uncomfortable discussing, even with care providers and partners.

Finally, a patient's personal and family mental health history can increase vulnerability for the development of a mood and anxiety disorder, not just during the perinatal stage, but at any time in life. Assessing a patient's familial mental health history is particularly important when the patient herself does not have a known history of symptoms, as perinatal mood and anxiety disorders can be inherited (Viktorin et al., 2016). Understanding which symptoms are prevalent in a patient's family history can support accurate diagnosis. Discussions about family history can also increase the clinician's awareness of a patient's personal biases or stigma associated with mental health care. For example, a patient may say, "My mother suffered so much from anxiety. I want to be proactive so my daughter does not have to deal with having such an anxious mom." Another patient may plead, "Tell me there is nothing wrong with me! My mother was so depressed when I was a child, and I can't bear the thought that I am like her. Everyone treated her like she was crazy and a bad mom." It is especially critical to inquire about any symptoms of bipolar disorders or psychosis when discussing a patient's personal and family history.

Patient Worksheet

BIOLOGICAL RISK FACTORS

This worksheet can help you recognize *biological* risk factors that increase your vulnerability for developing a mood and anxiety disorder while you are pregnant or postpartum. Check off any risk factors that are relevant to you, read through the identified risk management strategies, and consider what might get in the way of using one of these strategies. We then encourage you to share this worksheet with your health care provider.

☐ **History of thyroid changes, iron deficiency, or vitamin D deficiency**

Risk management strategies:

- Notify your health care providers of relevant medical history.
- Schedule routine assessments during and after pregnancy.
- Establish and maintain contact with primary care provider and any relevant specialists, like endocrinologists.

What could interfere with your ability to follow through with these strategies, and how might you overcome this difficulty?

_____

_____

_____

☐ **Poor nutrition and hydration habits**

Risk management strategies:

- Keep a basket of easy-to-grab nutritious snacks and water bottles in each room of your home and your car.
- Schedule a visit with a registered dietitian who can help you develop a detailed plan for managing your nutritional needs.
- Talk with a social worker or health care provider about any difficulties accessing adequate resources for nutrition.

Copyright © 2023 Hilary Waller and Karen Kleiman, *The Perinatal Patient*. All rights reserved.

What could interfere with your ability to follow through with these strategies, and how might you overcome this difficulty?

_____

_____

_____

☐ **Difficulty with infant feeding**

Risk management strategies:

- Establish care with an outpatient lactation consultant who can help you troubleshoot any breastfeeding or pumping difficulties (lactation consultants are helpful resources for bottle-feeding moms too).

- Make a list of feeding challenges you or your baby are having to discuss with your baby's pediatrician.

- Contact a peer counselor or review frequently asked questions (FAQs) through organizations like La Leche League and Kelly Mom.

- Fed Is Best is an especially helpful organization for moms who are bottle-feeding their babies using formula and/or breastmilk.

What could interfere with your ability to follow through with these strategies, and how might you overcome this difficulty?

_____

_____

_____

☐ **Pain related to pregnancy, labor/delivery recovery**

Risk management strategies:

- Tell your provider about any pain or discomfort you are experiencing (Be brave, and remember that obstetric providers are used to helping women with intimate and hard-to-discuss issues like pelvic prolapses, urinary and fecal incontinence, painful sex, and hemorrhoids).

- Talk with your partner about ways they can provide comfort during pregnancy and labor, like holding your hand, giving you a massage, or helping you advocate for yourself.
- Ask your obstetric provider about both medical (e.g., an epidural) and non-medical (e.g., use of a peanut ball) pain management strategies they recommend during labor.

What could interfere with your ability to follow through with these strategies, and how might you overcome this difficulty?

_____

_____

_____

☐ **Family history of a mood or anxiety disorder**

Risk management strategies:

- Notify your health care providers of your family history.
- Consider establishing care with a maternal mental health care provider who you can contact if you become symptomatic during pregnancy or postpartum.

What could interfere with your ability to follow through with these strategies, and how might you overcome this difficulty?

_____

_____

_____

☐ **Personal history of a mood or anxiety disorder**

Risk management strategies:

- Notify your health care providers of your personal history.

- If you are not currently working with a mental health care provider, consider reestablishing care with a therapist or seeking out a specialized maternal mental health care provider to contact if you become symptomatic during pregnancy or postpartum.
- Make a list of some of the tools you used to recover from your mood and anxiety disorder in the past and share it with your support system.

What could interfere with your ability to follow through with these strategies, and how might you overcome this difficulty?

_____

_____

_____

☐ **History of premenstrual syndrome (PMS) or premenstrual dysphoric disorder (PMDD)**

Risk management strategies:

- Notify your health care providers of your history of PMS or PMDD so they are aware that this is one of your risk factors.
- Consider establishing care with a maternal mental health care provider to contact if you become symptomatic during pregnancy or postpartum.

What could interfere with your ability to follow through with these strategies, and how might you overcome this difficulty?

_____

_____

_____

☐ **Lack of sleep due to insomnia, anxiety, or baby waking**

Risk management strategies:

- Develop a plan with members of your support system to protect your sleep by discussing who will handle the baby's nighttime waking.

- If you plan to breastfeed, consider ways to share the responsibility of other forms of care during the night, like having a partner change diapers and soothe between feedings.

What could interfere with your ability to follow through with these strategies, and how might you overcome this difficulty?

_____

_____

_____

☐ **History of fertility treatments, reproductive loss, or other major losses**

Risk management strategy:
- Use a journal, talk to a trusted support person, or meet with a provider who can help you recognize and cope with any lingering feelings of grief, loss, sadness, or anger you may have about these experiences.

What could interfere with your ability to follow through with these strategies, and how might you overcome this difficulty?

_____

_____

_____

☐ **Having multiples in pregnancy and birth, being an older mom (or a teen mom), or an unplanned pregnancy**

Risk management strategies:
- Search for a support group for peers who share this experience by asking friends, obstetric providers, or counselors for resources.
- Visit Postpartum Support International's website (www.postpartum.net) to search for online support groups that focus on your specific experience.

What could interfere with your ability to follow through with these strategies, and how might you overcome this difficulty?

_____

_____

_____

What additional risk factors are you aware of that could impact your well-being? How might you overcome them? What could stand in the way, and how could you address those difficulties?

_____

_____

_____

If you notice that implementing these strategies or identifying additional strategies for risk reduction is difficult for you, keep in mind that a mental health care provider can help.

Follow Up

- ☐ I am aware of my biological risk factors.
- ☐ I have shared this worksheet with someone who can support me in reducing my risk.
- ☐ I have shared this worksheet with my health care provider. That provider's name is:

_____

Patient Worksheet

PERINATAL PAIN

The experience of physical pain during the perinatal period is a risk factor for the development of a mood and anxiety disorder. Women tend to expect *some* lingering discomfort after giving birth, which leaves them feeling unsure about how much discomfort is normal and how long this discomfort should last. Some women find it difficult to talk to their providers about perinatal pain and aren't aware that the pain they are feeling can be reduced with treatment. This worksheet can help you communicate your needs and concerns to your provider.

Note any areas where you feel pain or discomfort.

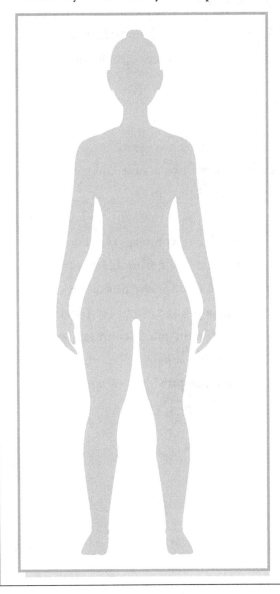
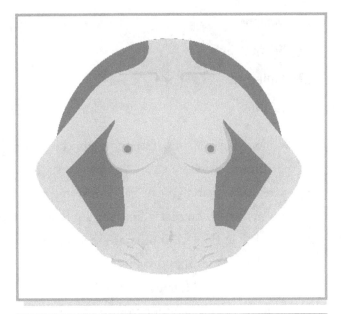
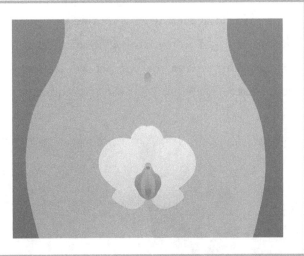

Copyright © 2023 Hilary Waller and Karen Kleiman, *The Perinatal Patient*. All rights reserved.

Note any specific sensations you are experiencing in these areas.

- ☐ Burning
- ☐ Feeling raw
- ☐ Numbness
- ☐ Itching
- ☐ Sensitivity
- ☐ Stinging
- ☐ Aching
- ☐ Leaking
- ☐ Bleeding
- ☐ Weakness
- ☐ Sharp pain
- ☐ Dull pain
- ☐ Bruising
- ☐ Tightness
- ☐ Pulling
- ☐ Pain during intimate touching
- ☐ Pain specifically during urination
- ☐ Constipation
- ☐ Feeling like something is falling out
- ☐ Feeling worried or insecure about how I look
- ☐ Feeling worried about what is different now from before
- ☐ Feeling worried that I am permanently changed and that I will feel like this forever
- ☐ Other: _____

While what you are feeling might be normal for your current stage of pregnancy or postpartum recovery, we encourage you to share your experience with your obstetric provider so they can assess what might be happening and help facilitate your healing process.

You may also consider asking for a referral to a pelvic floor physical therapist for additional support. Pelvic floor therapists are specially trained to treat pain, discomfort, and injury that impacts the muscles supporting the organs housed in the pelvis. Pelvic floor problems can cause organs to prolapse, difficulty controlling bowels or urine, and pain or difficulty during sex. Pelvic floor injuries are very common during pregnancy, and following both vaginal and cesarian births.

Pelvic floor therapy is a routine component of obstetric care in many countries around the world and is often covered by medical insurance. You can find a pelvic floor therapist by searching for one on the internet, contacting your health insurance provider, or asking one of your maternal care providers for a recommendation.

Social Risk Factors

There are several social risk factors that can increase the likelihood that a mother will develop a mood and anxiety disorder during the perinatal period. Social risk factors refer to aspects of the environment that influence a person's ability to access economic resources, physical and emotional safety, and community support. The *Social Risk Factors* worksheet at the end of this section provides a more detailed list designed to guide exploration of an individual patient's unique social risk factors, but here are some common themes:

- The increased *financial stress* associated with new parenthood can feel overwhelming regardless of a person's socioeconomic status, but it is especially challenging for families with low socioeconomic security or limited awareness of and access to financial support. Financial stress can impact access to household utilities, safe housing, food security, and childcare, as well as health care, hygienic supplies, and medicine for mothers, their babies, and other family members.

  For men, financial stress can increase vulnerability to *masculine gender role stress*, which is the type of stress men experience when there is a conflict between their perceived role as a male in society (e.g., being the primary breadwinner) and their new responsibilities as a parent (e.g., sharing in caregiving). This type of stress is another social risk factor for the development of mood and anxiety disorders during new parenthood (Chhabra et al., 2022).

- *Structural and institutional racism* are significant risk factors for the development of a perinatal mood or anxiety disorder. People who are BIPOC, gender non-conforming, LGBTQIA+, immigrants, and refugees are among the underrepresented and marginalized groups of parents. They routinely face bias and inequity that increase risk for a variety of adverse birth and health outcomes, including perinatal mood and anxiety disorders (van Daalen et al., 2022). It is noteworthy that despite increased risk and prevalence, racial and ethnic minorities in particular are less likely to start and complete treatment for mood-related symptoms in the perinatal period (Kozhimannil et al., 2011).

- Patients who have *trauma* in their history are more likely to experience disruptions to their mood during the perinatal period. This includes, but is not limited to, those with a history of child or pregnancy loss, difficult labor and delivery, adverse childhood experiences, intimate partner violence, and racial or cultural trauma.

- Strong feelings of *isolation* are an important social risk factor for the development of perinatal mood and anxiety disorders. Isolation may present as a feeling (e.g., "I have a lot of people around, but I have never felt so lonely") or may be logistical (e.g., "I live in a different state from my family, and they are unable to visit or help as much as I would like or need"). Isolation may also be experienced by mothers who are confronted with challenges that are not universal to all parents, such as having a baby admitted to the neonatal intensive care unit (the NICU), being a single parent, having an unplanned pregnancy, or becoming a parent as a teenager. Patients with unsupportive partners or complex relationships with their family of origin may also experience social isolation.

For many new mothers, feelings of isolation are both a common and confusing experience. On the one hand, people are attracted to pregnant women and small babies. Pregnant bellies and strollers can feel like magnets for curious glances and comments from loved ones and strangers alike. On the other hand, perinatal women frequently say that they have never felt more alone, even when surrounded by people. These feelings of isolation are reinforced by the amount of time that mothers actually do spend alone at all hours of the day and night tending to their babies and by the normal experience of postpartum adjustment and transition. Mothers spend time wondering whether others feel the same way they do about their bodies, themselves, and their babies, but they are often reluctant to initiate these conversations in their peer groups. As one patient told Hilary:

> How are you supposed to find out if your friends are still having hemorrhoids too at five months postpartum? Do you just bring it up over lunch with a friend one day while her baby is screaming in her face and mine is chewing on my nipple? I thought it would feel good to see a friend, but honestly, when I got in the car I had no idea how she was doing. I had no idea if how *I* was doing is normal, and I think I got to eat like two bites of food.

This patient's experience is recognizable to so many mothers who are trying to reconnect with their friends. It makes sense that mothers who miss some aspect of their old social lives would try to go back to it, even with a baby (and a diaper bag, portable highchair, baby food, and toys) in tow. But things *are* different after becoming a mother, and mothers often do not know how to articulate this difference to their friends, their partners, or even to themselves. Validating these differences is an important step toward grieving the losses associated with their former social life, accepting the changes occurring in reality, and eventually finding joy in the experience of motherhood.

In addition, cultural systems inform the expectations and fantasies that mothers bring with them to parenthood. For example, women in Latino cultures can be subject to *Marianismo* imagery, a gender role expectation that encourages them to embody the qualities of the Virgin Mary by practicing submissiveness, self-sacrifice, and chastity (Lara-Cinisomo et al., 2018). Similarly, Chinese culture endorses the practice of "sitting the month," where new mothers are expected to remain confined to their homes for the first month after giving birth and to adhere to strict rules, such as not showering, abstaining from cold food and drinks, and not using electronic devices (Lee & Brand, 2015).

The extent to which a woman relates with these cultural practices or finds them intrusive can increase development of a mood or anxiety disorder. The *Cultural Expectations* worksheet at the end of this section asks mothers to consider the rituals and traditions that have informed their expectations of parenthood, as well as the social messages they receive that influence these expectations.

The tools offered in this chapter can certainly support patients in developing coping skills to reduce their social risk factors. However, many patients will benefit from or even require specialized mental health care to address the overlapping vulnerability of the perinatal stage and the impact of these social risk factors.

Cultural Traditions and Rituals

The following is a list of common practices across various cultures that are related to welcoming a new baby. Although the traditions and rituals on this list are impressively diverse, it is by no means intended to be exhaustive. It is important to familiarize yourself with practices like these so you can better understand how a patient's culture can affect their vulnerability to developing a mood or anxiety disorder, and how it can even add logistical or emotional barriers to patients accessing the help that they need.

Cultural Traditions:

- **Marianismo:** Imagery among Latinas that reinforces traditional feminine gender role expectations (Lara-Cinisomo et al., 2018)

- **Superwoman mindset:** A mindset among African Americans that discourages emotionality, vulnerability, and dependency and encourages strength, determination, and help-giving despite one's own needs (Woods-Giscombé, 2010)

- **"Sitting the month" practice:** A practice in Chinese families that requires new mothers to be confined to their homes for the first month postpartum in adherence to rigid rules around hygiene, diet, and other behaviors (Lee & Brand, 2015)

- **La cuarentena tradition:** A tradition in Mexican families, a period of 40 days during which mothers are prescribed certain healing and rest practices in order to help a woman's body "close" after giving birth (Waugh, 2011)

- **Limited time for postpartum healing:** A limited value placed on perinatal social support in "technocentric" cultures, typically Western cultures that allot only a few days after giving birth to postpartum healing practices (Posmontier & Horowitz, 2004)

Ritual Celebrations:

- **Brit Milah:** A ritual circumcision ceremony among Jewish families (Glick, 2005)

- **Sutak:** Abstinence from participation in ceremonial or religious activities among Hindu families (Bhattacharya et al., 2008)

- **Tahneek:** The application of a softened date to a newborn's mouth among Muslim families (Shaikh & Ahmed, 2006)

Patient Worksheet

SOCIAL RISK FACTORS

This worksheet can help you recognize *social* risk factors that increase your vulnerability for developing a mood and anxiety disorder while you are pregnant or postpartum. Check off any risk factors that are relevant to you, read through the identified risk management strategies, and consider what might get in the way of using one of these strategies. We then encourage you to share this worksheet with your health care provider.

☐ **Significant lifestyle changes in addition to becoming a new mother (e.g., change in job, difficulties with other children, change in housing)**

Risk management strategies:

- Prioritize meeting your basic needs for adequate nutrition, hydration, and sleep.
- Find someone who will listen to you vent and offer emotional support, like a family member, friend, or group for new moms.
- Break down each stressor and identify ways others may be able help in each domain. For example, is your new employer willing to accommodate a later start date, some work-from-home days, or flexible shifts and hours? Can your older child's daycare teacher or school counselor offer you feedback on the difficulties you are having with them? Are there certain things about your new environment that you will find comforting to know right away and other things that can wait (e.g., finding out where the nearest grocery store is and organizing the living room sooner, but finding out where the library is and unpacking the garage later?).

What could interfere with your ability to follow through with these strategies, and how might you overcome this difficulty?

_____

_____

_____

- ☐ **Past or current history of drug and alcohol use**

    Risk management strategies:

    - If you are pregnant or postpartum and struggling with drug and/or alcohol use, it is essential for your health and for the health of your baby that you seek treatment. Disclosing substance use while pregnant can be quite terrifying. It may help to know that most states in the U.S. allow providers to refer pregnant patients to substance abuse treatment without reporting to authorities (Miranda et al., 2015) and that medical organizations such as the American Congress of Obstetricians and Gynecologists oppose prenatal substance use policies that punish a mother for seeking help (Meinhoffer et al., 2022).

    - Despite your fears, stopping any substance use on your own or with support is a necessity. If you have a history of substance use, the perinatal period is a time to proactively resume or continue any helpful self-care activities, such as attending support groups or working with a sponsor.

What could interfere with your ability to follow through with these strategies, and how might you overcome this difficulty?

_____

_____

_____

- ☐ **Complications with the baby's health related to or occurring after the birth**

    Risk management strategies:

    - Share updates, including any needs you may have with friends and family, or designate a support person to do this.
    - If your baby is in the hospital, ask to speak to a social worker on staff and request support and resources.
    - Ask as many questions of your baby's medical providers as you need to understand their condition, their prognosis, and ways you can participate in their healing.
    - Prioritize meeting your basic needs for adequate nutrition, hydration, and sleep.
    - Seek out groups in person or online for parents of babies with health complications, and ask for tips that were helpful for them.

What could interfere with your ability to follow through with these strategies, and how might you overcome this difficulty?

_____

_____

_____

☐ **Financial stressors**

Risk management strategies:

- Ensure that you have resources to meet the basic nutritional, hygiene, and safety needs of yourself, your baby, and your family.
- Recognize that asking for help when this is a struggle can be exceedingly difficult.
- Start by telling someone whom you feel most comfortable disclosing your need (a friend, family member, or provider) and ask them to help you gain access to resources.
- You may also consider searching online for local organizations that provide help to anonymous recipients.

What could interfere with your ability to follow through with these strategies, and how might you overcome this difficulty?

_____

_____

_____

☐ **Pressure from others in your social system to follow certain parenting practices (e.g., how to feed your baby or teach your baby to sleep)**

Risk management strategies:

- Practice setting boundaries.
- Practice advocating for your baby and their needs and communicate clearly about your decisions and preferences for your baby.

- Use affirmations like "I am my baby's parent, and I am capable of deciding when I need advice" to encourage yourself.

What could interfere with your ability to follow through with these strategies, and how might you overcome this difficulty?

_____

_____

_____

☐ **Difficult relationship with your family of origin**

Risk management strategies:

- Practice setting and maintaining boundaries, such as when family members may visit and in what contexts.
- Engage in self-care by giving yourself permission to reinforce your boundaries.
- Combat isolation or loss of support by expanding your idea of family beyond your family of origin to include in-law family, friends, and your community.

What could interfere with your ability to follow through with these strategies, and how might you overcome this difficulty?

_____

_____

_____

☐ **Being a member of a marginalized group (e.g., BIPOC, LGBTQIA+, teen, refugee, and single-parent communities)**

Risk management strategies:

- Seek out inclusive community spaces both locally and online.

- Nurture relationships with safe people whom you feel understand you, and proactively set up times to socialize with these individuals during the perinatal period (and beyond).
- Practice advocating for your needs to medical professionals, and consider asking a friend or a safe provider to help you role-play these conversations.

What could interfere with your ability to follow through with these strategies, and how might you overcome this difficulty?

_____

_____

☐ **Sensitivity to social media influences**

Risk management strategies:

- Establish social media–free periods in your home, such as during dinner, infant feeding times, or certain hours of the day.
- Spend social media time viewing reputable accounts that help you feel curious and empowered instead of inferior and distressed.
- Use helpful apps for meditating, journaling, or connecting with friends instead of social media apps.

What could interfere with your ability to follow through with these strategies, and how might you overcome this difficulty?

_____

_____

☐ **Tendency to "Google" symptoms or engage in reassurance seeking**

Risk management strategies:

- Identify trusted friends, family, or providers who can offer reassurance on a specific topic once (e.g., the pediatrician can be consulted about medical concerns, a mom-friend can give advice on sleep habits, a certain website can direct you to the best diaper brand) and then practice letting go of the worry once you have an answer.

- Practice mindfulness exercises to help you cope with the distress of not knowing or wanting more reassurance.

What could interfere with your ability to follow through with these strategies, and how might you overcome this difficulty?

_____

_____

_____

☐ **Intimate partner violence or a difficult relationship with your partner (or the baby's parent)**

Risk management strategies:

- Talk to a person you trust, like a friend, family member, or provider, about the difficulties you are having, and ask them to help you identify organizations that can help you navigate unsafe relationships.

- Find support urgently through such organizations if someone in your home is experiencing domestic violence or abuse.

- Consider seeking couples counseling with a family therapist or a perinatal mental health care provider who can help you through the adjustment to parenthood, even if you are safe in your relationship but are having a hard time.

What could interfere with your ability to follow through with these strategies, and how might you overcome this difficulty?

_____

_____

_____

☐ **Traumatic birth experience**

Risk management strategies:

- Request an opportunity to debrief or discuss what happened with the provider who delivered your baby or one who provides obstetric care.
- Let go of self-blame by recognizing the aspects of your birth that were out of your control.
- Seek a support group in-person or online for people who have experienced birth trauma.

What could interfere with your ability to follow through with these strategies, and how might you overcome this difficulty?

_____

_____

_____

☐ **History of trauma, recent or in childhood**

Risk management strategies:

- Practice good self-care by nourishing yourself, hydrating, and maintaining consistent sleep routines.
- Develop a meditation or mindfulness practice on your own, with a provider's support, or by using a website or app like Headspace or Calm.

- Reach out to a health care provider to explore professional treatment options if you are experiencing symptoms of PTSD, such as flashbacks, feeling easily startled or hypervigilant, or intrusive thoughts about the trauma.

What could interfere with your ability to follow through with these strategies, and how might you overcome this difficulty?

_____

_____

_____

What additional risk factors are you aware of that could impact your well-being? How might you overcome them? What could stand in the way, and how could you address those difficulties?

_____

_____

_____

If you notice that implementing these strategies or identifying additional strategies for risk reduction is difficult for you, keep in mind that a mental health care provider can help.

Follow Up

☐ I am aware of my social risk factors.

☐ I have shared this worksheet with someone who can support me in reducing my risk.

☐ I have shared this worksheet with my health care provider. That provider's name is:

_____

Patient Worksheet

CULTURAL EXPECTATIONS ABOUT PARENTHOOD

Parents often imagine what it will be like to become part of the social fabric of parenthood. They may find these fantasies exciting, appalling, or somewhere in between. Each parent will have different fantasies and expectations, depending on their individual upbringing and cultural environment. For some, the cultural traditions or rituals associated with childbirth can cause feelings of warmth and belonging. For others, it may feel archaic, stifling, and repressing. Often, parents will experience a blend of both kinds of feelings. This worksheet can help you make sense of some of the cultural pressures you might be experiencing.

Does your family or your partner's family acknowledge pregnancy, birth, the postpartum period, or new infant with certain rituals or traditions? If so, describe any cultural practices that you expect to participate in or have already been a participant of.

_____

_____

_____

_____

Are these practices shared by both your family of origin (and your partner's family of origin, if applicable) or by members of your social circle? How do you feel about this answer?

_____

_____

_____

_____

What emotions do you notice arise related to these practices? Circle any that apply and add your own:

Angry	Scared	Happy	Empowered	Calm	Sad
Hurt	Confused	Excited	Important	Nurtured	Guilty
Frustrated	Insecure	Hopeful	Included	Relaxed	Ashamed
Jealous	Embarrassed	Optimistic	Worthy	Grateful	Isolated

In what ways does your experience feel positive or negative?

_____

_____

_____

If you feel reluctant or even negative about these traditions, have you talked with your partner and family members about this? If not, what is standing in the way, and who (or what) might be able to help you communicate your feelings more clearly?

_____

_____

_____

Psychological Risk Factors

In addition to understanding biological and social factors, an important component of risk assessment is gathering information about a mother's psychological risk factors. Psychological risk factors refer to any personality traits, attitudes, or thinking patterns that reduce resiliency and increase susceptibility to mood and anxiety problems. This can include negative thinking, low self-esteem, or difficulty with flexibility.

The following is a more specific list of some of the most common psychological risk factors:

- *Perfectionism* is experienced by those who expect a level of accuracy, precision, and flawlessness in performance that exceeds appropriate or attainable limits. Perfectionistic people may feel significant internal pressure to meet high standards and believe that anything less than perfection will be a disappointment to themselves or others. Mothers with a tendency toward perfectionism may be especially vulnerable to self-comparison, self-criticism, and intrusive thoughts related to their perceived failure.

- People with *cognitive inflexibility* struggle to move between tasks, adjust to new circumstances, and engage in creative problem-solving. They may be rigid in their thinking, limit access to support, and may experience feelings of powerlessness in response to their symptoms. Mothers who have limited cognitive flexibility may have a difficult time using self-soothing strategies to shift their mindsets or adapt to the rapid changes that occur during the early years of parenthood. Like perfectionism, cognitive inflexibility can increase and reinforce negative self-talk and intrusive thoughts about the self.

- *Rumination* is a thinking style associated with depression. People who ruminate experience a pattern of repetitive thinking that involves a preoccupation with negative thoughts, distress, or symptoms. Perinatal mothers who ruminate, including those with and without depression, often tell us that the hardest part of new motherhood is their inability to stop thinking about what they perceive as their mistakes or failures.

- Locus of control refers to the extent to which someone believes that the actions they take can impact the outcome of a situation. People with an *external locus of control* are more likely to attribute both positive and negative outcomes to factors outside themselves. For example, a mother with an external locus of control who is having difficulty breastfeeding may attribute her difficulties to the shape of her nipples, the lactation consultant who first taught her to latch, the nurse who gave the baby a pacifier in the hospital, or the fact that the baby arrived via C-section. Because this mother believes that these circumstances are out of control of her, she is less likely to take steps to improve the situation. In contrast, a mother with an internal locus of control may recognize that she cannot change the shape of her nipples or the circumstances of her child's birth, while still recognizing that she can meet with a new lactation consultant to troubleshoot a wide variety of feeding issues. People with depression and anxiety are more likely to experience their locus of control as external.

- Finally, *hopelessness* is a well-known risk factor for the development of depressive symptoms, including suicidality. Perinatal mental health professionals must listen for hopelessness with a carefully trained ear. While some patients will declare, "I have never felt so hopeless in my life," more often they will quietly say things like "I am so tired," "I wonder if the baby will outgrow screaming every time we get in the car," or "I'm not sure I'll ever feel like myself again." When hope wanes in our patients, they may fail to see the value in therapy, their efforts, or the idea of tomorrow. Patients may lose confidence in the steps they are taking toward healing, the belief that things will change, and that they will feel better as their symptoms improve. For a population in which rates of depression, suicidal ideation, and suicide completion are so high, any expression of despair and despondency must be taken seriously. It is for this reason that the idea of building hope has been referenced many times throughout this book. Hope connects us to the future and the belief that there will be a tomorrow which will be, at best, joyful and exciting or, at the very least, worth waking up to see.

The following worksheet can help mothers gain greater insight into their psychological risk factors so they can communicate this information to their providers and address them during, or even before, pregnancy. We also encourage you to revisit *A Hopeful Letter to Myself* from chapter 2.

Patient Worksheet

PSYCHOLOGICAL RISK FACTORS

This worksheet can help you recognize *psychological* risk factors that increase your vulnerability for developing a mood and anxiety disorder while you are pregnant or postpartum. Check off any risk factors that are relevant to you, read through the identified risk management strategies, and consider what might get in the way of using one of these strategies.

☐ **Perfectionism or critical self-talk**

Risk management strategies:

- Make a list of positive affirmations, statements, or quotations that you can refer to easily and often.
- Practice recognizing your critical self-talk and respond with positive affirmations.
- Notice or inquire about how other people in your life cope with imperfection, disappointment, and failure.

What could interfere with your ability to follow through with these strategies, and how might you overcome this difficulty?

_____

_____

_____

☐ **Low self-esteem**

Risk management strategies:

- Keep a journal where you list your "wins" each day, such as things that caused you to feel proud of yourself, ways you have been helpful to others, or goals that you are meeting (no matter how small).
- Schedule time each week to do an activity that helps you to feel strong and capable, such as exercising, expressing yourself creatively, or volunteering.

What could interfere with your ability to follow through with these strategies, and how might you overcome this difficulty?

_____

_____

_____

☐ **Tendency to ruminate or worry**

Risk management strategies:

- Use distractions to shift your thinking, such as watching a TV show or movie you enjoy, playing with your baby, or listening to music or an audiobook.
- Write down the negative thoughts you are focused on and ask yourself whether there is something you can do to address these thoughts.
- Reach out to a family member or friend, or use affirmations, to receive support and compassion.

What could interfere with your ability to follow through with these strategies, and how might you overcome this difficulty?

_____

_____

_____

☐ **Difficulty adjusting flexibly to new changes**

Risk management strategies:

- Use affirmations to recognize and remind yourself that over time, changes will feel familiar ("Becoming a mother is hard, but I'll get used to being in this new role over time").

- Use affirmations to remember that you have adapted to change before ("I remember feeling uncomfortable at the start of the school year because getting to know a new class routine was hard, but I got through it").
- Reach out to a family member or friend to support you through the change.

What could interfere with your ability to follow through with these strategies, and how might you overcome this difficulty?

_____

_____

_____

☐ **Difficulty letting go of unmet expectations**

Risk management strategies:

- Acknowledge feelings of disappointment, anger, or unfulfillment.
- When things do not go as planned, remember that your ability to accept reality and let go of disappointment will provide relief from suffering (this is called radical acceptance).
- Explore ways you can create change when an opportunity exists. For example, if your baby's sleep schedule is more erratic than you expected, you could contact your pediatrician to learn strategies to help regulate your baby's sleep while also recognizing that infant sleep is sometimes unpredictable.

What could interfere with your ability to follow through with these strategies, and how might you overcome this difficulty?

_____

_____

_____

If you notice that implementing these strategies or identifying additional strategies for risk reduction is difficult for you, keep in mind that a mental health care provider can help.

Follow Up

☐   I am aware of my psychological risk factors.

☐   I have shared this worksheet with someone who can support me in reducing my risk.

☐   I have shared this worksheet with my health care provider. That provider's name is:

_____

Risk Reduction Via Self-Care

Now that you have learned a bit more about the various risk factors for perinatal mood and anxiety disorders, pause for a moment to consider what it might be like for a pregnant mother to be approaching motherhood in the context of these life experiences:

- Becoming a mother having grown up in a home impacted by the presence of a mood and anxiety disorder.

- Becoming a mother with the knowledge that your own mood and anxiety disorder could recur and impact your new baby or your own family in some way.

- Becoming a mother with the awareness that there is not much you can do about how your body behaves—that the circumstances of your birth and your hormonal reactions are out of your control.

- Becoming a mother while feeling isolated due to a lifetime of difficult relationships, a strained relationship with your parents or immediate family, domestic violence, racism, geographical limitations, socioeconomic factors, or public health and political circumstances.

- Becoming a mother and having no one who understands your experience or who can offer another set of helping hands.

- Becoming a mother as a BIPOC in the United States with the recognition that health outcomes for Black mothers and babies is exceptionally poor compared to those of White mothers and babies.

- Becoming a mother as a survivor of trauma and experiencing the intensity of pregnancy, birth, and the emotional transition to motherhood in a body and mind that has a history of being battered and violated.

As a provider, it is important to empathize with these various circumstances and to understand that women experience a major life adjustment when they become mothers, especially when they are carrying the load of these life experiences. Moreover, although certain women are at greater risk than others for developing a perinatal mood and anxiety disorder, *all* women are at some risk. As a result, all women should be mindful of these risk factors and take the appropriate steps to reduce their vulnerability as much as possible. However, we recognize that not all women will require or have the luxury of accessing therapeutic services, which is why we believe it is crucial to empower women with tools for self-care.

For many mothers, self-care feels like a luxury, one that is simply inaccessible at this life stage. Time is precious, with every moment consumed by some sort of work—motherhood-related or otherwise. Finances are limited. Self-care activities from pre-parent life feel unfulfilling, uncomfortable, or strange. Mothers' ideas about how a mother should behave clash with their longing for rest and reconnection with their pre-parent selves.

While it is true that some forms of self-care are luxurious and perhaps not attainable in this season of life (e.g., a child-free weekend getaway with friends), it is essential that mothers learn how to take care of themselves on a *daily* basis. Breaking down the broad concept of self-care into discrete categories can allow the idea of daily self-care seem more manageable and accessible. We find that mothers are often surprised when we point out that many kinds of activities fall under the category of self-care and find it comforting to know that it may not be as impossible to engage in self-care practices as they thought. Some categories we recommend sharing with mothers are:

- Attending to their physical needs (e.g., staying hydrated)
- Self-soothing when overwhelmed or in distress
- Establishing boundaries
- Finding time for enjoyable activities to do alone
- Finding time for enjoyable activities to do with a partner or friend
- Making time for relaxation and rest
- Advocating for themselves when they feel vulnerable

When mothers think about self-care in terms of *literally* taking care of themselves, it reframes the concept, reinforcing the importance of integrating self-care into daily habits and routines to shift attention away from the idea that self-care is an indulgence. Therefore, it is critical to encourage mothers to integrate self-care practices into their regular routine and problem solve any barriers to achieving this goal. While problem-solving through barriers is a critical part of this process, it is equally important for you to allow space for patients to express any feelings of loss, grief, and resentment they may be feeling toward their babies, partners, or other life circumstances that they feel have robbed them of their independence. Validate their pain while also helping them overcome any obstacles that may interfere with their self-care efforts.

Patient Worksheet

SELF-CARE CHECKLIST

When you are preoccupied with your pregnancy or your baby, it is easy to lose track of your own needs and well-being. Symptoms of exhaustion, burnout, or even illness can quickly sneak up on you. Maintaining your basic self-care needs is an important step toward reducing your risk of developing a perinatal mood and anxiety disorder. Review the items on this list and check off any self-care goals that you would be interested in incorporating into your daily routine.

☐ I will eat regular meals daily instead of snacking.

☐ I will ask my partner or another support person to care for my baby, or I will put my baby in a bouncer or swing, so I can sit down for one meal each day.

☐ I will ask someone else (like a neighbor, friend, family member, partner, or restaurant) to provide dinner one night.

☐ I will keep a water bottle nearby and stay hydrated.

☐ I will stretch for at least five minutes per day to soothe my sore muscles.

☐ I will use physical activities like dancing, walking, jogging, swimming, or playing a physical game to alleviate stress.

☐ I will use yoga, mindfulness, or meditation to soothe my frayed nerves.

☐ I will go out into the sunshine and notice the sounds, smells, and sights of nature.

☐ I will listen to music, sing, watch a funny show or movie, or get lost in an enjoyable book or podcast to improve my mood.

☐ I will make a short list of chores I can accomplish each day and check them off one at a time so I feel more organized.

☐ I will develop a system for keeping track of appointments, items I need to buy at the store, and other things I need to remember so I can worry less about forgetting.

☐ I will plant flowers, paint, make a scrapbook, or create arts and crafts so I can look at something beautiful and use my creativity.

☐ I will look for a class, book, or tutorial to learn a new skill, recipe, or technique that I will enjoy using.

☐ I will plan a date to go somewhere with a friend, family member, or my partner so that we can spend quality time together.

☐ I will take a moment to notice how it feels in my body when I am holding my baby and they are calm and relaxed, and I will remind myself then that I am a good mother.

Patient Worksheet

CARING FOR YOURSELF

As a new mother, taking care of your needs is often the last thing on your list, especially when the one person receiving all the attention is your baby—not you. Babies, symptoms of depression, and other stressors can get in the way of reaching your self-care goals. This worksheet will help you develop a plan for coping on days when your self-care goals are hard to reach.

What types of habits helped you maintain your well-being in the past? This can include habits related to nutrition, exercise, hygiene, spirituality, socializing, routine medical care, and more.

_____

_____

_____

_____

How is your pregnancy, baby, or mental health interfering with your ability to maintain these habits?

_____

_____

_____

_____

When you make self-care plans, it is very encouraging when these plans work out. Sometimes, however, your baby may not go down for the nap that allows you some time to read, you might have to work late and miss your evening walk, or your partner might get stuck in traffic, and you miss your opportunity for a long shower (or any shower). When this happens, try using one of these strategies to cope:

- Look for possible solutions to the problem. Could you read while your baby plays near you? Could you take the baby for a walk with you in the stroller or a carrier? Could your baby sit in a bouncer in the bathroom while you shower?

- Practice self-compassion by validating your frustration. Say out loud or in your mind that it is sad and disappointing to miss out on opportunities for self-care. Remind yourself that you can try again tomorrow and that giving yourself kindness will be more helpful than focusing on your failure.

- Try lifting your mood by choosing a different method of self-care that might be more accessible. For example, if you work late and miss your walk, could you listen to uplifting music or stop for a yummy snack on your way home?

With these tips in mind, what strategies can you use to overcome the barriers you identified earlier?

_____

_____

_____

_____

If these strategies don't work well enough, consider seeking support from a professional who can help you dive more deeply into the issue and help develop self-care plans that work.

CHAPTER 7

"What Can I Do for Relief?"

When mothers are struggling during the perinatal period, more than anything else, they want relief from the symptoms they are experiencing. They want to feel like good mothers and *be* good mothers. They want to feel reengaged with their partners, family, and friends. They want to feel like themselves again. They want to know how to achieve these goals and how they can immediately feel relief. In our years of clinical experience, we have come to recognize that mothers presenting for therapy in the perinatal period require two types of relief:

1. Relief from the uncertainty, overwhelm, and fragility inherent in the perinatal period
2. Relief from symptoms of perinatal mood and anxiety disorders

While separating these categories may seem unnecessary at first glance, consider the following example: Maya, a single mother to a five-month-old daughter, presented for therapy highly distressed and tearful. She reported having daily intrusive thoughts about her daughter's safety at daycare and envisioned terrible things happening to her daughter many times each day. As Maya explained it, "I worked so hard to find just the right daycare environment, and I know this place is perfect for her. I love her teachers, she has little baby friends, and they are so loving and attentive. There is no reason for me to worry. But I do worry—and constantly."

On the days Maya could bring herself to go to work, it took a long time to get ready to leave the house. She would check and recheck her daughter's outfits to make sure they weren't too tight and didn't have any loose strings. She would pack and repack her daughter's bottles to make sure they were clean, and she packed ample milk so her daughter would not be accidentally poisoned or starve. As soon as Maya arrived at work, she would become so distracted by the intrusive thoughts that she would call the daycare center frequently to check in, believing that her calls would somehow ensure her safety. At least one or two days each week, the obsessive thoughts were so distressing that she would call in sick.

Because Maya was so consumed by these thoughts, she had difficulty completing tasks at work and started receiving negative feedback from her supervisors as her performance suffered. Between her poor performance and frequent absences, Maya recognized that she was putting her job security in jeopardy, but she felt helpless to do things differently. On work nights, she would lay awake debating with herself: *Should I be a terrible mother tomorrow by sending my child to daycare where I am sure she will die? Or should I be a terrible mother tomorrow by missing work again and risking whether I will be able to put food on our table?*

As this example illustrates, Maya was suffering from OCD. She experienced recurrent and persistent intrusive thoughts that caused her high anxiety and distress, and when she failed to neutralize them, she developed compulsive behaviors that she believed would somehow prevent something terrible from happening to her daughter. These behaviors took up so much of her time that even her job was at risk.

While Maya clearly required treatment for OCD, which can be treated successfully by providers who do not specialize in perinatal mental health, she also needed help addressing the deep, dark worry that so many new mothers experience: the fear that she would be a bad mother. Maya's OCD symptoms were reinforcing this belief, and without addressing this perinatal-specific distress, she could not fully recover. Indeed, women who receive treatment for mood and anxiety disorders but who do not also address the nuanced distress of the perinatal stage (and the overlap between the two) report to us, even years after they recover, that their recovery feels "incomplete."

Therefore, this chapter includes worksheets designed to augment the work of mental health care providers who are treating perinatal patients for mood and anxiety disorders. The worksheets in this chapter are divided into four categories: (1) unmet expectations, (2) changes in identity, (3) loss of normalcy, and (4) symptom relief. The first three categories correspond to common themes reported by perinatal patients that contribute to their distress. The fourth category is intended to provide symptom relief for some of the most disruptive symptoms of perinatal mood and anxiety disorders.

Providers may use these worksheets to guide sessions with patients or assign them as homework between sessions. Mothers using this book on their own may find these worksheets useful for sorting through their feelings and decide that further exploration with a mental health care provider would be helpful. Keep in mind that none of these worksheets are intended to serve as treatment for a mood and anxiety disorder. What these worksheets are intended to do is increase attention to the patient's specific perinatal state, therefore offering a more comprehensive approach to treatment.

Worksheets Included in This Chapter by Theme

Developing Expectations:

- How I Imagined Motherhood Would Feel
- The "Good Enough" Mother
- Feeding Decisions
- Baby Steps

Identity Changes:

- Symptoms Experienced as Self
- Imagining the Future
- Becoming a Mother Changed Me
- What I Have Gained, What I Have Lost
- Planning Another Pregnancy

Finding a New Normal:

- Daily Routine
- How Will I Know When I Have Found a New Normal?
- Your Relationship with Change
- Understanding Changes
- Are My Symptoms Back?

Symptom Relief:

- Negative Self-Talk
- Strategies for Self-Soothing
- Talking with Providers and Support People about Scary Thoughts
- Thought Patterns of Perinatal Mood and Anxiety Disorders
- Breaking Down Hyperbole
- Rage
- Insomnia
- Coping with Perinatal Panic
- Making Sense of Birth Trauma
- Risk Management for Perinatal Bipolar Disorders
- Signs of Recovery

Patient Worksheet

DEVELOPING EXPECTATIONS: HOW I IMAGINED MOTHERHOOD WOULD FEEL

Unmet expectations are a challenging, but normal, part of becoming a parent. Your expectations for motherhood may be informed by your culture, childhood fantasies, stories told over generations by family members, the experience of your friends, or even social media. Understanding your expectations and where they come from is the first step toward accepting and coping with any disappointment you may feel. Use the following prompts to explore how becoming a mother is different from what you expected.

As a young child, what were your fantasies about becoming a mother? Some ideas to consider are:

- Who did you think would be part of your support system?
- How did you imagine you would feel about motherhood?
- How did you imagine you would feel about your baby?
- What did you envision your partnership or marriage would be like?
- Did you see yourself as a stay-at-home mom?
- Did you see yourself as career-focused or working outside the home?
- When you thought about what your baby would be like, what did you expect?
- How did you expect your body to look or feel?
- Do you recall having ideas about what becoming pregnant, giving birth, or being postpartum would be like?

What were some of your fantasies regarding motherhood?

_____

_____

_____

How did your parents' stories or cultural background influence the kind of mother you wanted to be?

_____

_____

_____

When you reflect on the movies, TV shows, or other social media influences that have contributed to your expectations, what comes to mind?

_____

_____

_____

How does your experience of motherhood compare to what you expected?

_____

_____

_____

Can you identify any examples of mothers in real life or fiction whose experiences relate to your actual experiences? If you cannot find any relatable influences, where might you look?

_____

_____

_____

Patient Worksheet

DEVELOPING EXPECTATIONS: THE "GOOD ENOUGH" MOTHER

To a baby, a good mother is a person who loves them, feeds them, soothes them, and plays with them. Babies neither require nor care about perfection in their mothers; they simply require a good enough mother. The idea of the "good enough" mother (or a "good enough" parent) was first developed in 1953 by Donald Winnicott, a pediatrician and psychiatrist. According to Winnicott, a good enough mother starts off being hyperresponsive to her new baby's every cry or whimper, responding with immediacy and urgency. However, as the baby grows older, the mother cannot give the child her full attention every waking moment—*and this is okay*. These small frustrations help the child develop the healthy independence they ultimately need to adapt to the realities of the external world.

Most parents feel relieved to know that being good enough *is* perfect. If this describes you, take a moment to think about a phrase, a quotation, an image, or even a photo that can remind you of this when you are questioning your ability as a mother. For example, a phrase like "Exactly who I am is good enough" can soothe you and make you feel anchored and able to find your confidence again. On the other hand, if learning about the good enough mother still doesn't provide you with relief or reassurance, answer the following questions to think about what might be getting in the way.

Think about your parenting role models. What qualities did they have that you would like to embody?

_____

_____

_____

Can you recognize ways your role model(s) might have been good enough instead of perfect? If they are available, you might ask them about their experience parenting and what they think about the idea of being good enough.

_____

_____

_____

What is your gut reaction to the idea that good enough parenting is truly what your baby needs? You may find it helpful to write down some of your thoughts and emotions related to this reaction.

_____

_____

_____

With this new awareness, consider ways you are meeting your baby's needs. Consider how you show love and provide care. Now review the introduction to this exercise, and think about how you would now answer the question, "Are you a good enough mother?"

_____

_____

_____

Patient Worksheet

DEVELOPING EXPECTATIONS: FEEDING DECISIONS

Feeding a newborn is an important, exhausting, and time-consuming activity. Mothers often feel tremendous pressure when deciding how their baby will be fed, whether they choose to breastfeed, bottle-feed, or both. This worksheet can help you think about how you will feed your baby and communicate with others about your decision.

How do you hope to feed your baby? What feeding options are available to you? What are some pros and cons of each option?

_____

_____

_____

What is influencing your decision-making? For example, what social or cultural messages have you received about feeding babies?

_____

_____

_____

Do you agree with these social or cultural messages? Fully? Somewhat? Not at all?

_____

_____

_____

How do you feel, or how do you expect you will feel, when you formula feed? Breastfeed? Pump breastmilk?

_____

_____

_____

What do you like, or think you will like, the most about feeding your baby? Will it be the experience of holding them? Listening to them gulp down milk or formula? Experiencing skin-to-skin contact? Do you think you can you enjoy this regardless of whether you breastfeed or bottle-feed your baby?

_____

_____

_____

Once your baby arrives and you start the feeding process (whether by breast, bottle, or a combination of both), observe your baby while they feed. How do they react when feeding?

_____

_____

_____

If you are still unsure what feeding options are right for you, we encourage you to contact your pediatrician or a lactation consultant. They can also discuss the option of combination feeding—when babies are fed some breastmilk and some formula.

Patient Worksheet

DEVELOPING EXPECTATIONS: BABY STEPS

It is difficult to imagine that the newborn you are cradling, the six-month-old you are rocking, or the one-year-old you are chasing will eventually become a person who is able to communicate with words, adhere to social expectations, and sleep, feed, and care for themselves independently. The journey from full dependence to independence is long, and for parents who are anxious, exhausted, or stressed out, it feels never-ending. It can help to recognize that some of your baby's most demanding and anxiety-provoking behaviors are actually signs that they are getting a little closer to independence.

Social-Emotional Development

Babies under the age of one are practicing relationship-building when they:

- Smile at you
- Begin to respond to or mimic the emotions they observe others are having
- Cling to you or to a favorite toy
- Purposefully try to solicit the attention of familiar people
- Avoid or behave shyly with strangers

In what ways do you recognize that your baby is forming relationships with others? In what ways is this joyful for you? In what ways is this anxiety-provoking?

_____

_____

_____

_____

_____

Communication and Language Development

Babies under the age of one are learning to express themselves when they:

- Cry
- Practice making consonant sounds like buh buh buh or da da da
- Copy others' movements and sounds
- Use recognizable words like *mama* or *dada*

In what ways is your baby learning self-expression? In what ways does this bring you joy? In what ways is this anxiety-provoking?

_____

_____

_____

_____

Cognitive Development

Babies under the age of one are trying to understand the world around them when they:

- Show interest in watching you move a certain toy in front of their eyes or focus on a mobile
- Turn toward sounds
- Put things in their mouths
- Learn to grasp and then pass items from one hand to another.
- Play games like peek-a-boo or throw-my-food-on-the-floor
- Follow simple directions like "hold your cup"

In what ways is your baby developing cognitively? Do you notice your baby's thinking is changing? In what ways does this bring you joy? In what ways is this anxiety-provoking?

_____

_____

_____

_____

Movement and Physical Development

Babies under the age of one are learning how their bodies work when they:

- Practice holding their heads up or turn their heads side to side
- Study their feet and hands
- Begin to sit independently
- Pull up on furniture or in their cribs
- Practice standing and moving from standing to sitting

In what ways is your baby's movement and body changing? In what ways does this bring you joy? In what ways is this anxiety-provoking?

_____

_____

_____

_____

Patient Worksheet

IDENTITY CHANGES: SYMPTOMS EXPERIENCED AS SELF

In the perinatal period, women often experience intense emotions that are expressed as *symptoms*, but that women experience as the *self*. That is, they believe whatever they are thinking or feeling is who they have become. As women with perinatal mood and anxiety disorders navigate the normal difficulties of motherhood, they begin to assume that feelings like incompetence, dependence, or failure must be a normal and miserable part of motherhood. Beliefs like "Now I am a failure" or "Now everything will always be out of my control" increase feelings of helplessness and despair. When you can understand that these beliefs are actually *symptoms* of a perinatal mood and anxiety disorder, even though they feel like *who you are*, it can be an important step toward healing.

Look through the list of negative thoughts commonly experienced by mothers with perinatal mood and anxiety disorders and check off any that apply to you. Then identify affirmations that you might find helpful in combatting these thoughts.

Common Negative Thoughts

- ☐ I am a bad mother.
- ☐ Everything is out of my control.
- ☐ I am powerless over how I am feeling.
- ☐ My loved ones will abandon me.
- ☐ This must be how motherhood feels; I will always feel this way now.
- ☐ Other: _____

Helpful Affirmations

- ☐ I am struggling with symptoms right now. As I work through my perinatal mood and anxiety disorder, I will begin to understand that I am doing the best I can and that I am not a bad mother.

- ☐ It is hard to feel in control when caring for a baby. If I really think about it, I realize there are a few things I can control, like asking my friend to come hold the baby for an hour so that I can take a shower today.

Copyright © 2023 Hilary Waller and Karen Kleiman, *The Perinatal Patient*. All rights reserved.

- ❒ My symptoms are so powerful that they cause me to feel powerless sometimes. If I take good care of myself today, even though I'm not feeling strong, I might start to feel a little better soon.

- ❒ Watching me experience a mood and anxiety disorder must be scary, but my loved ones are standing by me. I recognize this when I remember _____.

- ❒ My symptoms started almost as soon as I became a new mother, so of course I think this is how motherhood feels. I can't imagine it any other way. I am holding on to hope that as my symptoms improve, my experience of motherhood will improve too.

- ❒ Other: _____

Patient Worksheet

IDENTITY CHANGES: IMAGINING THE FUTURE

The literal and figurative noise of a baby makes it difficult to imagine what life might be like beyond this very moment. When you feel stuck in time—believing your life will never be anything different from what it is right now—it can help to think for a moment about what life might be like in the next year, or even five years. Here are some questions to help you consider what can change in the future.

How old will your baby be in one year (or five years)?

_____

_____

_____

_____

What are children like at that age? What activities can they do at that age that they cannot do now?

_____

_____

_____

_____

With this in mind, what family activities can you look forward to with a child at that age? What is something different you can plan with them that isn't realistic right now?

_____

_____

_____

_____

When you look into the future from this lens, what feelings arise for you? Does it shift how you are feeling about the current moment?

_____

_____

_____

_____

Patient Worksheet

IDENTITY CHANGES: BECOMING A MOTHER CHANGED ME

Many women feel that becoming a mother changes them in important ways. It changes their relationships, their sense of responsibility, their body, their autonomy, and their ability to think of anyone but themselves. These changes may be welcome or unwelcome—causing confusion and ambivalence for many mothers. When changes feel hard, tapping into your well of resiliency can help you cope with the challenges of your new identity as a mother. This worksheet can help you connect to your own strength and build on the resources you already have.

Think of a past challenge you were worried you might not overcome. What it was like to navigate that difficult time?

_____

_____

_____

_____

What qualities within yourself helped you get through this challenge?

_____

_____

_____

_____

Looking back now, how did this experience change you?

_____

_____

_____

Now think of some motherhood-related challenges that are worrying you. Describe them here.

_____

_____

_____

Consider your inherent qualities that helped you navigate this earlier challenge. How could these strengths help you now?

_____

_____

_____

What might be getting in the way of using these strengths now? Is there anyone or anything that could help you remove some of these barriers?

_____

_____

_____

Patient Worksheet

IDENTITY CHANGES: WHAT I HAVE GAINED, WHAT I HAVE LOST

Many people associate grief and loss with the death of a significant person in their life. And because it is common to associate motherhood with joy and gains, the paradox of finding relief in talking about motherhood-related losses may feel surprising. This worksheet can help you identify and work through feelings about your losses and also recognize some of the gains associated with motherhood. Keep in mind that gains may not cancel out losses, but maintaining awareness of both gains and losses can increase feelings of hope.

Losses

The following are some commonly experienced types of losses. Which ones can you relate to?

- ☐ Spontaneity
- ☐ Sleep and quiet meals
- ☐ Confidence in your body
- ☐ Sexuality and intimacy
- ☐ Expendable income
- ☐ Control and predictability
- ☐ The special attention of being pregnant
- ☐ The dream of being a perfect mother
- ☐ The dream of a perfect baby
- ☐ Other: _____

Copyright © 2023 Hilary Waller and Karen Kleiman, *The Perinatal Patient*. All rights reserved.

What feelings do you have about these losses?

_____
_____
_____

Know that it is normal to feel sad, angry, or resentful about these losses. Using comforting self-talk can help. For example: "I do not like how I am feeling, but these feelings are likely to pass" or, "Right now, I am having a hard time being physically intimate with my partner, but we can work on feeling connected in other ways."

Gains

What is one activity you enjoy doing with your baby and/or children?

_____
_____
_____
_____

What are three new skills you have mastered as a result of becoming a mother?

_____
_____
_____
_____

Compliment your body on one of its achievements since becoming a mother.

_____

_____

_____

Identify a way you have been able to relinquish control.

_____

_____

_____

Identify a most gratifying moment of your child's development.

_____

_____

_____

Identify a moment when you felt increased intimacy with your partner since becoming parents.

_____

_____

_____

Patient Worksheet

IDENTITY CHANGES: PLANNING ANOTHER PREGNANCY

After mothers begin to embrace their new identity, many start thinking about family planning again. However, planning another pregnancy can feel scary after experiencing a perinatal mood and anxiety disorder. It is normal for parents to worry about whether they will experience symptoms again and to wonder if there is anything they can do to prevent a recurrence. Mothers can use The Postpartum Pact to learn from their previous experiences and to communicate what they now know about their recovery. The pact is designed for mothers to complete alone or with a support person. Once complete, it can serve as a guide for your support people to use during a subsequent perinatal period.

The Postpartum Pact

We are reading this together because I need your help. It's possible that after the birth of our baby, I might not feel well. Since I'm at risk for depression again, we need to be alert for some of the signs so we address things right away.

I need to trust that you will be observant and candid about what you see and what concerns you.

You need to trust that I am a good judge of how I am feeling.

In the event that my symptoms interfere with my ability to determine how I am feeling or what is best for me, it is crucial that you solicit help from our family, our friends, my doctor, and my therapist. We both know that it is better to be overly cautious than to assume things will get better on their own.

I need you to tell me now that you understand how important all of this is and that you are prepared to act accordingly. Knowing this will give me great comfort.

These are questions that may help you determine how things are going after our baby is born. They all may not apply to us, but they will provide a general outline for us to follow. As we review each point together, we will highlight those that feel particularly relevant to our situation, so we don't miss a thing. If any feeling or experience that we went through has been overlooked, we will discuss that together and add it to the pact. After our baby arrives, I will depend on you to review these items a number of times at various stages since things can potentially change.

Here's what I need you to look for:

- ☐ Am I acting like myself?
- ☐ Is there anything I am saying or doing that seems out of character to you or not like my usual self? Am I too worried, too withdrawn, too talkative, too euphoric, too exhausted, too hyper, too unhappy, too uninterested? Do I seem confused?
- ☐ Am I crying all the time?
- ☐ Am I eating the way I usually do?
- ☐ Am I taking care of myself the way I typically do? Am I spending time with the baby?
- ☐ Am I reacting appropriately to the baby?
- ☐ Do I seem too worried or too detached regarding the baby? Am I less interested in things that used to interest me?
- ☐ Is my anxiety getting in the way of doing what I need to do?
- ☐ Do I seem preoccupied with worry or fear that seems out of proportion to you? Do I resist spending time with people who care about me?
- ☐ Do I seem too attentive or concerned with the baby's health? Am I having trouble sleeping, even when the baby is sleeping?
- ☐ Am I overly concerned with things being done perfectly with no room for mistakes? Are you noticing that I am isolating myself though I am fearful of being alone?
- ☐ Am I too angry, too irritable, too anxious, or too short-tempered?
- ☐ Am I having panic attacks where I say I can't breathe or think clearly?

Here's what I need you to listen for:

- ☐ Am I saying anything that scares you? Do I say I think something is wrong? Do I say I just don't feel like myself?
- ☐ Am I telling you I can't or don't want to do something that surprises you? Am I telling you I want to leave, or stop all this, or hurt myself?
- ☐ Am I asking you for things I don't usually ask for?
- ☐ Am I saying I'm too scared, too tired, or too unable to do what I need to do? Am I asking you to stay home with me all the time?

- ☐ Am I telling you I can't do this without your help?
- ☐ Am I expressing feelings of inadequacy, failure, or hopelessness?
- ☐ Do I keep asking you for reassurance or ask you to repeat the same thing over and over? Am I complaining a lot about how I feel physically (headaches, stomachaches, chest pains, shortness of breath)?
- ☐ Am I telling you we made a mistake, and I don't want this baby? Am I blaming everything on our marriage?
- ☐ Am I worried that you'll leave me?
- ☐ Do I tell you that you and the baby would be better off without me? Am I afraid I will always feel this way?
- ☐ Do I tell you I'm a bad mother?

Here's what I need you to do:

- ☐ Check in with me on a regular basis, several times a day. Ask me how I'm feeling and ask me what you can do to help.
- ☐ Enlist our friends and family to help whenever possible during the early weeks. Even if I resist, please insist that it's better for me to accept the help.
- ☐ Remind me that I've been through this before and things got better. Help me even if I don't ask.
- ☐ Insist that I rest even if I'm not able to sleep. Make sure I eat, even if I'm not hungry.
- ☐ Spend as much time caring for the baby as you can.
- ☐ If you are the slightest bit worried, encourage me to contact my doctor and therapist. If I protest, tell me that you will call them for me and come with me to the appointment.
- ☐ Remind me that even if everything's okay, it may be helpful and reassuring to make an appointment so we know for certain.
- ☐ Take a walk with me.
- ☐ Help with the baby during the night. If you're not able to, please make sure someone else is there to help out so I don't get sleep deprived, which would make everything worse.
- ☐ Trust your instincts if you are worried or you think something needs to be done differently. Talk to me. Tell me what you're thinking.

- ☐ Sit with me. Stay close even when there's nothing to say. Help me get professional help.
- ☐ Help me find the joy. Help me stay present and appreciate the little things. Help me find and feel the butterflies, the giggles, the hugs, the sunshine, the belly laughs, the smiles.

Here's what I need you to say:

- ☐ Tell me you will do whatever I need you to do to make sure I feel healthy. Tell me you can tolerate my anxiety, fears, irritability, and moodiness.
- ☐ Tell me you are keeping an eye on how I am feeling so things won't get out of hand. Tell me you love me.
- ☐ Tell me I'm a good mother.
- ☐ Tell me it's okay if things aren't perfect all the time.
- ☐ Tell me you are not going to leave me no matter what.

Here's what I need you to *not* do or say:

- ☐ Do not assume I am fine because I say I am.
- ☐ Do not leave everything up to me if I am feeling overwhelmed.
- ☐ Do not use this time to work harder, later, or longer if I need you home during the first few weeks. Do not tell me to snap out of it. I can't.
- ☐ Do not let my resistance or denial get in the way of what we need to do. Do not tell everyone how well I'm doing if I'm not doing well.
- ☐ Please do not tell me I am strong and that I can do this without help if I need help.
- ☐ Please do not sabotage any effort I might need to make to seek treatment, such as resisting medication or pressuring me about the financial strain.
- ☐ Do not complain about the cost of treatment.
- ☐ Do not pressure me to have sex while I'm feeling so bad.
- ☐ Please do not do anything behind my back. If you are worried, let me know. If you want to call my doctor, let me know you are doing this.
- ☐ Do not forget to take care of yourself during this time.
- ☐ Make sure you are eating well, resting as much as possible, and finding support for yourself from friends and family.

Here's what I need you to remember:

- ☐ I'm doing the best I can.

- ☐ Sometimes the big things that seem scary at first aren't as scary as more subtle things. For instance, if I have an anxiety attack or snap at you, even though it's upsetting, it may not be as troublesome as if I'm isolating myself in the bedroom and quietly withdrawing.

- ☐ If you're not sure about something regarding how I am feeling or how I am acting, please ask for help and tell me you will call my doctor or therapist.

- ☐ If I become symptomatic, chances are things will not get better on their own.

- ☐ Do not underestimate how much I appreciate the fact that I know I can count on you during difficult times.

Things we need to add to our list:

1. _____
2. _____
3. _____
4. _____
5. _____

Patient Worksheet

FINDING A NEW NORMAL: DAILY ROUTINE

There is no question that routines and schedules are important for mothers and babies, and many parenting websites, books, and experts focus on helping new mothers establish them. While many of these resources focus on helping *babies* settle into routines, it is equally important to find *your* new routine as well. Use this worksheet to create a routine for yourself, keeping in mind your baby's schedule and needs.

Begin by listing your baby's routine from morning through night, making sure to consider when your baby typically sleeps, eats, has appointments, plays with you, rests or plays alone in a bouncer or play area, and so on. Then look through items on the self-care essentials list and note when these activities might fit in your day. Keep in mind that some moms find it helpful to adhere to a schedule that corresponds to specific hours of the day or to parts of the day. Other mothers may find it more helpful to make a list of a few activities they would like to accomplish in a day, crossing items off as they go. Use the chart on the next page as a guide to help find the type of list that works best for you.

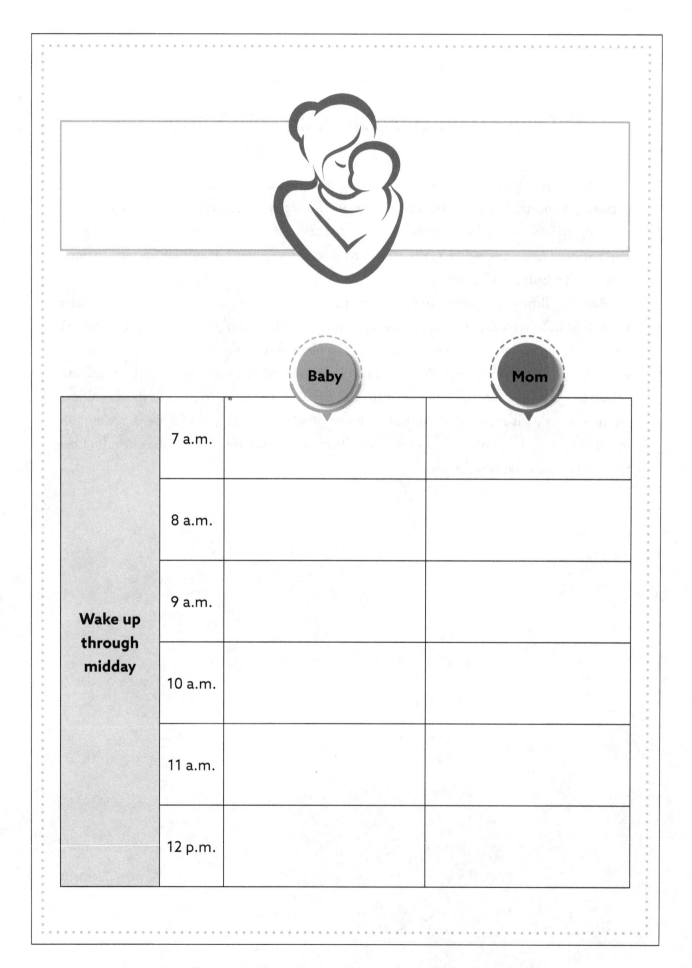

		Baby	Mom
Wake up through midday	7 a.m.		
	8 a.m.		
	9 a.m.		
	10 a.m.		
	11 a.m.		
	12 p.m.		

		Baby	Mom
Midday through early evening	1 p.m.		
	2 p.m.		
	3 p.m.		
	4 p.m.		
	5 p.m.		
Early evening through bedtime	6 p.m.		
	7 p.m.		
	8 p.m.		
	9 p.m.		
	10 p.m.		

		Baby	Mom
Overnight	11 p.m.		
	12 a.m.		
	1 a.m.		
	2 a.m.		
	3 a.m.		
	4 a.m.		
	5 a.m.		
	6 a.m.		

Self-Care Essentials List

- ☐ Meals (three per day)
- ☐ Snacks
- ☐ Sleep
- ☐ Fresh air or time outside
- ☐ Light exercise (e.g., short walk, stretching)
- ☐ Hygiene rituals (e.g., brushing teeth, showering)
- ☐ Quiet time
- ☐ Enjoyable activity time (e.g., putting on makeup, watching a show on TV, reading)
- ☐ Sleep
- ☐ Chores*

Tip: Notice how some of your self-care items can be combined. For example, you might find that a daily walk with your baby in a stroller or carrier meets your needs for fresh air, light exercise, and playtime with your baby. Regardless, hydrating with water is essential throughout your routine.

---

* **Disclaimer:** On the one hand, new moms are strongly encouraged to reach out for help with chores like dishes, laundry, bottle washing, and the like. On the other hand, routines can be good for your brain, so building in some time for chores is an important part of your daily activity. However, be sure to set specific and achievable goals. For example, if you would like to complete laundry, perhaps your goal can be to put one load of clothes in the washer in the morning, put those clothes into the dryer around midday, and fold and put away the clothes in the evening (or even the next morning). Breaking down the overall goal of "laundry" into smaller, specific, and achievable goals can help to reduce feelings of overwhelm and increase feelings of stability.

Patient Worksheet

FINDING A NEW NORMAL: HOW WILL I KNOW WHEN I HAVE FOUND A NEW NORMAL?

The term *new normal* can bring up complicated feelings during periods of enormous change. No one wants to be told that "this is the new normal" when things feel overwhelming, exhausting, and uncomfortable much of the time. When things feel upside down, try not to panic. Instead, be on the lookout for changes that feel consistent and familiar. This will help you see that life is slowly starting to feel normal again—a new normal. Here are some questions to consider.

Which parenting skills were challenging before that feel second nature now?

_____

_____

_____

_____

What kinds of baby behaviors used to feel overwhelming that now feel familiar?

_____

_____

_____

_____

What was it like to leave home with (or without) the baby when you first became a parent? In what ways is it easier now?

_____

_____

_____

_____

How do you feel like you and your partner are cooperating now compared to when you first became parents? How about regarding communication?

_____

_____

_____

_____

In what ways are your friendships evolving? Are you finding ways to connect with friends even though you now have a baby with you? Do you find that any of your friendships are enriched since your baby was born? Have you found some new friends since becoming a mother?

_____

_____

_____

_____

Is there a routine to your day now that was not there before?

_____

_____

_____

_____

What activities did you enjoy before your baby was born that you can return to now?

_____

_____

_____

_____

Keep in mind that you might not have adapted in all of these ways yet. That is not a bad thing. Finding a new normal takes time, and the best thing you can do is notice the progress you are making. If you feel stuck or like you are not progressing in a certain area, consider some of the reasons you may feel this way. Talking with a support person about this can help.

Patient Worksheet

FINDING A NEW NORMAL: YOUR RELATIONSHIP WITH CHANGE

While some embrace change and others avoid it at all costs, change is happening to us and around us all the time. During the pregnancy and postpartum period, your body, brain, and emotions are changing rapidly, as are your daily responsibilities. Sometimes these changes are welcome, like when the baby sleeps through the night, and other times less so, like when the dress you were intending to wear to a friend's wedding does not fit. Change can leave you feeling discombobulated at best or, at worst, depressed. This worksheet can help you understand how change challenges you while helping you develop a more hopeful outlook on change. Think of a situation related to change that you recently encountered, then use the prompts to explore how the change impacted your thoughts, emotions, and behaviors.

Situation: What was the change you had to deal with?

I woke up and my work pants did not button.

Thoughts: What were your immediate thoughts when you were confronted with the change?

I am getting so big, and nothing fits. I look terrible in my clothes, and I don't even look like I have a baby bump yet.

Emotions: What feelings did you experience when you had these thoughts?

I felt insecure, panicky, and sad.

Behaviors: What did you do when you were feeling this way and having these thoughts?

I called in sick.

Alternate thought: How could you view the situation differently to help you feel a little bit better about what happened?

The changes in my body are really uncomfortable, but I recognize my body is changing to make room for my growing baby. Maybe I will look up how my baby has changed this week, so I can focus on how my body is changing for my baby.

Copyright © 2023 Hilary Waller and Karen Kleiman, *The Perinatal Patient*. All rights reserved.

Situation: What was the change you had to deal with?

_____
_____
_____
_____
_____

Thoughts: What were your immediate thoughts when you were confronted with the change?

_____
_____
_____
_____
_____

Emotions: What feelings did you experience when you had these thoughts?

_____
_____
_____
_____
_____

Behaviors: What did you do when you were feeling this way and having these thoughts?

_____

_____

_____

_____

Alternate thought: How could you view the situation differently to help you feel a little bit better about what happened?

_____

_____

_____

_____

Patient Worksheet

FINDING A NEW NORMAL: UNDERSTANDING CHANGES

While women are well aware of the external changes that happen when they become pregnant, the internal changes they experience as mothers feel shocking and unexpected. Mothers are left to wonder what happened to the person they were before and ask themselves why they are like *this* now. As mothers notice how their hearts, minds, and spirits feel different, they sometimes worry that something is wrong. It may help to know that like your body, your heart, mind, and spirit are adjusting to the demands of your new baby. Also like your body, these emotional parts of you will readjust after some time, and you will start to feel like yourself again. This worksheet can help you consider reasons you might be experiencing these changes.

I used to be a person who: Never worried about travel.

Now I: Worry every time I leave home.

I am worried about this change because: Leaving home is so hard now. It's hard to run errands, let alone travel.

This change could be happening right now because: I love my baby and it's hard to leave without him. It's also hard to bring him with me sometimes.

On a scale of 1–5 (with 1 meaning "it can wait" and 5 meaning "I need this to change urgently") how important is it that you address this change in yourself? Why?

It's a 2. It's not that important for me to go out too often now. I have help with errands, and once I go back to work, I might get used to leaving without him more often.

Now decide whether you need to do anything about this change. You might decide to wait a while or start making a plan now.

I will need to do something about this if it never gets better, but for now I will just practice going out on short errands with him. Maybe in a few weeks, I can start to think about finding a babysitter so I can go out alone for a little while.

I used to be a person who: _____

_____

Now I: _____

_____

I am worried about this change because: _____

_____

This change could be happening right now because: _____

_____

On a scale of 1–5 (with 1 meaning "it can wait" and 5 meaning "I need this to change urgently") how important is it that you address this change in yourself? Why?

_____

_____

_____

Now decide whether you need to do anything about this change. You might decide to wait a while or start making a plan now.

_____

_____

_____

Patient Worksheet

FINDING A NEW NORMAL: ARE MY SYMPTOMS BACK?

When dealing with a perinatal mood and anxiety disorder, it can be hard to tell whether a period of moodiness or anxiety is a sign of a setback or a normal part of being a human with emotions. Learning the difference between a setback and a normal response to your environment (and developing a plan to cope with normal ups and downs) are important goals for recovery. Use this worksheet to think about some of your recent downs and brainstorm the factors that might have contributed to it.

When did you notice an increase in your symptoms?

_____

_____

How did you and your baby sleep the night before? Did you sleep for enough hours? Did you sleep well?

_____

_____

_____

How did you feel emotionally and physically in the morning?

_____

_____

_____

How did you feel emotionally and physically for the rest of the day?

_____

_____

_____

What were your interactions like that day? How did others treat you?

_____

_____

_____

What kind of mood was your baby in that day?

_____

_____

_____

How did you feel in response to your baby's mood?

_____

_____

_____

Did you have time to practice self-care that day? Why or why not?

_____

_____

_____

Did you encounter stressors like traffic, an unexpected bill, a problem with another child, an issue in your house, or something else that day?

_____

_____

_____

Did you feel as bad the day before? Did you feel better the day after?

_____

_____

_____

Reflecting on these answers, consider whether some of the normal stressors of parenthood triggered you to feel more moody or anxious that day. Keep in mind that down days happen. If you are having many down days in a row, or are having more down days than okay days over a week, reaching out to a maternal mental health care provider may be helpful.

Patient Worksheet

SYMPTOM RELIEF: NEGATIVE SELF-TALK

According to self-compassion expert Kristin Neff (2015), pain turns into suffering when you wish things were different than they are, *and* you resist accepting reality as it is. However, pain is like a gas, so if you simply allow it to be there—without fighting against it—it will eventually dissolve on its own. But if you try to box it up or push it away, the pressure will eventually build up until it explodes. If you are struggling with the pain of a perinatal mood or anxiety disorder, one way to help relieve the pressure of this pain is to practice self-compassion, which can help break any patterns of critical self-talk and release you from guilt and shame. To do so, try taking a self-compassion break (Neff, 2022).

First, think of a difficult situation in your life and say to yourself:

- This is a moment of suffering.
- Suffering is a part of life.

Then place your hands over your heart, or on another part of your body that feels soothing, and say to yourself:

- May I be kind to myself.

You can also adapt this script to fit your own circumstances:

- Choose a statement that mindfully acknowledges your current experience, without judgment. For example: "I am struggling with symptoms of depression or anxiety right now."
- Recognize that your experience is human. For example: "Many other mothers experience perinatal depression and anxiety. I am not alone."
- Ask yourself what words might bring you comfort. Consider what you might say to a good friend in this situation. For example: "I am a good mother, and sometimes good mothers struggle."

What other words or phrases might help you to experience kindness? Write some down so when you need to practice self-compassion, you are prepared:

1. _____

_____

_____

2. _____

_____

_____

3. _____

_____

_____

Patient Handout

SYMPTOM RELIEF: STRATEGIES FOR SELF-SOOTHING

Self-care is an important part of well-being that enhances your mental, emotional, and physical health. Although self-care often involves engaging in daily healthy habits that enhance your mental health, self-soothing is another important part of self-care that can provide relief when you are feeling stressed, overwhelmed, or depleted. Here are some self-soothing strategies that therapists often recommend.

Use Your Senses

- *Look* at something beautiful or comforting, like a flickering candle, a photo you love, or something in nature.
- *Listen* to favorite songs or sounds in nature; hum, sing, or play an instrument.
- *Smell* a lotion, perfume, or cologne that brings good memories; bake or cook something that smells delicious in your home.
- *Taste* a food you love or suck on a flavored candy. Savor the taste and feeling of that candy or food in your mouth.
- *Feel* warm water in the shower or bath, cold water in a lake or swimming pool, the soft fur of a beloved pet, a loving embrace, or the texture and comfort of a favorite blanket.

Calm Your Nervous System

- Take slow deep breaths, inhaling for a count of 2 and exhaling for a count of 4.
- Splash cold water on your face, hold an ice pack on your face, or suck on ice cubes.
- Practice exhaling slowly by gargling or blowing bubbles.
- Repeat a favorite quotation, meditation, or prayer.
- Increase oxytocin levels (your happy hormones) by hugging someone you love, playing with a pet or an animal, or spending quality time visiting with a friend or family member.

When a baby is in the picture, engaging in self-soothing behaviors can be very difficult. Parents often need to do things with divided attention, or one-handed while they attend to their babies and themselves simultaneously. Take a break if another caregiver is present and available to help. If not, think about some ways to use these strategies with your baby present.

For example:

- *Look* at something beautiful while taking your baby for a walk in nature.
- *Listen* to music or sing a song while rocking your baby.
- *Smell* baby lotion while giving your baby a massage.
- *Taste* a favorite smoothie or drink while holding your baby.
- *Feel* your baby's skin or soft hair with your hands, or your baby's weight settling against your chest.

You can also calm your nervous system and entertain your baby by blowing bubbles together or enjoying skin-to-skin contact while breastfeeding or bottle-feeding (or at any time). An added bonus: Skin-to-skin contact increases oxytocin for both mom and baby.

Patient Worksheet

SYMPTOM RELIEF: TALKING WITH PROVIDERS AND SUPPORT PEOPLE ABOUT SCARY THOUGHTS

Scary thoughts are negative, repetitive, unwanted, intrusive thoughts that can come out of nowhere at any time. They can present as ideas (*What if I drop the baby down the stairs?*) or images (*I can see myself dropping the baby down the stairs*). They may feature worries about something that might happen or could happen. They may even include thoughts of you causing harm to your baby on purpose (smothering your baby while changing their diaper). Talking with others about scary thoughts can feel understandably terrifying. Mothers often worry about how others will react if they disclose these thoughts. Giving this worksheet to your providers or support people can help you communicate clearly what you are experiencing.

My Scary Thoughts

Scary thoughts can focus on your baby, yourself, your partner, or your other children. They can come and go, or it can feel like they happen constantly. They can keep you awake at night and disrupt your concentration or focus throughout the day.

These are the scary thoughts I am experiencing:

_____

_____

_____

_____

_____

Copyright © 2023 Hilary Waller and Karen Kleiman, *The Perinatal Patient*. All rights reserved.

This is how often I am having these thoughts:

_____

_____

_____

These thoughts are distressing to me because:

_____

_____

_____

Facts About Scary Thoughts

Scary thoughts like these happen to most parents. When they happen very frequently and cause disruption to daily activities, they can be a symptom of a perinatal mood and anxiety disorder. Scary thoughts do not mean that you are going crazy, that you are a bad mother, or that you are dangerous to your baby. In fact, research shows that:

- There is no correlation between the presence of scary thoughts and harm coming to her baby (Collardeau et al., 2019).
- The prevalence of infant abuse among woman with unwanted intrusive thoughts of harming their infants is actually lower compared to levels of child abuse in the general population (Fairbrother, 2022).

Even though scary thoughts are not dangerous, they may cause you to experience feelings like hopelessness, fear, sadness, shame, guilt, and worry. If this happens, we encourage you to remind yourself that your scary thoughts are a symptom and that help is available. However, if you are feeling out of control, unable to tolerate how bad you are feeling, or are having urges to harm yourself or your baby, contact your health care provider immediately. If you feel that you are experiencing an emergency or are unable to keep yourself safe, call 911 or ask someone to accompany you to a local emergency room, and consider bringing this worksheet with you.

Patient Worksheet

SYMPTOM RELIEF: THOUGHT PATTERNS OF PERINATAL MOOD AND ANXIETY DISORDERS

Unwanted, intrusive thoughts are a common—and upsetting—symptom of perinatal mood and anxiety disorders. While these thoughts can present in many ways, there are some patterns. Understanding your own thinking styles can help you recognize any tendencies you might have had toward intrusive thoughts before becoming a mother. This worksheet describes some common thinking patterns associated with perinatal mood and anxiety disorders, and then asks you to explore how these relate to you. If you are working with a maternal mental health care provider, sharing your own observations can help them treat your symptoms more effectively.

Excessive Worry

People who worry excessively tend to experience a lot of "what if" thinking. They often believe that the act of worrying prevents their feared outcome from happening. They may have a difficult time coping with uncertainty or trusting their ability to solve problems. Excessive worry can also cause them to avoid the people, places, or situations that cause them to worry. For example:

> *What if I take the baby to the store and he starts to cry? Suppose he needs to eat? What would I do then? Suppose I can't find a private place to breastfeed or a clean place to make a bottle? Suppose he cries so inconsolably that I can't soothe him and he disrupts other shoppers? Maybe I shouldn't go.*

Rumination

Ruminative thinking involves getting caught up in cycles of negative thinking and may include brooding or intense focus on how you are feeling. This thinking style is strongly associated with depression.

> *What if I take the baby to the store and he starts to cry? I guess I could feed him, I could go to the car for that. But, ugh, that would be such a pain, and I would feel so embarrassed if people saw me running out of the store thinking I am a bad mother for having this screaming kid. Wow, I am a bad mother! What kind of mother is annoyed by her baby's crying? He's a baby—he cries. I cannot believe how selfish I am. There is no way other mothers are as selfish as I am.*

Obsessive Thoughts

Obsessions are recurrent and persistent unwanted thoughts in which people intensely focus their attention on things that they perceive as threatening. People with obsessive thoughts often believe that even thinking about a certain outcome will increase the likelihood of that outcome occurring. They may also believe that simply thinking about something bad is the equivalent of doing that bad thing. They may respond to these fears by working hard to avoid the thoughts, even when the cost of avoidance is high.

> *What if I take the baby to the store and he starts to cry? I would probably just pick him up and try to comfort him. But then maybe I would bump his head on the shopping cart and then drop him on the floor. Those linoleum floors at the grocery store would absolutely cause brain damage. We would end up in the emergency room and how would I ever explain this? They might flag me as abusive and take my baby away. I can't believe I go out with him at all. I should stop taking him out. It's not worth it.*

Intrusive Memories

An intrusive memory sweeps you up in the memory to the point that you become distracted or absorbed by it. Women who have experienced difficult childbirths or who have a history of trauma are more likely to experience this type of thinking. Intrusive memories can cause feelings of panic, overwhelm, or terror in the present, even if the memory is in the past and is not impacting the present.

> *What if I take the baby to the store and he starts to cry? I couldn't handle it if it was that loud, screaming cry. Every time that happens, I feel like I just get transported to his birth. I could hear he was crying, which was good because he was okay, but I couldn't get to him because he was across the room with the nurses, and I was still getting attention from all those doctors. It wasn't long after that I became so lightheaded and passed out, then things just got so much worse from there. Whenever I hear that cry, it's like I'm back in the delivery room about to have a medical crisis and unable to reach him.*

Catastrophic Misinterpretations

During pregnancy and the postpartum period, women tend to pay a lot of attention to how their bodies are feeling. People who are especially attuned to their bodies and sensitive to anxiety may interpret these symptoms as evidence of a physical catastrophe even though they are unrelated. For example, a mother might experience abdominal soreness related to pushing out a baby and misinterpret it as something terribly wrong with the healing process. Or she could have a headache due to poor sleep and misinterpret it as a brain tumor.

> *What if I take the baby to the store and he starts to cry? That would be okay, I guess. Let me grab some extra diapers, bottles, and supplies so I am prepared. Uh oh, why is my heart racing? I better sit down and take some breaths. It's not going away. What's going on with me? Something's not right. I can't go to the store right now. Do I need to go to urgent care? How will I get there? I can't drive in this state with the baby in the car!*

Now that you've learned about different types of thinking patterns, see if you notice any of these patterns in yourself.

Excessive Worry

I tend to worry excessively about: _____

_____

These things trigger my excessive worry: _____

_____

Rumination

Some of the thoughts that go around in circles in my mind are: _____

_____

My ruminations are worst when: _____

_____

Obsessive Thoughts

I can't stop thinking about (or seeing in my mind): _____

_____

When I have these thoughts, it is hard for me to: _____

_____

Intrusive Memories

My intrusive memories relate to: _____

_____

When these memories come to mind, I feel: _____

_____

Catastrophic Misinterpretations

The sensations in my body that make me worry the most are: _____

_____

When I feel these sensations, I think I might be: _____

_____

If you are experiencing any of these thought patterns and finding it difficult to break out of negative self-talk, consider seeking professional help from a maternal mental health care provider who can help you find relief.

Patient Worksheet

SYMPTOM RELIEF: BREAKING DOWN HYPERBOLE

New motherhood is intense, and some phases feel like they will last forever. While it makes sense that mothers sometimes think in all-or-nothing ways, this kind of exaggerated thinking can feel discouraging and eventually lead you to lose hope that things can and will get better. Use this worksheet to break down your own hyperbolic, or exaggerated, thoughts and come up with a more realistic way of thinking.

First, check off any of these common exaggerated thoughts that you have experienced:

- ☐ My baby never sleeps.
- ☐ I haven't eaten all day.
- ☐ I haven't had a shower in forever.
- ☐ I never exercise anymore.
- ☐ My marriage is ruined.
- ☐ I'll never feel like myself again.
- ☐ Other: _____

Then ask yourself, is this a feeling or a fact? Examine the available data to help you come up with an answer. For example, it may feel like your baby never sleeps, but if you examine the data closely, you might find that your baby has only been sleeping poorly for the last two nights.

_____

_____

_____

Now that you have a better understanding about what is happening, ask yourself what you can do (if there is anything you need to do at all). For example, if your baby is sleeping poorly, this is a problem. Mothers need to sleep, but every mother has a different limit for sleep deprivation, so ask yourself if you need help caring for your baby overnight or if you need to work on your baby's sleep routine. Then think about who can help you work on this. You might also decide that you can deal with another few nights of poor sleep and that you will reevaluate later.

___

Finally, recognize that your current situation will not last forever and see how that impacts your feelings. Then try practicing some self-compassion and engage in a self-care activity. For example, it helps to know that your baby has only been sleeping this badly for a few days and to remember that she might be teething. But you still feel exhausted, irritable, and frustrated, so take a moment to remind yourself that this is really hard right now *and* it will not last forever. Perhaps you could schedule time to take an evening bath to help soothe yourself before the nighttime chaos starts.

Patient Worksheet

SYMPTOM RELIEF: RAGE

In times of stress, you are sometimes able to remain calm despite the uncomfortable feelings you are having. Other times, however, stress and emotion build to the point of explosion, which can leave you feeling guilty, confused, and ashamed. Rage, an intense experience of anger, is one such emotion. Rage can be an uncontrollable and frightening experience, especially when it happens in response to interactions with your baby or child. Learning to recognize signs that an eruption might be coming and identifying triggers for rage can help you to feel more in control.

Recognize Body Signs

Put a check mark by any warning signs your body gives you that anger is building:

- ☐ Facial flushing
- ☐ Shakiness
- ☐ Feeling out of control
- ☐ Dizziness or lightheadedness
- ☐ Racing heart
- ☐ Rapid breathing
- ☐ Muscle tension
- ☐ Other: _____

Recognize Emotions

Check off any emotions that are associated with your rage. Often, mothers with postpartum anxiety or depression find that several feelings are expressed explosively as rage.

- ☐ Frustrated
- ☐ Sad
- ☐ Anxious
- ☐ Overwhelmed
- ☐ Trapped
- ☐ Disappointed
- ☐ Obligated
- ☐ Lonely
- ☐ Isolated
- ☐ Ignored
- ☐ Dismissed
- ☐ Exhausted
- ☐ Misunderstood
- ☐ Disrespected
- ☐ Criticized
- ☐ Insecure
- ☐ Foolish
- ☐ Incompetent

Copyright © 2023 Hilary Waller and Karen Kleiman, *The Perinatal Patient*. All rights reserved.

☐ Guilty   ☐ Threatened

☐ Ashamed   ☐ Other: _____

Recognize Triggers

Sometimes it is possible to recognize events or circumstances that trigger rage. Check off any triggers that apply to you:

☐ Lack of sleep

☐ Hunger or thirst

☐ Loud or overstimulating environment

☐ Comments about your parenting or unsolicited advice

☐ Scrolling through social media

☐ Advice or stories about motherhood on the internet

☐ Disagreements with your partner

☐ When things are not working out

☐ When you can't get everything done

☐ When your house feels messy

☐ When your baby is difficult to soothe

☐ When you are not sure why your baby is upset

☐ When your baby will not sleep at night

☐ When your baby only wants your partner

☐ When your baby only wants you

☐ When your older children, pets, or other family members are competing for your attention

☐ Disruptions while you are trying to concentrate or accomplish something

☐ Disruptions while you are trying to relax or use coping strategies

☐ Support people letting you down

☐ Other: _____

Practice Healthy Coping Skills

If you are able to identify some of your own triggers, make a plan to increase your support during these times or try one of the following coping skills:

- Take deep breaths, breathing in for a count of 4 and exhaling for a count of 8.

- Visualize yourself in a peaceful place, imagining any sights, smells, and sounds you might experience if you were actually there.

- Practice progressive muscle relaxation, tensing and relaxing the muscles in each part of your body one at a time, starting from your toes and working your way up toward your head.

- Hold an ice cube in your hands or splash cold water on your face.

- Raise your heart rate by doing 10 pushups or 10 jumping jacks.

- Listen to, sing, or hum a comforting or upbeat song.
- Remind yourself that the noise and responsibility of parenthood can be overstimulating for mothers. Forgive yourself for losing your patience or needing extra rest.

Patient Handout

SYMPTOM RELIEF: INSOMNIA

Many women experience sleep disruptions during their pregnancies and the postpartum period. These disruptions are often caused by the normal discomforts of pregnancy, the needs of a baby, or a toddler who is still learning to sleep. While this is typically an expected part of parenthood, you can practice several *sleep hygiene* habits to reduce the discomfort of sleep deprivation. Sleep hygiene is important for all people and is particularly important when sleep habits are disrupted by stressors, like pregnancy or a baby. Here are some tips to improve your sleep hygiene. Mothers who are at risk for or who are struggling with a perinatal mood and anxiety disorder should pay especially close attention to their sleep hygiene.

Increasing Physical Comfort

- Ask your obstetric provider for advice to manage any nausea, vomiting, heartburn, constipation, or other gastrointestinal discomforts that occur during pregnancy or the postpartum period.
- Use pillows to increase comfort when you lie down. Resting on your side and placing pillows under your abdomen, behind your back, and/or between your knees can reduce pressure and discomfort in your body, especially during pregnancy.
- Even when you are exhausted, regular movement can alleviate physical discomfort and improve sleep quality. Check with your obstetric provider to find out how to safely include a short period of movement, like walking, exercising, or stretching, into your daily routine.

Improving Sleep Patterns When a Baby Is Disruptive

Sleeping for a few hours in a row at night is essential for good postpartum health. During your pregnancy, talk with your partner about developing routines around infant care that allow you both to have a nightly opportunity for uninterrupted sleep. Here are some tips to consider, but remember that for most babies, periods of hourly sleep disruption are brief. These disruptions often last only the first few weeks or months of life (or for a few days at a time after that, during developmentally appropriate sleep regressions or illnesses). If you are worried about how your baby is sleeping, or the length of a sleep regression, reach out to your pediatrician for guidance.

- Avoid screens two hours before bedtime and throughout the night. Since many mothers use screens to help them stay awake while caring for their babies, try some of these alternatives before turning to a screen:
  - Use earbuds to listen to a podcast, music, or book.
  - Try singing or talking to your baby in a soothing voice.
  - Use a small reading light to read a book or magazine instead of exposing yourself to the blue light of digital devices.
- For mothers who are bottle-feeding, talk with your partner and other support people about taking feeding shifts during the night. Try to maintain the same shifts night after night if you can, as lying down to sleep and rising from sleep at consistent times is helpful in establishing healthy sleep patterns.
- For mothers who are breastfeeding and who have not yet integrated the use of a bottle, consider sharing overnight feeding responsibilities by having your partner wake with the baby and bring the baby to you to eat. You may also wake your partner after a feeding is over so they can soothe baby back to sleep, allowing you to return to bed and rest.

Improving Sleep Patterns When You Can't Fall Asleep

- Keep your bedroom dark and consider covering windows and lights on electronics.
- Try to maintain a comfortable temperature in your bedroom.
- Avoid eating large or heavy meals before bed and limit caffeine intake, including coffee, teas, and sodas.
- Maintain as regular a sleep-wake schedule as you can by developing a schedule for overnight childcare.
- Create an evening ritual to reduce anxiety, panic, or worry and increase feelings of calm.
  - Take a warm bath
  - Drink herbal or caffeine-free tea or warm milk
  - Listen to a guided meditation
  - Stretch
  - Do some breathing exercises
  - Practice some restorative yoga before bedtime.

- If unwanted or intrusive thoughts are keeping you up, consider talking with a support person or a maternal mental health professional to determine whether professional intervention for anxiety or depression might be helpful.

Do not underestimate the importance of sleep during pregnancy or the postpartum period. If you do not like how you are feeling and you believe that the sleep you are getting is inadequate, talk to your provider about additional strategies to improve your sleep.

Patient Worksheet

SYMPTOM RELIEF: COPING WITH PERINATAL PANIC

When mothers experience symptoms of panic during pregnancy or the postpartum period, it can be distressing and cause them to worry that something terrible is happening to them. While the symptoms of panic can feel life threatening, panic does not indicate that a major medical crisis is happening. Panic is simply a form of anxiety, which can range from mildly uncomfortable to fully overwhelming. Recognizing panic and understanding why it is happening can help you cope and reduce its symptoms more quickly.

What Is Panic?

Panic is a physiological reaction that can occur in response to triggers or without warning.

Symptoms of panic include intense fear, dread, or nervousness; trembling; racing heart, numbness, and tightness in chest. These symptoms can start gradually or suddenly and tend to increase in intensity before they subside.

What Can You Do about Panic?

- Cold temperatures can help reduce symptoms of panic, so try holding an ice pack, taking a cold shower, washing your face with cold water, or placing a cold towel around your shoulders.
- Wrap yourself tightly in a blanket.
- Try holding something heavy, like a weighted blanket, in your lap.
- Distract yourself with an enjoyable activity.
- Reach out for social support by calling a friend.
- Practice taking deep breaths, inhaling for a count of 2 and exhaling out for a count of 4.
- Talk with your medical or mental health care providers for additional tools.

Getting to Know Your Panic

How do you typically react when you feel unsafe? Alone? Unloved? Out of control? Unheard? Overwhelmed?

_____

_____

_____

Did you often experience panic before having a baby? If so, in what ways?

_____

_____

_____

The next time you experience panic, think about what was happening in your day before your symptoms started. Can you identify any stressors, thoughts, or emotions that felt overwhelming, confusing, or provoking? If so, write them down here when you are feeling calmer. Then evaluate these triggers on your own, or with the help of a professional, to determine what you can do to cope with or eliminate these triggers.

_____

_____

_____

If you can't identify any triggers for your panic, try not to worry. Remember that panic can occur spontaneously, and your efforts to increase your feelings of calm will still work to help you feel better.

Panic When Caring for a Baby

Symptoms of panic can feel like they are hijacking your body, mind, and mood. Taking care of yourself during this time can be difficult, let alone when you are taking care of a baby. If you are dealing with perinatal panic, it may be comforting to have a plan for managing your baby's needs if symptoms occur when you don't have a support person nearby.

Where can you safely place your baby while you use your calming strategies (e.g., buckled into a stroller or bouncer, or in a bassinette or crib)?

_____

_____

_____

Write down three people you can call if you feel unable to tolerate your symptoms or feel unsafe. Post this list somewhere you can easily find it if you need support.

1. _____

2. _____

3. _____

Choose a phrase you can use to remind yourself that your baby is safe and that your panic will pass shortly. Post this phrase somewhere visible so you are more likely to see and remember it when panic is happening.

_____

_____

_____

Patient Handout

SYMPTOM RELIEF: MAKING SENSE OF BIRTH TRAUMA

After giving birth, many women describe their experiences as traumatic. They often feel confused or conflicted about their emotions related to birth and wonder how to make sense of what they are feeling. This handout can guide your thinking about your birth and help you find the support you need to feel better.

What Is Birth Trauma?

Psychologically speaking, birth trauma refers to any experience of giving birth that results in emotional distress for the mother. Medically speaking, birth trauma refers to certain medical outcomes resulting in certain injuries to the mother or baby. Medical birth trauma is one of many risk factors that can cause a mother to experience psychological birth trauma. Other risk factors include a mother's unmet expectations for her birth, feelings of overwhelm and confusion in response to normal birthing situations, medical interventions even with healthy mother and baby outcomes, and poor support during labor and delivery. BIPOC and non-binary mothers may also experience birth trauma in response to systemic racism and discrimination.

What Is PTSD?

Some mothers who experience birth trauma will develop posttraumatic stress disorder or PTSD. Although it is normal to experience some emotional distress, intrusive thinking, and even nightmares or flashbacks after experiencing or witnessing a traumatic event, PTSD is diagnosed when symptoms interfere with your ability to function over a certain amount of time. If you are worried that you are experiencing PTSD, do not hesitate to contact a maternal mental health care provider who can help you sort out what might be happening and offer options for treatment.

How to Cope with Birth Trauma

- **Make a list of experiences you had after giving birth that felt positive to you.** When the birthing experience is complicated, it can be comforting to focus on other first motherhood memories that bring you joy, such as holding your baby for the first time, arriving home with your baby, breathing fresh air after the hospital stay, or seeing your baby smile.

- **Allow yourself time to grieve.** It is normal to feel sadness and loss after a birth trauma. Writing in a journal, talking with a loved one, or sitting quietly and processing your feelings and thoughts can help.

- **Honor the feelings you are having without judgment.** When you associate negative feelings with your birth, the transition to motherhood, or your baby, it can cause feelings of guilt, shame, or grief. Accepting these feelings as real and valid can help you move through them. Practicing mindfulness on your own, using a mindfulness app, or working with a counselor or mindfulness teacher can help you develop this skill.

- **Release stress through physical movement.** Many people experience feelings of anxiety and panic in their bodies, especially after a traumatic experience. To physically release these symptoms, you can practice stretching, yoga, walking, or other forms of light aerobic exercise. Discuss your physical limitations and abilities with your provider.

- **Ask your obstetric provider to debrief with you about your birth.** Understanding the events that happened during and after your birth from your provider's perspective can help you gain clarity and establish a path toward feelings of closure.

- **Reach out to a professional who can help you navigate your feelings and support your healing process.** Mental health professionals can help you whether or not you are experiencing clinical symptoms of PTSD, no matter the severity of your symptoms.

A Final Note

Keep in mind that partners who witness traumatic events in the labor and delivery process may be impacted significantly by this experience. If this is the case for your partner, we also encourage them to reach out for professional support from a perinatal mental health specialist.

Patient Worksheet

SYMPTOM RELIEF: RISK MANAGEMENT FOR PERINATAL BIPOLAR DISORDERS

If you are pregnant or postpartum and have a history of bipolar disorder, maintaining your mental health is an important part of your perinatal care. This worksheet can help you communicate crucial information to members of your support system who can help you access care if you experience symptoms of bipolar disorder.

Recognizing Symptoms

Describe what you are like when you are in a *depressed* state. Consider behaviors others might observe, what you might say to yourself or others, and how you might feel physically and emotionally.

_____

_____

_____

Describe what you are like when you are in a *manic* state. Consider behaviors others might observe, what you might say to yourself or others, and how you might feel physically and emotionally.

_____

_____

_____

Describe what you are like when you are in a *balanced* state. Consider ways others might see you behave, what you might say to yourself or to others, and how you might feel physically and emotionally.

_____

_____

_____

List any early warning signs that a depressive episode could be starting.

_____

_____

_____

List any early warning signs that a manic episode could be starting.

_____

_____

_____

How Others Can Help

If someone in your support system notices changes in your mood and behavior, it would be helpful for them to:

_____

_____

_____

If you are dealing with symptoms of depression or mania, it would be helpful for people in your support system to:

_____

_____

_____

Self-Care

If you have experienced bipolar symptoms in the past, list the self-care habits and routines that have helped you recover:

_____

_____

_____

Then consider how you may need to adapt these habits while pregnant or postpartum. For example, how could a baby interfere with maintaining this habit? What could you do to reduce this interference?

_____

_____

_____

Sleep

Ensuring adequate sleep is essential for perinatal wellness and is particularly important for mothers who are vulnerable to symptoms of bipolar disorder. Do your best to ensure that you get at least 5 hours of uninterrupted sleep each day, even in the early postpartum days. Discuss ways to achieve this goal with your partner. For example, list any support people or professionals who could help in the evening and overnight hours.

People who can take a childcare shift during the evening/overnight hours:	Contact information:	Potential availability:
_____ _____ _____	_____ _____ _____	_____ _____ _____

Professionals I can contact for help so I can nap during the day or sleep at night (e.g., postpartum doulas, baby nurses, childcare providers):	Contact information:	Cost for services:	If financial support is needed, could anyone help?
_____ _____ _____ _____	_____ _____ _____ _____	_____ _____ _____ _____	_____ _____ _____ _____

In addition, list any routines or habits that can help you relax when it is time to sleep.

_____

_____

_____

Finally, needing many hours of consecutive sleep can interfere with breastfeeding if you are a breastfeeding mother. It will help to identify the name of an internationally board-certified lactation consultant who can help you overcome these challenges. Ask one of your providers for a referral or search for one at www.uslca.org. Write down any referrals you find here:

_____

_____

_____

Medications

List any medications, treatments, and providers that you have had in the past that have helped you recover from an episode of bipolar symptoms.

Medication (including dosage):	Provider:	Any concerns resuming this medication when pregnant or postpartum?
_____	_____	_____
_____	_____	_____
_____	_____	_____

Discuss treatment options with your obstetric provider or a mental health care provider who has expertise in treating perinatal bipolar disorders. Ask for referrals to providers who specialize in this area if yours do not. You may wish to contact The Postpartum Stress Center (www.postpartumstress.com) or Postpartum Support International (www.postpartum.net) for additional resources if your providers do not have referrals local to you or with availability. Write down any referrals you receive here.

Referrals for therapy:

_____

_____

_____

Referrals for reproductive psychiatry:

_____

_____

_____

Patient Handout

SYMPTOM RELIEF: SIGNS OF RECOVERY

The road to recovery from a perinatal mood and anxiety disorder is long and can be difficult to endure. The light of hope can appear dim or even impossible to find at the end of the tunnel. When this happens, it might help to recognize some signs that improvement is happening.

When you are feeling depressed or anxious, are you **trying to use healthy coping skills** like asking for help, trying to connect with friends or other moms, using a journal or artwork for self-expression, stretching or exercising? *Even if you do not find that these strategies provide great symptom relief, notice if they help reduce your symptoms somewhat, even if from a 10 to a 9. If so, that is important progress—you are on your way! If you are not noticing small improvements yet or it is not happening consistently, simply engaging in these coping activities is a sign of progress.*

Even though things still feel overwhelming, are you **making plans** to see family and friends? Beginning to imagine taking your baby to fun places like the playground? Considering doing something enjoyable for yourself, like getting a beauty treatment, rejoining a club, resuming exercise routines, or taking a class in something that interests you again? *Planning for the future is a sign of healing. It shows that you recognize this difficult time will not last forever.*

Do you notice that you are **making jokes or laughing** from time to time? Are you finding humor in some aspects of parenting? Do new things, like the sounds your baby makes, make you giggle or even belly laugh? *It is true that laughter is medicine. Laughter is a wonderful stress reliever and releases powerful feel-good chemicals in the body. In addition to its medicinal effect, laughter can remind you that you are feeling more like yourself again, even if only for a few minutes at a time.*

As terrible as you might be feeling, are you starting to **trust the process of your treatment** and believe that you are receiving the support you need to feel better? *A very scary part of a perinatal mood and anxiety disorder is the worry that your symptoms will never improve. When you find the right provider, you will notice a trusting, hopeful feeling that grows from a flicker to a bright light over time. You might find yourself looking forward to sessions, thinking about things you discussed between sessions, or changing your priorities to accommodate some of the things that have been recommended to you for healing.*

Remember, recovering from a perinatal mood and anxiety disorder is different from recovering from a mental health condition at any other time in life; there is a baby in the mix! Your progress will be impacted day to day by your baby's mood. Progress is not measured in a straight line but in trends across time. Notice how you feel week to week instead of minute to minute. In addition, try to remember that how you are feeling is separate from how your baby is feeling. A fussy baby will cause most people to feel a little (or a lot!) fussy themselves. You can be making great progress toward recovery while simultaneously experiencing a wide range of emotions in response to the normal stressors of motherhood. A mental health professional can help you differentiate between the two if it's difficult to do this yourself.

CHAPTER 8

"What If I Am Navigating Infertility, Loss, or Other Pregnancy or Postpartum Complications?"

The transition to parenthood is destabilizing by nature. For some families, though, this already tenuous set of circumstances is further complicated by a series of unexpected outcomes during the pregnancy and postpartum periods—outcomes that can involve tremendous loss, grief, and confusion. This includes the experiences of infertility, the onset of perinatal mood and anxiety disorders in the non-gestational parent, miscarriage, stillbirth, and a child's stay in the neonatal intensive care unit (NICU). In this chapter, we aim to increase awareness of these experiences so providers can use the information to facilitate a safe and trusting space for patients, and so parents struggling with these circumstances can feel seen and validated. If you're not confronting these issues personally, we still encourage you to read ahead, as this information will help you become a stronger support for family members and peers who are navigating these challenges.

Before moving on, we feel obligated to provide some disclaimers for context. First, you will notice that the information in this chapter is presented in a straightforward and matter-of-fact style. Readers who have experienced infertility, perinatal loss, or a child's stay in the NICU may find that our descriptions of these devastating experiences move too quickly through the difficult emotions. In our clinical, and also personal, experiences, we have come to recognize a serious lack of education about what infertility, miscarriage, stillbirth, and the NICU actually entail. Many people do not know basic facts about what happens when a baby is born still or what a visit to the reproductive endocrinologist (i.e., infertility specialist) involves. Our patients find this lack of knowledge exasperating and exhausting, especially when their own professional providers lack this information. This chapter serves to directly communicate facts so providers and support people will be better equipped to help individuals who are living through one of these nightmares with understanding, empathy, and compassion.

Second, this chapter does not intend to answer all questions or guide comprehensive treatment for families struggling with these complex issues. While we believe it is important for providers to have a general awareness of the special circumstances that complicate the perinatal period for their patients, we do not believe it is necessary for every provider to become an expert in every area. Instead, we encourage providers to convey with confidence that they are capable and willing to find the information they need in order to support their patients.

Disenfranchised Parenting

One of the many reasons every potential patient inquiry to The Postpartum Stress Center is returned by a trained clinician (as opposed to an answering service) is to provide an on-the-spot, rapid assessment of the patient's current state and presenting problem. Our clinical director often hears statements like "I'm not sure if your center can help me with this but . . ." What often follows is a story involving a person who is struggling with issues related to parenthood but does not have a baby due to difficulty conceiving, a history of one or many pregnancy losses, or a stillbirth or infant death. In these cases, the person calling may recognize that their emotional difficulties are related to their parenthood status but feels unsure about whether they belong in the perinatal community.

These parents are experiencing *disenfranchised grief*, or grief that is often left unacknowledged by the general public and unrecognized by social rituals. Parents who are faced with complex challenges like these often describe having intense and pervasive feelings of isolation and exclusion. They are not only experiencing disenfranchised grief, but can also feel like *disenfranchised parents*—people who relate to a child as a parent, but who may not have a child to parent.

No one expects that they will be unable to conceive a child. No one expects that their baby will die. As those navigating infertility or perinatal loss will tell you, talking about these topics can cause others to quickly change the subject or become avoidant. Discomfort around these topics is understandable, given that some cultures avoid talking about medical issues, reproduction, and death. But for those who encounter these losses, it can feel alienating and disorienting to search for people and places who can offer support and healing. If you want to support parents confronting infertility and loss, what helps most is to provide a safe space for these parents to express their feelings and to talk about their experiences. While you may not feel you are doing much, your open ear and heart allow those who are dealing with loss to navigate the difficult terrain of grief.

Fertility and Infertility

Most patients who are receiving treatment for infertility have been wishing for a child for a long time. While they wait for a successful pregnancy, people often fantasize about what it will be like to become pregnant and share their pregnancy with others. They may fantasize about the baby they are hoping for, imagining who that baby will be and how life will change. As months or years pass and the baby is not conceived or born, the light of hope dims and each opportunity for a pregnancy feels like a loss. Many parents with infertility have also experienced failed *transfers*, which occurs when a healthy embryo is transferred into a mother's prepared uterus, only to discover that the embryo did not implant. Many have experienced one or more miscarriages or stillbirths. These individuals have related to an imagined baby, an embryo, or a baby as its parent, but a child has not come to fruition, leaving them to wonder where they fit among parents.

Approximately 11 percent of reproductive age Americans are impacted by infertility (Lepkowski et al., 2010), which is defined as the inability to conceive after one year of unprotected intercourse. However, many infertility specialists will begin working with women who are 35 years of age or older after six months of unsuccessful attempts to become pregnant (CDC, 2022a).

> ### Who Seeks Infertility Treatment?
>
> In addition to patients who have difficulty conceiving within a certain period, there are many other types of individuals who seek out the help of a reproductive endocrinologist:
>
> - Same-sex and transgender couples
> - Women with a history of multiple miscarriages
> - People whose fertility has been compromised by other medical conditions, such as cancer and related treatments
> - Women whose previous births have severely compromised their reproductive organs (e.g., those who have had a hysterectomy) and are pursuing a gestational carrier for a subsequent pregnancy
> - Couples who are carriers for genetic disorders and who wish to have embryos tested before they pursue a pregnancy

It may surprise you to learn that while *in vitro fertilization*, or IVF, is a commonly discussed treatment for infertility, only 3 percent of fertility patients actually undergo IVF (American Society for Reproductive Medicine, 2017). Equally surprising is that while many people believe that IVF will surely result in the birth of a healthy baby, success rates vary widely and depend on many factors, such as maternal age, overall reproductive health of both parents, and the quality of the embryo that is used in each attempt. Most patients who are in the care of a reproductive endocrinologist will receive treatments that integrate a variety of medications, testing, medical procedures, and surgical procedures that are likely to involve some degree of physical discomfort or pain.

It is interesting to note that many patients whose fertility treatments are successful, resulting in a healthy pregnancy and baby, are still at an increased risk for perinatal mood and anxiety disorders (Raguz et al., 2014). This association is likely because, despite the high motivation to have a child, the logistical and emotional toll resulting from treatment can be overwhelming. It's an enduring process that is hard on both partners. In fact, it is not uncommon for parents to have difficulty complying with treatment protocols or to end treatment early due to this extraordinary stress (Wadadekar et al., 2021).

Logistically, fertility treatments require an incredible amount of time and financial commitment from patients. Typically, patients are monitored in accordance with their menstrual cycles, a factor that is largely out of their control, and may need to present to their doctors' offices as often as daily for their treatments. Lab work is needed regularly during a cycle, leaving patients waiting with bated breath for hours or days to find out whether their treatments have been successful, or whether they will need to wait another month for another chance to become pregnant. Reproductive endocrinologists do what they can to increase convenience by offering early morning office hours and by developing close relationships with patients. Still, scheduling many in-person appointments is extremely taxing on the schedule of a working adult, particularly when they prefer privacy around personal and medical issues.

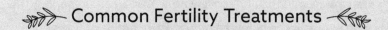

Common Fertility Treatments

Assessments

Patients undergo a variety of assessments when establishing care with a reproductive endocrinologist or when starting a new *cycle* or attempt to conceive. Some patients undergo a *hysterosalpingogram*, or an HSG, an in-office procedure that examines the fallopian tubes and shape of the uterus. Some will need a *hysteroscopy*, a procedure in which a small light is inserted through the vagina to examine the inside of the uterus. Patients can usually expect to be monitored via *ultrasound* (*including transvaginal ultrasounds*, in which an ultrasonography probe is inserted into the vagina) and *blood tests*. Male partners will likely be asked to provide a semen sample for *semen analysis*, a test that can identify male factor infertility by evaluating sperm count and quality.

Treatments

- *Fertility drugs* are prescribed to increase chances of conceiving. Many different oral or injectable drugs may be used as part of fertility treatment, and each woman's prescription will be individualized for her specific needs. These medications are often very expensive, require women to use specialized pharmacies, and may not be covered by health insurance.

- *Timed intercourse* involves patients having intercourse on specific days in response to their physician's assessment of fertility.

- *Intrauterine insemination (IUI)*, also called artificial insemination, involves placing sperm into the vagina, uterus, or fallopian tubes via medical intervention instead of via sexual intercourse. IUI protocols may include the use of fertility medications.

- *In vitro fertilization (IVF)* is a process in which fertility drugs are used to prepare a woman's body for an *egg retrieval*. During an egg retrieval, mature eggs are removed from a mother's body and are subsequently combined with sperm in a laboratory. As the eggs fertilize in the lab, patients are updated regularly on the survival rates of the eggs, the number of successfully fertilized eggs, and the number of fertilized eggs that become embryos viable for *embryo transfer*, which is the surgical insertion of an embryo into the uterus. In some cases, mothers will decide to use *cryopreservation* to freeze embryos so the embryos can undergo further genetic testing or be transferred to the mother's body later in a *frozen embryo transfer*.

Patients may also need to acquire medications from specialty pharmacies with limited hours that are far away from where they live or work. Sometimes, they may need to purchase medications that they don't even end up using, as treatment protocols can change based on the doctor's observation of how the patient's body is responding to the prescribed medications. The cost for these medications, whether they are used or not used, and the treatments themselves are astronomical, and there is no guarantee that the costs will be covered by health insurance policies in the United States (RESOLVE: The National Infertility Association, 2022).

Psychologically, the experience of infertility is quite complex. Patients tell us they feel misunderstood by family and friends who view infertility as an inconvenience or a small bump in the road toward parenthood. However, the reality is that infertility is a major medical condition that involves extensive medical care, a roller coaster of bad and good news, use of medications that can significantly impact both mental and physical health, and for many, feelings of defectiveness and failure. Patients often struggle with anger and resentment that may be directed toward themselves, their bodies, aspects of their personal or medical history, or their partners, especially when it is the partner whose fertility is compromised (about half of all infertility cases are influenced by male factor infertility; Ferlin et al., 2022).

Therefore, it should come as no surprise that infertility increases the risk of developing a perinatal mood and anxiety disorder, even among those who end up conceiving a child. This can be a harrowing juxtaposition for parents, who feel extreme guilt and shame for having symptoms while caring for a baby who was so badly desired. It is crucial for providers and support people to be aware of the many nuances of infertility so they can be better positioned to provide empathy and comfort to parents experiencing these unexpected emotions. The Learning and Sharing About Infertility Journeys worksheet can give you some insight into how to start a conversation with individuals who are struggling with infertility, whether or not they have conceived a child. It can also help patients explore their own thoughts and serve as a means to share these thoughts with others.

Patient Worksheet

LEARNING AND SHARING ABOUT INFERTILITY JOURNEYS

When you are experiencing infertility, it can be difficult for others who have not had this experience to understand what you are going through, which can feel isolating and disappointing. Use the questions here to clarify what you are thinking and feeling for yourself. You may find it helpful to use these questions as journaling prompts or conversation starters with support people, medical providers, or your partner. If you are a provider or support person, you can also use this list of questions to guide discussions with patients and loved ones.

What triggers you in your day-to-day life (e.g., seeing gender reveal announcements on social media, receiving an invitation to a baby shower)?

_____

_____

_____

What is the hardest part of your fertility journey right now?

_____

_____

_____

_____

How has your fertility journey impacted your body image?

_____

_____

_____

How has your fertility journey impacted your relationships?

_____

_____

_____

How has your fertility experience impacted you spiritually?

_____

_____

_____

What do you wish others knew about infertility?

_____

_____

_____

What is the hardest part about waiting for a baby?

_____

_____

_____

What losses, in addition to pregnancy losses, have you experienced because of your fertility journey?

_____

_____

_____

What do other people say about your fertility journey that is upsetting to you?

_____

_____

_____

What do you wish people would say instead when you tell them about your fertility journey?

_____

_____

_____

Are there people who are trying to support you but who are saying the wrong things? What could they say to you instead that might feel supportive?

_____

_____

_____

Is there anything else your closest family, friends, or partner are doing or could do to help you through this time?

_____

_____

_____

Non-Gestational Parents

A non-gestational parent is a parent who did not carry or give birth to their children. Non-gestational parents include fathers, one or more parents in a same-sex or trans partnership who did not carry their baby themselves, parents who employ a gestational carrier or surrogate, and adoptive parents. Many parents and providers alike mistakenly believe that perinatal mental health is only relevant to people who have given birth. Therefore, when non-gestational parents experience symptoms of mood and anxiety disorders during the first one to two years of parenthood, they wonder where to turn for help and often don't receive the prenatal and postpartum care they need.

The reality is that many non-birthing parents experience symptoms of depression and anxiety in response to the transition to parenting. Studies show evidence of depressive and anxious symptoms in more than 11 percent of new fathers (O'Brien et al., 2017) and in up to 26 percent of adoptive parents (Foli et al., 2016). While these numbers are astoundingly similar to the prevalence of perinatal mood and anxiety disorders in birthing parents, treatment and social support options are limited for non-gestational parents compared to cisgender birthing mothers. In turn, non-gestational parents often feel uncertain, marginalized, and invalidated.

Although there are several common risk factors for depression across birthing and non-birthing parents, including social support, mental health history, marital satisfaction, and expectations for parenthood (Foli et al., 2016), unique to the experience of adoptive parents is the process of adoption itself and the social, psychological, and financial scrutiny under which families are placed during the process of applying to become an adoptive parent. It's also important to keep in mind that some adoptive parents have experienced a history of infertility, pregnancy, infant losses, or the loss of a potential child to adopt, further complicating their stories.

Non-gestational parents sometimes identify with other marginalized or underrepresented communities as well, leading them to face multiple forms of discrimination, alienation, and isolation. This is especially relevant for those in the LGBTQIA+ population who are regularly confronted with discrimination related to parenting, challenges related to finding competent health care providers for themselves and their families, and worries about how their children will be accepted into their own communities.

Given the entrenched stigma, gender expectations, and stereotypes that non-birthing parents face, it is no surprise that they report feeling as if they are not entitled to experience the symptoms of a perinatal mood and anxiety disorder (Eddy et al., 2019). Providers can work to correct these biases by offering equitable services that recognize and validate the need for *all* new parents to have support and access to mental health care.

> ### ～ Language of Diverse Families ～
>
> Parents whose reproductive journey requires donated genetic material or a third person to conceive the baby wrestle with feelings about the involvement of this additional person and how, whether, or to what extent they might be involved in their child's life. Some important terms to know include:
>
> - **Birth parent:** The individual who carried and gave birth to a child who was placed for adoption.
>
> - **Donor parent:** The individual whose egg or sperm was donated for use by another person to conceive a child.
>
> - **Gestational carrier:** A woman who carries a pregnancy for another parent in which she does not have any genetic relationship to the child.
>
> - **Intended parent:** Individuals or couples who choose to become parents through a gestational carrier or traditional surrogate.
>
> - **Traditional surrogate:** A woman who carries a pregnancy for another couple in which the woman's own egg is fertilized with sperm in a medical procedure.

Ways to increase accessibility include:

- Adding a diversity, equity, and inclusion (DEI) statement to your website and marketing. Post this in your waiting room as well.

- Adapt language on your practice forms so they convey inclusivity of parents across the gender spectrum and from a wide variety of racial, ethnic, and socioeconomic backgrounds.

- Recognize that, as the provider, you set the tone for the patient-provider relationship. Use your status in your professional space to convey that keeping patients safe from discrimination is a priority for you and your colleagues.

If you are a non-gestational parent experiencing symptoms of a perinatal mood and anxiety disorder (or your partner is), allow yourself to seek care. If you are unsure about how to find resources that feel safe for you in your local area, the *Maternal Mental Health Resources* worksheet from chapter 5 is a great place to start. In addition, you can complete the following worksheet, which provides information about mood and anxiety symptoms during the postpartum period, and can guide conversations with potential support people, including your partner and health care provider.

Perinatal Mood and Anxiety Disorder Prevalence Among LGBTQIA+ Parents

Currently, research specific to perinatal mood and anxiety disorders among LGBTQIA+ parents is extremely scarce. Research in the non-perinatal population shows that lesbian, gay, trans, and bisexual individuals are at a higher risk for developing a mood and anxiety disorder in their lifetime than their cisgender or heteronormative counterparts (McDonald, 2018). We believe strongly that empirical information to help us understand increased risk for perinatal mood and anxiety disorders among LGBTQIA+ parents is forthcoming. At this time, our qualitative understanding of the challenges this community faces is sufficient to support the position that LGBTQIA+ parents are entitled to, in need of, and deserving of reproductive mental health services provided with respect, gentle care, and humility.

Patient Worksheet

SUPPORTING ALL PARENTS EXPERIENCING PERINATAL MOOD AND ANXIETY DISORDERS

If you are a new parent experiencing symptoms of depression or anxiety, but you have not given birth yourself, it can be confusing and difficult to figure out where to find support. First, know you are not alone. Many fathers, adoptive parents, and partners of non-birthing parents experience mood and anxiety disorders during the first few months and years of parenthood. While it is true that people who have not given birth will not experience the full biological impact of pregnancy and birth, *all* new parents are vulnerable to the overwhelming social and psychological changes that occur during early parenthood.

In addition, parents who have not given birth face some unique challenges, as they must:

- Provide emotional and physical support to a partner who is recovering from pregnancy and birth
- Confront the stigma of experiencing mood and anxiety symptoms during new parenthood without having given birth
- Find providers skilled at treating non-gestational parents with perinatal mood and anxiety disorders
- Overcome cultural or gender-related reluctance to seek mental health care

The following information and questions may help to clarify what symptoms you are having and can guide conversations with your partner and health care provider. If you do not have a provider whom you trust with information about your mental health, consider searching for a specialist in parental mental health through organizations or counseling centers that specialize in perinatal or maternal mental health. These providers receive general training in parental mental health and will be able to provide therapy services, referrals, and/or additional information that can facilitate your healing.

What Are Your Symptoms?

Put a check mark by any symptoms you might be experiencing right now. While any of these symptoms can be a normal part of adjustment during the first months of parenthood, if you are uncomfortable with what you are feeling, reach out to a health care provider or other supports.

☐ Feelings of sadness, anxiety, overwhelm, fear, or frustration

- ☐ Feelings of regret, including regret about having a baby
- ☐ Feelings of hopelessness or helplessness
- ☐ Feelings of guilt, shame, or self-doubt
- ☐ Feelings of rage, anger, or irritability
- ☐ Feeling dependent on others for physical help and/or emotional support
- ☐ Worry or fear that disrupts sleep or makes it difficult to leave the house or be alone with the baby
- ☐ Intrusive anxious thoughts about yourself or your baby (e.g., "What if I drop the baby down the stairs?")
- ☐ Difficulty with decision-making, concentration, memory, or maintaining daily routines
- ☐ Upset stomach
- ☐ Changes in appetite or eating habits
- ☐ Consuming more caffeine than usual
- ☐ Consuming more alcohol than usual
- ☐ Shortness of breath or tightness in chest
- ☐ Heart palpitations
- ☐ Racing heart
- ☐ Dizziness
- ☐ Feeling shaky or nervous
- ☐ Headaches
- ☐ Urges to isolate from family, friends, and social environments
- ☐ Loss of interest or enjoyment in activities that were previously pleasurable

How Disruptive Are Your Symptoms?

It is normal to experience transient and mild symptoms of depression or anxiety every once in a while. However, the more your symptoms disrupt your daily routine, the greater the likelihood that you will benefit from some additional support. Answer these questions to determine how disruptive your symptoms are. If you are unsure, reach out to a provider to gain some clarity.

How often do your symptoms occur? Once in a while? Daily? Only at night? Almost constantly?

_____

_____

_____

How intense are your symptoms? Are they fleeting, or can you overcome them within a few minutes?

_____

_____

_____

How long have you been feeling this way? A few days? A week? A few months?

_____

_____

_____

To what extent do your symptoms interfere with your day-to-day functioning? For example, are you unable to complete tasks at work due to distraction or low motivation?

_____

_____

_____

Symptoms That Require Support

Some symptoms of mood and anxiety disorders are serious and require more support. If you are experiencing any of the following symptoms, seek help as soon as possible. Consider contacting your health care provider or calling a suicide or crisis hotline like 988 if you are in the United States.

Examples of symptoms that may require more support include:

- ☐ Thinking that your partner, baby, or family would be better off without you
- ☐ Thinking you might harm yourself
- ☐ Feeling an urge to run away
- ☐ Thoughts or fantasies of suicide

Conversation Starters

You may consider disclosing to your partner, support system, or health care provider:

- ☐ The hardest thing about parenthood right now
- ☐ How becoming a parent has impacted your self-esteem
- ☐ How you feel becoming a parent has impacted your relationships
- ☐ Any thoughts or memories you are having about your childhood, your earlier life, or your own parents and caregivers
- ☐ Whether you are feeling isolated right now
- ☐ Whether you are feeling connected to your baby and partner right now
- ☐ Some of the things you are stressed about (e.g., job security, finances, whether you are doing a good job supporting your partner and baby)

You may also think about:

- ☐ What you wish people would say when you tell them about the difficulties you are having
- ☐ What others could say that might feel supportive
- ☐ Whether there is anything your closest family, friends, or partner are doing or could do to help you through this time

Bereavement: Pregnancy Loss and Stillbirth

The first few hours, days, and weeks of a baby's life are filled with moments emblematic of the transition to parenthood. Parents share common experiences, such as using a car seat for the first time, spending the first night at home, giving the first bath, and making first introductions between babies and pets or siblings. When pregnancies end prematurely and when babies die, it is hard to know how to embrace the role of parent, or even if one is entitled to hold this title. Questions like "Do you have children?" or "How many children do you have?" become fraught with anguish and doubt. In therapeutic spaces, one important goal is to help people develop a narrative for their losses that reduces disenfranchisement by empowering them to find answers to difficult questions like these.

In the perinatal field, the term *perinatal loss* applies to early and late-term miscarriages, stillbirths, neonatal/infant deaths, and maternal deaths. While the frequency at which perinatal losses occur is extremely high—with roughly 1 in 4 pregnancies ending in miscarriage (Dugas & Slane, 2022) and 1 in 160 ending in stillbirth (CDC, 2020)—perinatal bereavement remains a topic shrouded in stigma and taboo. Women often describe feeling confused by mixed messages about how they should handle a perinatal loss. While the experience of miscarriage is becoming more normalized on social media, there remains prominent superstition and reluctance to disclose pregnancy news during the earlier stages of pregnancy.

Types of Perinatal Loss

Miscarriage: Loss that occurs before 20 weeks gestation, occurring in an estimated 26% of pregnancies and 10% of clinically recognized pregnancies (Dugas & Slane, 2022)

Recurrent pregnancy loss: Two to three consecutive pregnancy losses; approximately 2% of women will experience two consecutive losses and 0.5% of women will experience three consecutive losses (Yale Medicine, 2023)

Primary recurrent pregnancy loss: When a mother experiences recurrent losses with no history of viable pregnancy

Secondary recurrent pregnancy loss: When a mother experiences recurrent pregnancy loss following a live birth

Stillbirth: Death of a fetus, typically after 20 weeks gestation or after 14 ounces birth weight, which can occur in utero or during the process of delivery and impacts 1 in 160–200 births per year (Tsakiridis et al, 2022).

Neonatal death: Death occurring after a live birth and before 28 days of life

Early neonatal death: Neonatal death occurring within the first week of life

Late neonatal death: Neonatal death occurring within the first 7-27 days of life

SIDS: Refers to sudden infant death syndrome, when sudden death occurs in infants during the first year of life

Miscarriage

Many women will experience an early pregnancy loss, or a miscarriage that occurs within the first trimester of pregnancy (i.e., before 13 weeks). Miscarriages are often perceived as "common" or "no big deal." Parents are told that "they can always try again" or that "it's better it happened early." However, the reality is that miscarriages involve physical pain, discomfort, and sometimes medical complications and procedures, as well as emotions that can run the gamut from relief to despair. It is important to support parents going through this experience by allowing them to explore any thoughts and feelings they might have by listening without assumptions or expectations. The questions on the *Talking About Miscarriage* handout offer guidance for those who want to provide an open ear for someone experiencing this type of loss.

While the best thing you can do for a person grieving an early pregnancy loss is to offer emotional or logistical support, it is also helpful to understand what it means to have a miscarriage. Miscarriages usually happen for reasons that are far beyond a mother's control, often occurring due to genetic issues that disrupt development (American College of Obstetricians and Gynecologists, 2022). Some mothers may experience signs of miscarriage, like bleeding, spotting, and severe cramping, while others may learn about their miscarriage at an early doctor's appointment when they discover that embryonic or fetal growth has stopped. For some, a pregnancy will progress normally during the first part of the first trimester and a heartbeat may even be detected at an early ultrasound—only to be followed by a loss toward the end of the first trimester.

Since miscarriages are not unusual during the first trimester, women commonly experience anxiety about pregnancy loss during this early period of development. For many women, the experience of imagining their baby and viewing themselves as mothers begins the moment they learn the news of their pregnancy. Therefore, even a miscarriage at this stage can leave a mother feeling blindsided and grief stricken as she copes with the loss of both her pregnancy and the hopes and dreams she imagined for herself and her baby.

While the risk of miscarriage is greatly reduced for women who reach the second trimester, up to 3 percent of women will experience a miscarriage during the second trimester (Odendaal et al., 2019). Signs of miscarriage at this stage also include bleeding, spotting, and cramping—and, for women who can feel their babies moving, a change in fetal movement. By this stage in pregnancy, many women begin to develop pregnant-looking bellies and have begun to share news of their pregnancy with family, friends, and coworkers. They have started imagining what motherhood will feel like and are aware that the baby inside them is beginning to look less like a gummy bear and more like the little newborn they imagine holding in a few more months.

Treatment for miscarriage in both the first and second trimesters may include a combination of surgeries and medications, but mothers having a later miscarriage may need to present to labor and delivery for an induction of labor followed by the birth of the fetus. In these cases, mothers may have an opportunity to hold or interact with their babies, an experience that can be healing and also inconceivably difficult. Sometimes parents request medical testing on the embryo or fetus in hopes of discovering a reason for the loss. Some parents request that any fetal remains be cremated and returned to them. In some cases, there are no remains to be salvaged or women may miscarry outside of a hospital setting.

Provider Handout

TALKING ABOUT MISCARRIAGE

Asking the wrong questions or saying the wrong thing to someone who has experienced a miscarriage can be alienating and isolating for that person. If someone in your life is navigating this type of loss, consider using the following questions to initiate conversation and help the other person clarify what they are thinking and feeling.

- How do you remember feeling when you thought about building a family before miscarriage?
- Since your miscarriage, how have these feelings changed?
- What has been the worst part about having a miscarriage?
- Has anything surprised you about having a miscarriage?
- Is there something you wish you had known before your miscarriage?
- Is there something you wish others knew about miscarriage in general?
- Is there something you wish others knew about your miscarriage?
- Is there a ritual or practice you are doing to remember your baby? Is there a way that others could support you in this?
- Is there anything others could do to help you feel more supported, emotionally or logistically? For example, do you need help getting to follow-up appointments or do you need a break from errands and housework?

Medical providers can provide support through these heartbreaking experiences by providing education about what patients can expect regarding their bodies during a miscarriage and by offering education about family planning when the parents are ready to receive this information. As always, this conversation should be handled gently with clarity and compassion. Make no assumptions about how parents will or should feel about a miscarriage. Show your empathy by making an effort to normalize feelings of grief without patronizing the patient and by providing bereavement resources. It is also important to be mindful of emerging symptoms of mood and anxiety disorders, as risk for these conditions is increased for women who have experienced a miscarriage (Bicking Kinsey et al., 2015; Nynas et al., 2015).

Stillbirth

Although miscarriages have received increased attention in the media in recent years, with more women coming forth to describe their experiences, the experience of a stillbirth is less discussed, leaving parents whose baby has been born still to wonder what other people know or think about their loss. Stillbirth is defined as a fetus who is delivered at or after 20 weeks of gestation showing no signs of life (The American College of Obstetricians and Gynecologists, 2020). In the United States, rates of stillbirths vary according to the race or ethnicity of the mother, with rates of 4.89 per 1,000 births in White women and 10.32 per 1,000 births in Black women (CDC, 2020). Additional risk factors for stillbirth include younger and older maternal age, pregnancy and non-pregnancy related medical conditions, obstetric history (such as prior stillbirths), pregnancy with twins or multiples, and inadequate prenatal care. Aside from follow-through with good medical and self-care, there is not much a mother can do to reduce her risk of stillbirth. Nevertheless, self-blame, guilt, and shame are very commonly experienced by mothers following a stillbirth.

It is important for providers to recognize that stillborn babies are typically birthed in traditional labor and delivery settings and that the process of inducing labor, laboring, and giving birth is physically the same whether a mother is giving birth to a live or dead infant. Parents of stillborn children often comment on the excruciating complexity of this experience—the excitement and adrenaline of birth, coexisting with the horror of tragedy and the expectation that their baby's cries will never be heard. After giving birth to a still infant, mothers will still require the same postpartum medical care as mothers who have given birth to a living baby. Their bodies will still need to heal from pregnancy, labor, and delivery. They will still lactate, as their bodies are hormonally unaware that the infant they carried has died. Some mothers decide to maintain lactation to donate their breastmilk, while others choose to stop lactation using a combination of techniques that may also be used by mothers who are not able to or choose not to breastfeed their living children.

While the American College of Obstetricians and Gynecologists recommends that an autopsy be performed to collect any available data to explain the reason for stillbirth (Oliver et al., 2020), parents are encouraged to spend time with their stillborn babies. Many hospitals utilize techniques for cooling the baby's body to prolong the amount of time that parents can spend with them. These moments, while agonizing, are important opportunities for parents to get to know their babies. This time allows parents to count fingers and toes, bathe and clothe their newborns, and notice their babies' unique features.

Racial Health Disparity

In the United States, mothers and babies who are BIPOC are three times more likely to die from perinatal health complications than White mothers and babies (CDC, 2022b). Risk of death increases with maternal age and persists regardless of factors that we may expect to be protective, like level of education (Carvalho et al., 2021). This racial disparity in obstetrics is not a recent or passing problem. In the 1800s, when obstetrics and gynecology emerged as a medical discipline, Black women were subject to experimentation and unethical research (Chinn et al., 2021).

Given that the Black community has endured the chronic stress of racism over the course of multiple generations, a theory known as the *weathering* hypothesis has proposed that poor maternal and infant health outcomes among Black women are a result of this constant discrimination and oppression (Patterson et al., 2022). Indeed, research shows that it is systemic oppression, bias, and discrimination that lead to racial differences in equal access to health care (Chinn et al., 2021).

Given that mortality rates decrease dramatically when newborns are cared for by physicians of the same race (Greenwood et al., 2020), as a health care provider, you have a moral and ethical duty to educate yourself on this significant public health problem and pursue additional anti-racism training to address your own implicit biases and provide equitable and nondiscriminatory patient care. Two in three perinatal deaths are preventable, so we implore you to seek out continuing education courses, books, and other resources to help you identify and address the ways that racial biases may impact your work. If you take a moment to search the internet for diversity and anti-racism resources, you will find thousands of free and low-cost options to begin this essential journey.

Parents who experience stillbirth question whether to talk about their pregnancy and birth, show photos of their child, or notify others about their child's birth and death. Any therapist working with patients who have experienced perinatal bereavement will benefit from specialized training in this area, but here are a few recognized best practices for supporting bereaved parents:

- If you are present at the baby's birth, encourage parents to spend time with their babies. If you are supporting the family after the baby has been born and died, ask about any time they spent with their babies. Often, parents will take photos of their babies and appreciate when others ask to see them.

- Recognize the baby as an individual—a human being whose existence has meaning and purpose.

- Validate for parents their incomplete transition to parenthood, whether they are first-time parents or have older children.

- Validate the complexity of witnessing the transitions of birth and death simultaneously.

- If you are a medical provider, answer questions regarding the baby's physical condition both before and after birth.

- Babies should be treated like living babies by those who meet them. They should be recognized as beautiful, caressed, held, and cared for. Nurses and other medical providers who are present can facilitate this process.

- Encourage parents to engage in any memory-making rituals with the child, such as taking photos. Many hospitals offer professional photography services and will keep the photographs for parents who do not wish to keep them at the time of the birth. This allows parents to return for their child's photos at any time in the future (Lindh Jorgenson et al., 2021).

Grief After Perinatal Loss

After a miscarriage, stillbirth, or infant death, parents may experience an array of emotions associated with the grief process, including sadness, guilt, shame, and anger, as well as uncertainty around family planning and fertility. This grief can be all consuming and touch every aspect of their lives as they learn to adapt to life again, gradually accept the loss, and reorganize their reality to accommodate the loss. After some time—the length of which will vary from person to person—normal grief will feel less constant and less urgent, which creates space for hope and future planning. Eventually, these parents will become able to reconsider family planning and may look forward to conceiving another pregnancy. The grief these parents feel related to their loss will still be present but will interfere less in everyday activities.

> ### Conceiving After a Loss
>
> When parents are trying to conceive after a loss, grief can often manifest as a heightened sense of anxiety about the anticipated baby. Certain dates or milestones in pregnancy, like dates associated with the loss or ultrasound appointments, can exacerbate this stress and trigger feelings of intense grief.

However, some parents may experience symptoms of prolonged grief disorder, also known as complicated grief, in which the feelings of loss remain severe, persistent, and disabling for 12 months or more after the loss. Counselors who treat prolonged grief aim to help patients return to their daily routines, increase acceptance of their loss, and restore feelings of hope and meaning. Other forms of support, such as parental bereavement groups, peer counseling, and debriefs with health care providers, can help parents process their grief and enable the intensity of their grief to abate over time. The following handouts can also help you support parents after a perinatal loss.

Patient Handout

SUPPORTING PARENTS AFTER STILLBIRTH AND NEONATAL DEATH

Bereaved parents often feel unsure about how to talk about their grief with people who have not experienced stillbirth or infant loss. They often notice that others, even those closest to them, are unsure about what words and questions will be supportive. If you have lost a child, you can provide your loved ones with some of the tips below to guide their interactions with you as you navigate this process.

- Provide condolences (e.g., "I am so sorry for your loss.")
- Consider ways you can help logistically (e.g., "I am available to bring your toddler home from daycare tomorrow and the next day. Would that be helpful?" or "I am grocery shopping; is it okay if I drop off some snacks? Is there anything specific you need?")
- Connect with both parents, recognizing that both are grieving and may have different needs during this time.
- Keep in mind that stillborn babies are delivered just like living babies and that mothers will be recovering from giving birth and lactating after their baby has died.
- If you feel comfortable, ask whether the parents have any photos or mementos from the time they spent with their baby after their baby was stillborn. You may decide to ask whether they feel comfortable sharing these mementos with you.
- Be sensitive to the fact that bereaved parents may feel upset by things happening in your family. For example, many bereaved mothers need some time to heal before attending baby showers or visiting postpartum friends again. While this may hurt your feelings, try to keep in mind that this is a part of their healing. Let them know you understand their need to heal to honor their loss and grieving process.
- Many bereaved parents prefer to talk about the babies they lost and to integrate them into their family story. For example, you may notice that bereaved parents use a certain symbol in honor of their child or include the name of their child on a family holiday card. Ask directly how the family plans to honor this child's memory and their role in the family, and ask what you can do to be mindful of this.

- Remember that important dates will trigger more intense feelings of grief and loss. Try reaching out to bereaved parents to offer support on holidays, dates relevant to their loss, and on the child's birthdate.
- Ask whether parents are participating in a ritual or practice to remember their baby. Ask whether there is a way you could be supportive of this.

Provider Handout

HELPING PARENTS PROCESS STILLBIRTH AND NEONATAL DEATH

There is no good way to help parents prepare for the death of their baby or child. When this happens, a parent's entire world collapses. It becomes hard to think straight and impossible to make decisions, even though many need to be made. The points below can help providers guide bereaved parents through some of these difficult moments.

- Explain to parents what services your hospital or practice offers bereaved parents. For example, are cooling cots available to preserve the baby's body so parents can spend more time with them?

- Provide resources for both in-person and virtual support groups, and educate parents on the importance of social support in navigating this time.

- Discuss what parents can expect when their baby is born. Help them prepare for what their baby may look like and what kinds of things can happen to the baby's body over the first few days.

- Discuss options for honoring their baby in the short term (e.g., holding a memorial service or a burial). Some parents may want to create a birth-and-death announcement, or a stillbirth announcement, to send to family and friends, in which case they may appreciate guidance around wording.

- Initiate conversation about how parents will answer questions about their baby. How might they answer questions about how many children they have? Where will they consider this baby in their children's birth order? Who will they talk with about their baby in more detail and who will receive a brief explanation of their circumstances? For example, when the bereaved parent goes to have a haircut, what will they tell their stylist about their baby?

- Express curiosity about how parents spent time with their babies after birth. Allow parents space to describe what their baby looked like, what they did during this precious time, and how they felt.

- When navigating all these conversations, use clear, plain language. Although this may feel uncomfortable at times, providing parents with specific information can increase their understanding of their circumstances and rights.

Neonatal Intensive Care Unit (NICU)

After a baby is born, new parents are charged with the daunting responsibility of learning to care for their baby. While the enormity of this duty can elicit feelings of terror, stepping into this new role represents the natural order of things. A baby is born, a parent is born. This natural course is upset when a baby is whisked away to the NICU immediately or soon after birth. When a baby is admitted to the NICU, teams of doctors, nurses, and other practitioners take over, administering indispensable and lifesaving treatments that parents are simply not equipped to provide. Parents come and go, adhering to the instructions of their baby's medical team—the baby's primary caretakers who are not them. While parents understand that it is in their baby's best interest to receive this care, the routine of following others' directions, witnessing others care for their new baby, and leaving the hospital empty handed for days, weeks, or months in a row can leave parents feeling undermined, invisible, and invalidated. Parents may find healing by using the following worksheet to explore these feelings and by talking with each other, their loved ones, or their providers about their experience.

Approximately 10 percent of newborns delivered in the United States are admitted to the NICU following birth (Grunberg et al., 2019). A newborn may be admitted to the NICU for complications related to congenital anomalies (also called birth defects), prematurity (delivery before 37 weeks gestation), the circumstances of their birth, and a wide variety of medical complications. The length of stay may be short (ranging from a few hours or days), or it may be long (lasting many weeks or months), depending on the complexity and severity of the baby's needs. Infants are discharged from the NICU when they reach specific medical milestones, but they are at a higher risk for additional hospitalizations, developmental delays, and ongoing medical complications that may require monitoring in the short or long term (Treyvaud et al., 2012).

The psychological burden of a NICU stay on a family system can be profound. Research validates what we have learned anecdotally from the many NICU parents we have worked with over the years: that a stay in the NICU imposes extraordinary stress on the adjustment to parenthood in many ways. Here are just a few:

- As many as half of all parents whose newborns require NICU care will experience clinically significant symptoms of depression, anxiety, and trauma (Grunberg et al., 2022). Both parents should be screened for mental health complications when their newborn is admitted to the NICU, as both mothers and partners are deeply affected by this experience.

- Learning to use and understand medical devices both in the hospital and outpatient setting can be stressful and upsetting. Many of our patients identify the sounds and sights associated with medical devices and interventions as triggers for trauma reactions.

- The NICU setting requires parents to defer their newborn's care to a medical team of neonatologists, nurses, and other specialists. This experience can interfere with parent-infant attachment, as well as a parent's development of confidence, efficacy, and agency (Davis & Tesler Stein, 2012).

- After the mother is discharged from the hospital, the family functioning must shift to accommodate the needs of the infant who remains hospitalized. For example, parents must navigate whether and how to take extended time off work (if this is even available to them) and how to juggle childcare responsibilities for any other children, especially if the hospital is a distance from home. Many babies, both during their NICU stay and after their discharge, require extra protection from germs due to compromised immune systems, physical immaturities, and other medical conditions. This can limit parents' access to practical and social support from loved ones and visitors and can impact the lives of older children who attend school, playdates, and other activities.

Often, parents describe their NICU experience as an emotional roller coaster, with ups and downs informed by the frequent reports they receive from their baby's medical providers. Parents watch other families come and go and fantasize about their own child's discharge. In many cases, parents will learn that plans for discharge are being made, only to learn at the last minute that their babies will require another night, or a few nights, of monitoring. To outsiders, it may be comforting to know that babies are observed closely and are only allowed to leave the NICU when they are absolutely ready. For parents, this back and forth can feel like a form of cruel torture, with the excitement of finally bringing a car seat to the hospital squashed over and over again. When homecoming finally does happen, parents must overcome the normal learning curve presented by newborn life as well as the challenges unique to post-NICU life.

We strongly encourage parents to seek out support from other parents who have gone through similar postpartum experiences and, when possible, whose infants have similar medical complexities. When an infant requires NICU care, providers should also be proactive about screening parents for symptoms of perinatal mood and anxiety disorders throughout the child's hospitalization and should provide resources for peer and professional support regardless of screening outcomes. Above all, we encourage providers to remain mindful of the role they can play in facilitating the parent-newborn relationship in the NICU setting. Although, as the patient, a newborn deserves their medical team's full attention, when you empower parents with support and education, it ultimately strengthens the overall psychosocial health of NICU babies and has life-long positive impact on their parents' mental health and family functioning.

Patient Worksheet

A NICU PARENT'S LOSSES

The first hours, days, and weeks of a baby's life are filled with firsts. From first breaths to first meetings with siblings and other family members, to first pediatrician appointments and first snuggles at home, these moments often feel exciting and to be expected. However, when babies require NICU care, these moments may not happen. Although it is a priority for babies to receive this essential and lifesaving care, it is often normal for feelings of loss and disappointment to coexist. Use this worksheet to explore your experiences in navigating your child's stay in the NICU.

What are some disappointments you have experienced due to your baby's stay in the NICU? For example, are there any memories you anticipated making that you have missed out on?

_____

_____

_____

_____

What logistical stressors do you have to deal with because of your baby's time in the NICU? What feelings do you have about this?

_____

_____

_____

_____

Are you experiencing any worries that you might not have had you if your baby did not require NICU care? If so, what types of worries?

_____

_____

_____

_____

Are you experiencing any symptoms of PTSD, including flashbacks, nightmares, or hypersensitivity to certain items, places, or sounds? If so, describe them here.

_____

_____

_____

_____

A Final Note to Providers

In the pages that follow, you will find handouts for each set of circumstances we discussed in this chapter, which contain essential information you may need at a glance when interacting with patients affected by infertility, loss, and other postpartum complications. These sheets include a glossary with basic definitions, key questions to ask, validating phrases to use, and resources for parents who need additional support. You will also find recommended resources for your own ongoing education and development, some of which may be offered free of charge. If you hope to work with parents who feel marginalized or experience disenfranchised grief, we strongly encourage you to seek out this added training to become a true participant in helping these parents to feel fully seen, understood, and accepted.

Provider Handout

INFERTILITY CHEAT SHEET

What is infertility?

Infertility is defined as the inability to conceive after one year of unprotected intercourse. However, many specialists will begin working with women who are 35 years of age or older after six months of unsuccessful attempts to become pregnant (CDC, 2022a).

Who experiences infertility?

Approximately 11% of reproductive age Americans are impacted by infertility (Lepkowski et al., 2010), including both men and women who may require treatments to increase the likelihood of conception, as well as single parents and same-sex parents who may require donor gametes (donor sperm or eggs) to conceive.

What should I say to a patient experiencing infertility?

- *Do* ask your patients about whether they are undergoing treatment for infertility and how this is impacting them. *Do not* make assumptions about what kinds of treatments your patients are seeking.

- *Do* ask your patients how they are feeling about their infertility journey. Respond by listening, expressing that you care, and asking whether they feel well cared for by any specialists that they are working with. *Do not* try to make your patient feel better by giving advice or pointing out that they can adopt, already have one child, may choose a child-free life, or can try a different approach to treatment.

- *Do* validate any feelings your patients are having and give feedback within the scope of your practice if requested. While it is important to validate feelings of grief, loss, sadness, and anger, be mindful that the risk of mood and anxiety disorders is increased in infertility patients. *Do not* lose sight of the very nuanced experience of parents experiencing mood and anxiety disorders during or after an infertility journey. If you have not pursued specialized training in this area, give your patients appropriate mental health care resources. A list of mental health care providers who have completed training in reproductive difficulties can be found at www.asrm.org.

- *Do* remind patients that even if infertility is not your area of specialty, you care about their well-being and will do what you can to be supportive and helpful. *Do not* compartmentalize a patient's fertility experience. Infertility impacts, and is impacted by, many aspects of a patient's emotional and physical health. Knowing that all providers are on their side and willing to be supportive in any ways necessary is a relief to patients.

What Resources Are Available for My Patients?

- Resolve: The National Infertility Association: https://resolve.org

What Continuing Education Resources Are Available for Me?

- American Society of Reproductive Medicine: www.asrm.org
- Fertility Counseling Postgraduate Course: www.covingtonandhafkin.com

Provider Handout

NON-GESTATIONAL PARENTS CHEAT SHEET

What is a non-gestational parent?

A non-gestational parent did not carry or give birth to their children. This can include fathers, one or more parents in a same-sex or trans partnership who did not carry their baby themselves, parents who employ a gestational carrier or surrogate, and adoptive parents.

Can a non-birthing parent experience a perinatal mood and anxiety disorder?

Yes. Some providers use different terminology for mood and anxiety disorders that emerge in non-gestational parents. The terms postadoption depressive syndrome, postadoption depression, paternal postpartum depression, and postnatal depression all refer to the emergence of mood and anxiety symptoms during the transition to parenthood.

What should I know about perinatal mood and anxiety disorders in non-gestational parents?

- Non-gestational parents can identify with other marginalized and underrepresented communities, such as those in the LGBTQIA+ community, and are vulnerable to many forms of discrimination, alienation, and isolation. Do your best to provide resources that are sensitive to these unique needs by looking for providers who value equity, social justice, and inclusion.

- Educate your patient on the psychosocial factors that contribute to the onset of mood and anxiety disorders in the perinatal period, such as a personal history of mood and anxiety disorders, lack of sleep, complications related to the baby's health or the mother's health, cultural pressures, difficult family-of-origin relationships, and a history of trauma, whether related or unrelated to the baby's birth. When parents understand that perinatal mood and anxiety disorders are not exclusively caused by hormonal changes related to giving birth, it can help them feel entitled to receiving support and treatment.

- If your patient is the parent who has given birth, ask how their partner is doing and educate your patient on the topic of mood and anxiety symptoms in non-gestational parents. Provide referrals for your patient's partner, and also for your patient, if either are having a difficult time.

What resources are available for my patients?

- For Fathers:
  - The Good Men Project: www.goodmenproject.com
  - The Center for Men's Excellence: www.menexcel.com

- For LGBTQIA+ Parents:
  - PFLAG: www.pflag.org

- For Adoptive Parents:
  - Creating a Family: www.creatingafamily.org

- For Birth Parents:
  - BirthMom Buds: www.birthmombuds.com

What continuing education resources are available for me?

- Creating a Family Curriculum Library: www.creatingafamily.org
- *Parental Mental Health: Factoring in Fathers* (Honikman & Singley, 2020)
- National Council for Adoption: www.adoptioncouncil.org

Provider Handout

PERINATAL LOSS CHEAT SHEET

What is perinatal loss?

Perinatal loss applies to early and late-term miscarriages (loss of a pregnancy before 20 weeks gestation), stillbirths (death of a fetus after 20 weeks gestation), neonatal/infant deaths (death of a newborn up to 28 weeks gestation), and maternal deaths.

How often do perinatal losses occur?

- Miscarriage occurs in 26% of all pregnancies and 10% of clinically recognized pregnancies.
- Stillbirth occurs in 1 out of 160–200 births annually.
- Neonatal death occurs in 18/1,000 live births globally (UNICEF, 2023).
- Maternal death occurs in 23.8 out of 100,000 live births, with a much higher rate of 55.3 deaths in 100,000 live births among Black mothers (Hoyert, 2022).

How should I address perinatal loss with patients?

- *If you see your patient in the hospital setting*: Recognize that regardless of gestational age, any loss can bring up intense feelings of grief. Express your condolences and set aside time for your patient to debrief their experience with you. If your patient experienced a stillbirth or early neonatal death, encourage them to see and spend time with their baby, and help them to access any available hospital services (e.g., use of cooling blankets, infant photography, pastoral care, social work, or funeral arrangements).

- *After hospital discharge*: Follow up with your patient to discuss any physical discomfort and to offer resources for grief support. Keep in mind that patients may find it difficult to speak with you or to return to your office. When they do come in or have contact with your staff, make sure that their loss is noted clearly on their medical charts.

- *If your patient is pregnant or would like to become pregnant after a perinatal loss*: After a perinatal loss, patients tend to experience more feelings of anxiety about their pregnancies, particularly when approaching milestones related to their loss. For example, mothers whose miscarriage was recognized at her 12-week ultrasound often report high anxiety around this time and specifically around attending a subsequent 12-week ultrasound. Make discussions about post-loss anxiety a regular part of prenatal care for bereaved parents, as this can encourage help-seeking behavior and foster a strong patient-provider relationship.

What resources are available for my patients?

- MISS Foundation: www.missfoundation.org
- Star Legacy Foundation: www.starlegacyfoundation.org
- Return to Zero HOPE: www.rtzhope.org
- Unite Grief Support: www.unitegriefsupport.org

What continuing education resources are available for me?

- MISS Foundation Compassionate Bereavement Care Certification: www.missfoundation.org
- Resolve through Sharing Bereavement Training: www.resolvethroughsharing.org
- Return to Zero Hope Webinar Series: www.rtzhope.org
- Star Legacy Foundation Stillbirth Summit/Education: www.starlegacyfoundation.org
- Unite Grief Support Facilitator Training: www.unitegriefsupport.org

Provider Handout

NICU EXPERIENCES CHEAT SHEET

What is the NICU?

The neonatal intensive care unit (NICU) is a specialized department within a hospital that provides newborns and infants with a high level of medical care when needed.

Why are newborns admitted to the NICU?

A newborn may be admitted to the NICU for complications related to congenital anomalies (also called birth defects), prematurity (delivery before 37 weeks gestation), the circumstances of their birth, and a wide variety of medical complications.

How long do babies stay in the NICU?

The length of stay can range from a few hours or days to weeks or months, depending on the complexity and severity of baby's needs.

What are some difficulties experienced by parents of babies admitted to the NICU?

- Separation from their babies at the time of or shortly after birth.
- Increased likelihood that the events of pregnancy, labor, and birth have been traumatic.
- Logistical challenges associated with traveling back and forth to the NICU at various hours and accommodating the needs of other children and family members.
- Learning about and becoming comfortable with medical devices needed to manage their newborn's health conditions.
- Tolerating emotional stress of deferring newborn care to medical professionals and feeling limited in their parental authority.
- Coping with stress of witnessing the medical interventions of other infants who are also hospitalized.
- Uncertainty about when their child may be discharged from the NICU and understanding that discharge or decision not to discharge can happen suddenly and unexpectedly.

Be mindful that risk for the onset of mood and anxiety disorders is increased in NICU parents. We encourage you to supply your patients with mental health resources in addition to those provided by hospital staff.

What resources are available for my patients?

- *Intensive Parenting: Surviving the Emotional Journey Through the NICU* (Davis & Tesler Stein, 2012)
- Hand to Hold: www.handtohold.org
- March of Dimes: www.marchofdimes.org
- Project NICU: www.projectnicu.com

What continuing education resources are available for me?

- NICU Parenting: A Practitioner's Guide to Working with Families in the NICU and Beyond (available at https://www.touchstoneinstitute.org/trainings/nicu-parenting)
- NIDCAP: www.nidcap.org

Section III

Therapy with Perinatal Patients

How to Support and Care for Perinatal Patients

CHAPTER 9

The Art of Holding Perinatal Women in Distress

The world of a perinatal mother is too busy. There is too much to learn, too much to think about, too much to process. When symptoms of a perinatal mood and anxiety disorder are in the mix, so much feels insurmountable.

The world of a health care provider is also too busy. Sometimes things go as planned, and we witness healing and joy. Those days fill us with gratitude and purpose, motivating us to keep going when we feel overwhelmed and depleted. Still, we know that the well-being and lives of our patients hang in the balance. Every day, we face grief, sorrow, trauma, and pain, and we carry the responsibility of maintaining our own strength to care for others. We do this despite our awareness that, at any time, the tides could turn and we could be faced with similar suffering. Even when we are suffering, we must still rise to the needs of our patients.

Interestingly, when we interview therapists with years of experience in maternal mental health, we find that they overwhelmingly rely on supportive psychotherapeutic methods for the treatment of perinatal women. This is despite the existence of evidence-based treatments like CBT and IPT, which have been adapted for perinatal patients and receive considerable empirical attention. This raises the question: Why do so many perinatal specialists lean on supportive therapeutic techniques when evidence endorsing its use for perinatal distress is so sparse? It's because we know it works, and we see women get better. The healing power of supportive psychotherapeutic interventions is indisputable, despite the lack of rigorous research. It is true that supportive interventions are difficult to operationally define, measure, and manualize, but if positive outcomes alone were enough to determine the efficacy of supportive psychotherapy for perinatal distress, its use and merit in the professional community would be unchallenged.

We believe supportive therapy as a primary intervention for perinatal distress is clearly worthy of further study, which has been the focus of Karen Kleiman's work. The Art of Holding Perinatal Women in Distress is a theoretical approach informed by psychodynamic schools of thought designed to respond to the specific needs of perinatal women. **The Art of Holding offers therapists directives and skills for tuning in, not only to what a perinatal patient is saying, but to what she is not saying as well. To what she cannot say. To what she does not want to say. To what she is afraid to say.**

By understanding the complex psychology of perinatal women and recognizing patterns of response and tendencies, Holding can increase the likelihood that patients will feel safe disclosing the depths of their suffering, rendering whatever therapeutic interventions a therapist applies more effective. Stating what is perhaps obvious, therapy is only as effective as what patients will disclose and explore. Therefore, it is imperative that perinatal therapists become skilled at (1) familiarizing themselves with perinatal-specific psychodynamics and vulnerabilities; (2) understanding the patterns of resistance that both protect and interfere with the therapeutic process; and (3) learning how to gain access to the heart of perinatal suffering to open pathways to recovery.

For the purposes of this book, we devote this chapter to a broad overview of the Holding approach. We briefly review the theoretical underpinnings of the approach and discuss the six holding points that serve as skills for increasing attunement within the therapeutic relationship. Please note that while this chapter largely focuses on the work of therapists, at its core, the Holding approach prioritizes active listening, sensitive interactions between patient and provider, empathy, and cultural humility—tenets of care that are requisite for all caretaking professions. For this reason, we encourage all maternal care providers to consider The Art of Holding as a relevant and applicable approach to their work with perinatal patients.

As you read ahead, consider that we are aware of the many therapeutic orientations and accompanying techniques that therapists use to promote symptom relief in their patients. The use of the Holding approach is not intended to take the place of these other interventions, but to augment them by maximizing relational attunement to promote patient disclosure.

The Holding Environment and The Good Enough Mother

The concept of the *holding environment* was first introduced by Donald Winnicott (1960, 1965), a renowned pediatrician and psychoanalyst whose work has deeply impacted developmental psychology. Winnicott proposed that the development of self-regulation, trust, and safety in relationships—and a strong sense of self—requires an approach to care that balances reactivity with space for expression. For example, in a holding environment, when a baby cries, the mother responds by listening and making various attempts to soothe her baby. She will check to see that her baby is clean, warm, and fed and will attend to any of these basic needs. If the baby continues to cry, she will attempt to soothe her child in a calm manner by rocking, patting, or singing softly. She works hard to maintain her own regulation to continue to stay attentive to her baby's needs.

Within Winnicott's holding environment exists the concept of the good enough mother. Although many mothers equate good mothering with a baby who is content and happy all or most of the time, when infants are expected to fit this presentation, mothers may experience a low level of tolerance for infant frustration. This can lead mothers to inadvertently limit their baby's range of self-expression. Winnicott's good enough mother, on the other hand, encourages mothers to actively respond to their infants' frustrations rather than trying to prevent or squelch them. He validates that during the course of infancy and babyhood, children can and need to learn to tolerate a wide range of emotions, and he views the mother's ability to remain responsive to, but not controlling over, her infants' emotions as helpful in facilitating this process.

In his great wisdom, Winnicott further recognizes that providing children with empathic, regulated, and attentive round-the-clock care will not be sustainable over long periods of time. He encourages mothers to trust their nurturing instincts and to be aware that when they falter, they are teaching children an important life skill: to tolerate disappointment and imperfection.

> ### Sharing Holding Responsibilities
> It is important for mothers to know that they are not the only person who can provide the type of comfort that characterizes a holding environment. All loving parents and parental figures can provide good enough parenting in a holding environment, regardless of sex, gender, or gestational status. Therefore, when mothers become tired, impatient, or experience their own distress, encourage them to take a break and ask for help from another person who loves their baby.

The Holding Environment for Perinatal Distress

Winnicott (2002) himself applies the concept of the holding environment to the therapeutic relationship by recognizing that, like parents, therapists teach self-regulation, build trust and safety, and strive for attunement with their patients. Karen Kleiman elaborates on this analogy by applying Winnicott's holding environment specifically to the needs of the perinatal mother. In her work, Kleiman recognizes the poignant similarities between a vulnerable newborn and its new mother. Inspired by Winnicott's attention to the benefits of attunement for infant development, The Art of Holding Perinatal Women in Distress focuses on increasing therapists' ability to mindfully and skillfully attend to the acute and specific distress of perinatal patients.

In addition, Kleiman explores the unique impact of the primal, sometimes excruciating, needs of the perinatal patient on the therapeutic relationship. Whether therapists work in general practice or specialize in reproductive health, working with perinatal patients can be triggering, and the risk of overidentification and transference are daily pitfalls. Although therapists are typically familiar with these pitfalls, what is harder to anticipate is how deeply impacted they can feel when they're deep in the trenches of such intimate and personally relevant work. As human beings, therapists have their own reproductive experiences that raise a wide variety of complex emotions. Kleiman's Art of Holding requires therapists to examine their personal experiences and prepare themselves for these critical moments.

The Holding Points

Central to The Art of Holding are six holding points: grounding, current state, expert, design, presence, and safeguarding. The holding points highlight six aspects of the therapeutic process that Kleiman views as essential for building an attuned alliance between the therapist and a perinatal patient. In the following section, we define each holding point and include an example of its clinical application.

Grounding

Grounding refers to the therapist's use of self, including modulation of voice and nonverbal cues, to restore balance to a patient's activated state (Kleiman, 2017). Grounding recognizes how difficult it is for perinatal women to reach out for support and validates the range of feelings they may have about needing help and about their mothering experience. When we encourage a patient to sit comfortably, utilize therapeutic silence, or offer a moment to take a deep breath within the holding framework, we observe their level of comfort or discomfort with these activities. Our observations may reveal a lack of self-regulation skills, resistance to self-regulation skills, or confusion about how to engage in self-regulation while caring for a baby.

> ### Grounding in Session
>
> When mothers arrive for a therapy session, they are often juggling a diaper bag, a purse, and an infant still buckled into their car seat. They come into the office, sit on the edge of the chair, and give us a halfhearted smile. Then they say something like "Hey, sorry I'm a mess today and he hasn't slept" while gesturing to their baby. They start to tell us about their week while they fumble with objects designed to soothe or distract the baby. In response, we take a deep breath, settle back in our chairs, and say, "Let's take a minute together. Sit back. Just breathe for a second. Let's see what happens." If a mother is able to take this moment to rest, breathe, or sit back in her seat, that's wonderful. If she fidgets in her chair, looks anxiously around the room, or preoccupies herself with her baby, we become curious about whether, and why, this is hard for her. That is where we begin, exploring what it is about her current situation that is getting in the way of her feeling more grounded.

Current State

Current state is the therapist's ability to attend to symptoms and initiate a rapid evaluation of the patient's physical safety, level of distress, and level of functional impairment (Kleiman, 2017). Current state recognizes that perinatal women often conceal the severity of their symptoms and feel dismissed by people who rush to normalize their distress or who overlook their distress altogether. It demonstrates sensitivity to how the perinatal state, the mother's physical and emotional depletion, and the presence of her baby impact her mental well-being. When an assessment of current state occurs within the holding environment, we convey that we value the mother's own perception of her distress and understand that what she is showing us or others on the outside may not fully capture how bad she is feeling on the inside. When a patient feels understood in this way, it increases the likelihood of her disclosure, enabling providers to more accurately assess her impairments, symptom severity, and degree of urgency.

> ### Current State in Session
>
> It isn't unusual for mothers to come into our offices and say that they are doing fine. Sometimes, therapy is their only real opportunity to interact with another adult, and they simply want to connect with someone. Other times, mothers might want us to think that they are doing okay, or they might be having a truly okay morning during an otherwise difficult week. Either way, when we ask mothers how they are doing, and the answer is vague or non-specific, we pause to wonder if they are telling us how bad they have truly been feeling. We always have in mind that perinatal women want so badly to feel better that they will cling to any sign of improvement.
>
> We also never lose sight of how much new moms don't want to feel like they are falling apart, even though therapy welcomes all emotions. We listen carefully to what they are saying, closely observe their affect, and respond with something like "You know, it looks like you are feeling so much better today. Have you felt this way all week? Can you tell me if there have been low points this week?" After mothers describe their low points, we then follow up with, "Can you put into words how bad you were feeling in that moment? Did anyone know how bad you were feeling then?" Even when a mother does clarify how she is doing, we remain aware that there may still be information she is not ready to disclose, and we continue to listen for that.

Expert

Expert refers to the therapist's capacity to exude competence and confidence in their ability to carry high levels of distress (Kleiman, 2017). This skill requires therapists to tap into their own sense of self to ensure they are projecting themselves as someone who can help. When a therapist is mindfully aware of how a mother's perinatal state is impacting her—and the therapist, in turn, reflects this awareness to the mother—it reinforces the mother's decision to ask for help and begins to build trust in the relationship. Experts do not have all the answers. But perinatal women have many questions, and one of our tasks is to reassure them that we have resources and access to information to address their concerns. Our confidence is an essential part of their investment in this process.

> ### ✤ Expert in Session ✤
>
> One of the most powerful gifts we can give to our patients is hope. Hope comes from a true belief that perinatal mothers will get better, and we instill this hope by empowering them with knowledge. When a mother comes to our offices feeling like a failure or expressing hopelessness about herself and her experience, we help her see that these feelings are symptoms that will improve with treatment. We'll often say something like "Your symptoms are unique, and as we work together, we'll explore exactly how they are affecting you. But I want you to know that lots of mothers come to this office with similar thoughts and feelings and recover completely. They feel better, like themselves again. We need some time together to find this path for you, but I am confident that we can get there together." In response, we see her demeanor change. She holds her head higher, she makes eye contact, and she exhales.

Design

Design is the therapist's blueprint of an initial treatment plan—aimed at symptom relief—which centers the patient's stated needs and evolves collaboratively (Kleiman, 2017). Design recognizes that perinatal women require opportunities to build personal agency and self-esteem during the adjustment to motherhood. Design can take the form of a structured plan for treatment or can simply be the problem-solving strategies you use to help her get through the day.

> ### ✤ Design in Session ✤
>
> We are always mindful of the great longing perinatal women have for control. One of the ways we can help them regain feelings of control is by helping them set small, achievable goals aimed at building their confidence in mothering, engaging in self-care, nurturing their relationships, or enhancing other aspects of their lives that foster healing. For example, mothers often report feeling trapped at home. We acknowledge these feelings and then work with them to identify a solution to their problem, like making a plan to get out of the house. But helping them overcome their fears, anxiety, and resistance to following through with the solution is the key to them feeling held in the therapy environment. We patiently work through their fears, carefully addressing any emotional or practical difficulties they may be experiencing. At the end of the session, they have a plan to follow when they feel trapped, and they feel supported in their efforts to make this plan.

Presence

Presence is the therapist's capacity to establish and sustain the therapeutic connection while simultaneously maintaining self-awareness, relational attunement, and boundaries (Kleiman, 2017). Presence recognizes a perinatal patient's need to be heard by someone who doesn't have an agenda or a bias toward fixing or mollifying them. Presence further calls to attention the unique ways that treating perinatal distress challenges the therapeutic alliance, as it illuminates issues of countertransference and tests our professional boundaries. Remaining fully present with a perinatal patient in distress may be our most important task, and it is arguably our most difficult.

> ### Presence in Session
>
> Working with perinatal patients was challenging when Hilary was pregnant herself. Early in her pregnancy, she was working with a patient who experienced a miscarriage at 10 weeks. Every week, she would come into Hilary's office and talk about how blindsided she felt when she found out her baby had stopped growing at her 12-week ultrasound appointment and how much anxiety she had about becoming pregnant again one day. It took every iota of strength that Hilary had to listen to this patient without becoming completely self-involved. She took a lot of deep breaths in those sessions to remain engaged and worked hard to focus on the patient's words. And she always needed to schedule this appointment at the end of the day. After each session, Hilary would take some time to process her own anxiety. Her supervisor and her own therapist were invaluable during this time as well. Hilary felt so relieved when she passed her own 12-week ultrasound.

Safeguarding

Safeguarding refers to the therapist's role in balancing a mother's need for protection and support while facilitating her autonomy and sense of agency (Kleiman, 2017). Safeguarding recognizes the dangers and urgency of the perinatal period while focusing on protecting both the patient (and baby), as well as the integrity of therapeutic alliance, to ensure full recovery. Safeguarding reminds us to never make risky presumptions about a patient's well-being and to regularly monitor her vulnerabilities along with her progress.

> ### ❧ Safeguarding in Session ❧
>
> One striking feature of perinatal anxiety is the very high distress mothers experience in response to their intrusive thoughts. To perinatal mothers, these thoughts signify a crisis—that something must be terribly, terribly wrong with them. As their therapists, though, we realize that while it is terrifying to experience scary thoughts, the presence of these thoughts does not signify a crisis. We also know that symptom relief will be forthcoming. When a mother is having scary thoughts about smothering her baby or crashing her car, it can be hard to convince her that not only is she okay, but that she *is* a safe caretaker for her baby. We start by carefully assessing the patient's symptoms to demonstrate that we are taking her distress seriously, but we are careful not to overreact to her fear. We then share our perspective on her symptoms and let her know that we will keep an open dialogue about how she is feeling. Our goal is to reinforce that while we are not distressed by her symptoms, we will remain vigilant on her behalf, safeguarding against her worst fears coming true: that she is alone and will lose all control.

Engaged Empathy and the Holding Points

Therapists who attend trainings on The Art of Holding Perinatal Women in Distress often ask, "How will I know if I am using the holding points correctly? How will I know if she is feeling held?" Karen reassures them that they will *know*. Karen refers to that intuitive knowing as "engaged empathy," which occurs when the therapist and patient feel a certain magic in the therapeutic space—when they feel that therapy is working. As Karen's student, and a student of Holding, Hilary is extremely familiar with this feeling and describes it best as "the ineffable magic of relational therapy."

However, recent research on burnout has begun to operationally define, or at least articulately describe, engaged empathy. In their book, *Burnout: The Secret to Unlocking the Stress Cycle*, Emily and Amelia Nagoski (2019) describe how the search for meaning is protective against burnout, where they define meaning as our connection to something greater than ourselves. For therapists, this greater purpose is often found in witnessing our patients find relief from their suffering. Many maternal health care providers, in particular, find special meaning in knowing that when patients experience this relief, they are better positioned to care for infants who will become the next generation of stewards for our world. When providers recognize the far-reaching potential for their work to be impactful, it can fill them with meaning.

In the context of Holding, engaged empathy occurs when the use of the holding points results in a moment of shared meaning between provider and patient. When the holding points converge and the patient experiences a palpable relief from suffering, she simultaneously experiences a surge of hope. In witnessing this relief, the therapist simultaneously experiences an increased connection to their reasons for doing this hard work. When these moments happen, the therapist can feel reassured that they are holding and that they are holding well.

Hard to Hold

It comes as no surprise that there is a negative correlation between the depth of the therapeutic relationship and therapist burnout (Zarzycka et al., 2021)—meaning that the higher the quality of the therapeutic relationship, the lower the level of therapist burnout. When the therapeutic relationship is strained or patients are not progressing, therapists can begin to doubt their efficacy, which increases vulnerability to burnout. One well-utilized resource to prevent efficacy-related burnout is professional consultation groups, where therapists help each other problem solve ways to reduce patient resistance and increase progress. In consultations that focus on The Art of Holding Perinatal Women in Distress, this is described as a patient or a presentation that is *hard to hold*.

In Karen's experience with the Holding approach, patients can present as hard to hold for a variety of reasons, including a history of trauma, difficulties with attachment, the presence of mood or anxiety symptoms, or general propensity toward resistance. No matter the reason, when a patient is hard to hold, it can interfere with the development of a secure holding environment within which the therapeutic relationship can flourish. In this section, however, we explore a therapist's individual vulnerabilities that can render a patient hard to hold.

As therapists, we are well trained to maintain our focus on our patients and to overcome any moments of distraction we experience in session. However, the work between a therapist and a perinatal patient is uniquely intimate, as the content of sessions has relevance to the experience of *all* human beings. We all have a reproductive system. We all have parents. We all wonder about whether we will have children. If we have children, we wonder if we are good parents. No matter how strong our boundaries are or how aware we are of our countertransference, listening to a new mother whose experience so closely mirrors our own can be uniquely agitating and unnerving. To prevent these moments from taking us by surprise (though this will still occur from time to time), it can help to prepare in advance by identifying our specific vulnerabilities, developing a plan for coping in session, and learning to reflect on instances when we are caught off guard. The pages that follow can guide this exploration.

Provider Handout

HARD TO HOLD: PROVIDER PERSONAL HISTORY

Therapists know that remaining present in session is essential for building a strong therapeutic relationship. When patients feel that they have their therapist's full attention, the therapeutic alliance blossoms and relational healing can take place. Although all therapists strive to remain attentive and grounded in sessions—tuning out other stressors and stimuli that could be distracting—even seasoned therapists find that the content of a session or an interaction with a patient can activate their own vulnerability.

Increasing awareness of your own vulnerabilities can help you identify aspects of your life that may require further examination in your own therapy or in professional supervision so that you are better positioned to establish a secure and supportive holding environment for your patients. Consider the questions below to explore any factors that might be making it more difficult for you to hold certain patients. Discuss your answers with a support person or professional supervisor, use them as journal prompts, or ponder them on your own. Note any items or topics that bring up an intense emotional, cognitive, or physical response.

Reproductive History

What is your reproductive story?

_____

_____

_____

What emotions do you experience when you think about your reproductive story?

_____

_____

_____

What feelings do you notice in your body when you think about your reproductive story?

_____

_____

_____

Are there certain parts of your story that bring up difficult or intense emotions or bodily feelings?

_____

_____

_____

Are there certain parts of your story that you find especially distracting or preoccupying?

_____

_____

_____

Do you have a history of reproductive (or any) trauma?

_____

_____

_____

When you think about others' reproductive stories, do any bring up difficult or intense emotions or bodily sensations? For example, infertility journeys, miscarriage stories, terminations of pregnancy, stillbirths, NICU experiences, or adoptions?

_____

_____

_____

Yourself as a Parent and as Your Parents' Child

If you are a parent, how do you feel about yourself as a parent? Or, if you are not a parent at this time, how do you feel about this?

_____

_____

_____

What are some of the stressors related to your status as a parent, or as a person without children, at this time?

_____

_____

_____

What is your relationship like with your own parents?

_____

_____

_____

What are some of the stressors related to your status as an adult child to your parents?

_____

_____

_____

Have you experienced any disappointments or losses in your relationships with your parents?

_____

_____

_____

Partners and Friends

If you have a partner, what is the quality of your relationship? Or if you do not have a partner at this time, how do you feel about this?

_____

_____

_____

Are you supported by friends? If so, what is the quality of your friendships?

_____

_____

_____

Have you experienced any disappointments or losses in your relationships, either with your partner or friends?

_____

_____

_____

Self-Esteem

Do you feel confident in your roles? As a partner? As your parents' child? As your children's parent? If not, what issues might you need to confront that could arise in the context of a session?

_____

_____

_____

Do you feel confident in your ability to tolerate the normal process of rupture and repair in therapy? Why or why not?

_____

_____

_____

Do you notice that your own feelings of guilt and shame accompany you into your sessions? In what ways?

_____

_____

_____

Would you recommend yourself as a therapist? Why or why not?

_____

_____

_____

Do you believe in your ability to help your patients recover? Why or why not?

_____

_____

_____

When you are finished, review the items that elicited stronger feelings from you, and identify three people or resources you can trust to help you explore your reactions and develop coping plans to use in session should these emotions surface.

Provider Handout

SELF-CARE IN SESSION AND AFTER SESSION

Whether you anticipate feeling activated by the content of a session, or whether the dysregulation catches you by surprise, knowing how to care for yourself in the aftermath is important. Reflect on the ways you already implement self-regulation strategies in your life, then consider how you might apply those skills, or the skills listed below, to moments in session that are hard to hold.

- **Transition your focus with your breath:** When your mind wanders, try taking a slow, deep inhale to bring your attention back to the moment. Try to hear the whooshing sound of your breath as it fills your lungs, feel your belly and chest expand, and notice the gentle coolness of your breath on the tip of your nose.

- **Expose yourself to temperature changes:** Keep a cold glass of water or hot cup of tea near you. Exposing your body to cold conditions, in particular, can increase feelings of calm when you're feeling anxious (Niehues & Klovenski, 2019).

- **Write down your trigger:** Reach for a note pad or scrap of paper and write yourself a quick reminder to revisit your trigger after the session. For example, if you find it difficult to listen to a patient describe her miscarriage, write down "miscarriage" and then return your focus to the story of your patient. Remind yourself that you can explore the feelings you are having as soon as the session is over.

- **Practice using boundaries:** When you are planning to meet with a patient whose story you often find activating, consider scheduling this patient at the end of the day or before a scheduled break. Plan to give yourself some space to recover afterward. If you are caught off guard in a session and do not have a scheduled break between sessions, consider asking your next patient to wait a few minutes so you can take a bathroom break. Then use those few minutes to self-soothe. Remember, you owe it to yourself and to your patients to engage in this self-care.

- **Plan scheduled professional supervision or personal therapy:** If you wait until you feel triggered to schedule a meeting with a supervisor or therapist, you'll be adding something to your to-do list when you already feel stressed. Instead, maintain regular appointments with this person to help you work through triggering situations.

- **Journal:** Take time after your session or at the end of your day to journal about the triggering experience. Note any specific emotions, body sensations, or thoughts that came up during this time. Consider bringing your journal to a support person for further exploration.

Provider Handout

SELF-DISCLOSURE IN PERINATAL WORK

Perinatal patients in distress often present with such intense feelings of isolation and longing for connection that therapists can become tempted to use self-disclosure as a means for building the therapeutic alliance. While this population can benefit from slightly more self-disclosure, therapists must engage in careful and ethical decision-making to guide their disclosures. Use this handout to consider whether self-disclosure might be appropriate for a particular patient or situation.

1. First, be mindful of the various types of self-disclosure. Disclosures may be:

    - **Deliberate:** Information you decide to share, ideally with great consideration and care.

    - **Unavoidable:** Information you may or may not wish to share but may be obliged to disclose for any number of reasons. For example, you might need to disclose your own pregnancy and subsequent maternity leave.

    - **Accidental:** Information patients discover accidentally, such as when a patient bumps into a therapist with their family at the grocery store.

    - **A result of the patient's actions:** Information that patients discover about their therapists intentionally, for example, by researching a therapist on social media.

2. Before engaging in any purposeful self-disclosure, consider:

    - How might self-disclosure *benefit* your patient right now? Will it challenge stigma? Reduce isolation? Provide role-modeling? Instill hope?

    - How might self-disclosure *negatively* impact your patient right now? Will it deter focus from the patient? Cause patients to become worried about your needs? Compromise your professionalism? Make patients feel unsure about their role in the therapeutic relationship?

    - Could this disclosure upset the therapeutic alliance by positioning you as a friend/peer?

    - Is there secondary gain for you in making this disclosure? For example, are you in need of a therapist, confidant, or friend to talk through this right now?

    - Is there a different way to help your patient achieve the same therapeutic goal? For example, if your goal is to reduce stigma around your patient's experience, are there ways other than self-disclosure that you might try first?

Copyright © 2023 Hilary Waller and Karen Kleiman, *The Perinatal Patient*. All rights reserved.

Cultural Humility: A Prerequisite for Holding

We cannot conclude this chapter on The Art of Holding Perinatal Women in Distress without discussing cultural humility. In the context of psychology and medicine, cultural humility is a two-pronged practice aimed at increasing sensitivity, appreciation, and trust between providers and patients. Those who practice cultural humility experience a willingness and desire to engage in self-reflection on their own cultural context. Moreover, they feel a sincere desire to increase their understanding and appreciation of others' cultural environments and experiences. Individuals who practice cultural humility may be described as embodying open-mindedness, curiosity, and inquisitiveness (Zhang et al., 2021). The concept of cultural humility applies to all forms of culture, including but not limited to race, ethnicity, nationality, gender expression, sexual orientation, and physical ability.

In your work as a maternal health care provider, you must realize that cultural humility is not only a best practice but a prerequisite for establishing the holding environment. Therapists who are unaware of how their own lived experiences, prejudices, preferences, and implicit biases impact their work risk damaging the therapeutic relationship. Perinatal women who are resistant to attend therapy, limited in resources, or reluctant to engage may simply be unable to tolerate these ruptures. In contrast, when you practice cultural humility, you show up with a genuinely eager willingness to learn, which positions you to uphold your ethical duties to protect the welfare of your patients and do no harm. Consider how the holding points themselves can serve as a guide:

- **Grounding:** What topics or statements cause you to feel dysregulated or judgmental in session? Can you identify aspects of your own expectations or cultural norms that inform your reaction?

- **Current state:** Are you aware of how you feel in the presence of someone whose skin color, body, religion, or values system is different from yours? What emotions or body sensations do you notice when you're in their presence?

- **Expert:** Do you find it difficult to maintain your expert stance when interacting with someone who is different from you? Do you feel threatened? Defensive?

- **Design:** What trainings, therapy, or professional consultation can you seek to help you explore the cultural dynamics in your sessions? Identify your options and make a commitment to follow through.

- **Presence:** Practicing cultural humility can be uncomfortable. Remind yourself that learning to sit with your own discomfort during this process is a credit to who you are as a provider and that you are practicing cultural humility in the service of your patients.

- **Safeguarding:** Remind yourself that it is okay for this process to be difficult and uncomfortable. Personal growth, change, and adjustment are not painless processes. Try to take comfort in knowing that as you are growing, you are expanding your capacity to hold and to hold well.

A Final Word from
Karen Kleiman

I am encouraged and hopeful about the direction that perinatal education, trainings, research, and advocacy are moving in recent years. Perinatal mood and anxiety disorders, and the interference they impose on growing families, have finally received the academic and clinical attention they deserve. The aspect that remains elusive is *how* to uncover what the perinatal woman may not be telling you. This is the precious piece that lives silently inside each perinatal woman in distress— the piece that reinforces the enduring stigma and stifles her cry for help. As much as we try, our words and our efforts have fallen short of a woman's innate urge to silence and protect herself and her baby from a society that she believes doesn't understand, doesn't support, and doesn't really get it.

Those of us who have dedicated our professional lives to the study of perinatal women in distress believe we *do* get it. We believe that women suffer in silence for many reasons, but first and foremost, they are terrified that they will be misunderstood, that their baby will be taken away, and that they are losing their mind. Although they are not losing their mind, and their baby won't be taken away, they are far too often completely misunderstood. Health care providers, including many therapists, *think* they know, *hope* they understand, and *believe* they have studied enough to effectively intervene on behalf of a pregnant or postpartum woman who is struggling with depression and anxiety.

Unfortunately, this is often not the case. Why? Because it's not enough to read a book. It's not enough to have experienced perinatal depression and anxiety yourself. It's not enough to listen to and believe that what your patient tells you is true. Training matters. Training that focuses on what lies beneath the surface, beneath the shroud of perfection and bliss. Training that emphasizes tuning in to the subtle and excruciating feelings and thoughts that are *not* being expressed. That is the beginning of healing. Maternal health care providers who are trained in holding techniques are finally in a position to listen, *really* listen, to agonizing details from a mother who cannot bear her own thoughts and feelings. When we access this authentic suffering, we have succeeded in helping her feel heard. To date, there is no antidepressant, no manualized therapy guide, and no certificate of achievement that comes close to helping a perinatal woman in distress feel cared for. In this important way, holding is the gateway to healing.

I am completely honored and immeasurably grateful that Hilary Waller demonstrates such mastery of this subject and sees the value of carrying on my work. This book is a testament to her indescribable capacity to translate my gut-wrenched creations and turn them into constructive formulations. Simply put, she has taken my magic and put meaning behind it. If you are a serious perinatal therapist, or if you are a maternal health care provider who wants to enhance your clinical work, this book is a must-read. Because if you don't understand what is *not* being said, you will provide insufficient treatment. For women who are having difficulty adjusting to motherhood, not receiving excellent care can be disappointing and frustrating. But for women who are experiencing a serious perinatal mood and anxiety disorder, missing the mark can mean the difference between life and death. We implore you to be informed about and dedicated to this population if you take on this specialized and exceptionally rewarding work.

References

Aktas, S., & Calik, K.Y. (2015). Factors affecting depression during pregnancy and the correlation between social support and pregnancy depression. *Iranian Red Crescent Medical Journal, 17*(9), Article e16640. https://doi.org/10.5812/ircmj.16640

American Psychiatric Association. (2013). *Diagnostic and statistical manual of mental disorders* (5th ed.). https://doi.org/10.1176/appi.books.9780890425596

American Society for Reproductive Medicine. (2017, March 8). *Quick facts about infertility*. https://www.reproductivefacts.org/faqs/quick-facts-about-infertility/

Anderson, J. K., Howarth, E., Vainre, M., Jones, P. B., & Humphrey, A. (2017). A scoping literature review of service-level barriers for access and engagement with mental health services for children and young people. *Children and Youth Services Review, 77*, 164–176. https://doi.org/10.1016/j.childyouth.2017.04.017

Arampatzi, C., Spyropoulou, A., Antoniou, E., Orovou, E., Michailidou, E.M., & Eskitzis, P. (2022). The effect of postpartum psychosis on partner's and infant's life. *World Journal of Advanced Research and Reviews, 15*(1), 122–127. https://doi.org/10.30574/wjarr.2022.15.1.0676

Arnautovic, T. I., & Dammann, C. (2022). The neonatal perspective of paid family medical leave (PFML). *Journal of Perinatology*. Advance online publication. https://doi.org/10.1038/s41372-021-01300-6

Barnes, D., & Brown, J. (2016). Understanding postpartum psychosis and infanticide. *Forensic Scholars Today, 1*(4).

Bauer, N. S., Ofner, S., Pottenger, A., Carroll, A. E., & Downs, S. M. (2017). Follow-up of mothers with suspected postpartum depression from pediatrics clinics. *Frontiers in Pediatrics, 5*, Article 212. https://doi.org/10.3389/fped.2017.00212

Bhat, A., Nanda, A., Murphy, L., Ball, A. L., Fortney, J., & Katon, J. (2022). A systematic review of screening for perinatal depression and anxiety in community-based settings. *Archives of Women's Mental Health, 25*, 33–49. https://doi.org/10.1007/s00737-021-01151-2

Bhattacharya, A., Dwivedy, R., Nandeshwar, S., De Costa, A., & Diwan, V. K. (2008). 'To weigh or not to weigh?' Sociocultural practices affecting weighing at birth in Vidisha, India. *Journal of Neonatal Nursing, 14*(6), 199–206. https://doi.org/10.1016/j.jnn.2008.07.009

Biaggi, A., Conroy, S., Pawlby, S., & Pariante, C. M. (2016). Identifying the women at risk of antenatal anxiety and depression: A systematic review. *Journal of Affective Disorders, 191*, 62–77. https://doi.org/10.1016/j.jad.2015.11.014

Bicking Kinsey, C., Baptiste-Roberts, K., Zhu, J., & Kjerulff, K. H. (2015). Effect of previous miscarriage on depressive symptoms during subsequent pregnancy and postpartum in the First Baby Study. *Maternal and Child Health Journal, 19*(2), 391–400. https://doi.org/10.1007/s10995-014-1521-0

Browne, H. D. (2020). *Depression and awareness of mental health resources among minority and non-minority college students* [Doctoral dissertation, Walden University]. Walden University ScholarWorks. https://scholarworks.waldenu.edu/cgi/viewcontent.cgi?article=9952&context=dissertations

Byatt, N., Biebel, K., Friedman, L., Hosein, S., Lundquist, R., Freeman, M., & Cohen, L. (2014). *Depression screening algorithm for obstetric providers*. Massachusetts Child Psychiatry Access Program (MCPAP). https://www.mcpapformoms.org/Docs/AdultProviderToolkit_2019.pdf

Carvalho, K., Kheyfets, A., Maleki, P., Miller, B., Abouhala, S., Anwar, E., & Amutah-Onukagha, N. (2021). A systematic policy review of Black maternal health-related policies proposed federally and in Massachusetts: 2010–2020. *Frontiers in Public Health, 9*. https://doi.org/10.3389/fpubh.2021.664659

Centers for Disease Control and Prevention. (2020). *Stillbirth: Data and statistics*. https://www.cdc.gov/ncbddd/stillbirth/data.html

Centers for Disease Control and Prevention. (2022a). *Infertility FAQs*. https://www.cdc.gov/reproductivehealth/infertility/index.htm

Centers for Disease Control and Prevention. (2022b, April 13). *Infographic: Racial/ethnic disparities in pregnancy-related deaths—United States 2007–2016*. https://www.cdc.gov/reproductivehealth/maternal-mortality/disparities-pregnancy-related-deaths/infographic.html

Chhabra, J., Li, W., & McDermott, B. (2022). Predictive factors for depression and anxiety in men during the perinatal period: A mixed methods study. *American Journal of Men's Health, 16*(1), 1–15. https://doi.org/10.1177/15579883221079489

Chimbo, C., Sunday, O. O., Oriji, S., Erohubie, P. O., James, B. O., & Lawani, A. O. (2021). Pain and depression among adult outpatients with osteoarthritis in Nigeria: A cross-sectional study. *Asian Journal of Social Health and Behavior, 4*(3), 116–121. https://doi.org/10.4103/shb.shb_15_21

Chinn, J. J., Martin, I. K., & Redmond, N. (2021). Health equity among Black women in the United States. *Journal of Women's Health, 30*(2), 212–219. https://doi.org/10.1089/jwh.2020.8868

Clark, C. T., & Wisner, K. L. (2018). Treatment of peripartum bipolar disorder. *Obstetrics and Gynecology Clinics of North America, 45*(3), 403–417. https://doi.org/10.1016/j.ogc.2018.05.002

Cohen, L. S. (2019, May 8). *Bipolar disorder during pregnancy: Lessons learned*. MGH Center for Women's Mental Health. https://womensmentalhealth.org/posts/bipolar-disorder-during-pregnancy-lessons-learned/

Collardeau, F., Corbyn, B., Abramowitz, J., Janssen, P. A., Woody, S., & Fairbrother, N. (2019). Maternal unwanted and intrusive thoughts of infant-related harm, obsessive-compulsive disorder and depression in the perinatal period: Study protocol. *BMC Psychiatry, 19*(1), Article 94. https://doi.org/10.1186/s12888-019-2067-x

Corrigan, C. P., Kwasky, A. N., & Groh, C. J. (2015). Social support, postpartum depression, and professional assistance: A survey of mothers in the midwestern United States. *Journal of Perinatal Education, 24*(1), 48–60. https://doi.org/10.1891/1058-1243.24.1.48

Daly, D., Higgins, A., Hannon, S., O'Malley, D., Wuytack, F., Moran, P., Cusack, C., & Begley, C. (2022). Trajectories of postpartum recovery: What is known and not known. *Clinical Obstetrics and Gynecology, 65*(3), 594–610. https://doi.org/10.1097/GRF.0000000000000726

Davis, D. L., & Tesler Stein, M. (2012). *Intensive parenting: Surviving the emotional journey through the NICU*. Fulcrum Publishing.

De Sousa Machado, T., Chur-Hansen, A., & Due, C. (2020). First time mothers' perceptions of social support: Recommendations for best practice. *Health Psychology Open, 7*(1). https://doi.org/10.1177/2055102919898611

DeAngelis, T. (2015, March). In search of cultural competence. *Monitor on Psychology, 46*(3). https://www.apa.org/monitor/2015/03/cultural-competence

Dugas, C., & Slane, V. H. (2022, June 27). Miscarriage. In *StatPearls*. StatPearls Publishing. https://www.ncbi.nlm.nih.gov/books/NBK532992/

Eddy, B., Poll, V., Whiting, J., & Clevesy, M. (2019). Forgotten fathers: Postpartum depression in men. *Journal of Family Issues, 40*(8) 1001–1017. https://doi.org/10.1177/0192513X1983311

Fairbrother, N., & Abramowitz, J. S. (2007). New parenthood as a risk factor for the development of obsessional problems. *Behaviour Research and Therapy, 45*, 2155–2163. https://doi.org/10.1016/j.brat.2006.09.019

Fairbrother, N., Collardeau, F., Albert, A., Challacombe, F. L., Thordarson, D. S., Woody, S. R., & Janssen, P. A. (2021). High prevalence and incidence of obsessive-compulsive disorder among women across pregnancy and the postpartum. *The Journal of Clinical Psychiatry, 82*(2), Article 20m13398. https://doi.org/10.4088/JCP.20m13398

Fairbrother, N., Collardeau, F., Woody, S. R., Wolfe, D. A., & Fawcett, J. M. (2022). Postpartum thoughts of infant-related harm and obsessive-compulsive disorder: Relation to maternal physical aggression toward the infant. *The Journal of Clinical Psychiatry, 83*(2), Article 21m14006. https://doi.org/10.4088/JCP.21m14006

Fawcett, E. J., Fairbrother, N., Cox, M. L., White, I. R., & Fawcett, J. M. (2019). The prevalence of anxiety disorders during pregnancy and the postpartum period: A multivariate Bayesian meta-analysis. *The Journal of Clinical Psychiatry, 80*(4), Article 18r12527. https://doi.org/10.4088/JCP.18r12527

Ferlin, A., Calogero, A. E., Krausz, C., Lombardo, F., Paoli, D., Rago, R., Scarica, C., Simoni, M., Foresta, C., Rochira, V., Sbardella, E., Francavilla, S., & Corona, G. (2022). Management of male factor infertility: Position statement from the Italian Society of Andrology and Sexual Medicine (SIAMS). *Journal of Endocrinological Investigation, 45*, 1085–1113. https://doi.org/10.1007/s40618-022-01741-6

Freeman, M. P., & Goldberg, J. F. (2022). The pursuit to recognize bipolar disorder in pregnant and postpartum women. *The Journal of Clinical Psychiatry, 83*(5), Article 22ed14399. https://doi.org/10.4088/JCP.22ed14399

Foli, K., South, S., Lim, E., & Jarnecke, A. (2016). Post-adoption depression: Parental classes of depressive symptoms across time. *Journal of Affective Disorders, 200*, 293–302. https://doi.org/10.1016/j.jad.2016.01.049

Gilden, J., Poels, E. M. P., Lambrichts, S., Vreeker, A., Boks, M. P. M., Roel, A. O., Kahn, R. S., Kamperman, A. M., & Bergnik, V. (2021). Bipolar episodes after reproductive events in women with bipolar I disorder, A study of 919 pregnancies. *Journal of Affective Disorders, 295*, 72–79. https://doi.org/10.1016/j.jad.2021.08.006

Glick, L. (2005). *Marked in your flesh: Circumcision from Ancient Judea to Modern America*. Oxford University Press.

Gorrell, C. (2021, May 19). *We need to talk about postpartum bipolar disorder*. PsyCom. https://www.psycom.net/postpartum-bipolar-disorder

Greenwood, B. N., Hardeman, R. R., Huang, L., & Sojourner, A. (2020). Physician-patient racial concordance and disparities in birthing mortality for newborns. *Proceedings of the National Academy of Sciences, 117*(35), 21194–21200. https://doi.org/10.1073/pnas.1913405117

Grunberg, V. A., Geller, P. A., Bonacquisti, A., & Patterson, C. A. (2019). NICU infant health severity and family outcomes: A systematic review of assessments and findings in psychosocial research. *Journal of Perinatology, 39*, 156–172. https://doi.org/10.1038/s41372-018-0282-9

Grunberg, V. A., Geller, P. A., Hoffman, C., Njoroge, W., Ahmed, A., & Patterson, C. A. (2022). Parental mental health screening in the NICU: A psychosocial team initiative. *Journal of Perinatology, 42*, 401–409. https://doi.org/10.1038/s41372-021-01217-0

Hameed, S., Naser, I., Al Ghussein, M., & Ellulu, M. (2021). Is iron deficiency a risk factor for postpartum depression? A case-control study in the Gaza Strip, Palestine. *Public Health Nutrition, 25*(6), 1631-1638. https://doi.org/10.1017/S1368980021003761

Hatters Friedman, S., Resnick, P. J., & Rosenthal, M. B. (2009). *Postpartum psychosis: Strategies to protect infant and mother from harm*. Current Psychiatry. https://cdn.mdedge.com/files/s3fs-public/Document/September-2017/0802CP_Article2.pdf

Hirschfeld, R. M., Williams, J. B., Spitzer, R. L., Calabrese, J. R., Flynn, L., Keck Jr, P. E., Lewis, L., McElroy, S. L., Post, R. M., Rapport, D. J., Russell, J. M., Sachs, G. S., & Zajecka, J. (2000). Development and validation of a screening instrument for bipolar spectrum disorder: The Mood Disorder Questionnaire. *American Journal of Psychiatry, 157*(11), 1873–1875. https://doi.org/10.1176/appi.ajp.157.11.1873

Honikman, J. I., & Singley, D. B. (2020). *Parental mental health: Factoring in fathers*. Independently published.

Hoyert, D. L. (2022). *Maternal mortality rates in the United States, 2020*. National Center for Health Statistics. https://dx.doi.org/10.15620/cdc:113967

Kabir, K., Sheeder, J., & Kelly, L. S. (2008). Identifying postpartum depression: Are 3 questions as good as 10? *Pediatrics, 122*(3), e696–e702. https://doi.org/10.1542/peds.2007-1759

Kennedy, E., & Munyan, K. (2021). Sensitivity and reliability of screening measures for paternal postpartum depression: An integrative review. *Journal of Perinatology, 41*, 2713–2721. https://doi.org/10.1038/s41372-021-01265-6

Kimura, L. F., Novaes, L. S., Picolo, G., Munhoz, C. D., Cheung, C. W., & Camarini, R. (2021). How environmental enrichment balances out neuroinflammation in chronic pain and comorbid depression and anxiety disorders. *British Journal of Pharmacology, 179*(8), 1640–1660. https://doi.org/10.1111/bph.15584

Kleiman, K. R. (2017). *The art of holding in therapy: An essential intervention for postpartum depression and anxiety*. Routledge.

Kleiman, K. R. (2019). *Good moms have scary thoughts: A healing guide to the secret fears of new mothers*. Familius LLC.

Kleiman, K. R., & Raskin, V. D. (1994). *This isn't what I expected: Overcoming postpartum depression*. Bantam.

Kleiman, K. R., & Wenzel, A. (2010). *Dropping the baby and other scary thoughts: Breaking the cycle of unwanted thoughts in motherhood*. Routledge.

Kozhimannil, K. B., Trinacty, C. M., Busch, A. B., Huskamp, H. A., & Adams, A. S. (2011). Racial and ethnic disparities in postpartum depression care among low-income women. *Psychiatric Services, 62*(6), 619–625. https://doi.org/10.1176/ps.62.6.pss6206_0619

Lara-Cinisomo, S., Clark, C. T., & Wood, J. (2018). Increasing diagnosis and treatment of perinatal depression in Latinas and African American Women: Addressing stigma is not enough. *Women's Health Issues, 28*(3), 201–204. https://doi.org/10.1016/j.whi.2018.01.003

Leahy-Warren, P., Newham, J., & Alderdice, F. (2018). Perinatal social support: Panacea or a pitfall. *Journal of Reproductive and Infant Psychology, 36*(3), 219–221. https://doi.org/10.1080/02646838.2018.1477242

Lee, A. T., & Haskins, N. H. (2020). Toward a culturally humble practice: Critical consciousness as an antecedent. *Journal of Counseling and Development, 100*, 104–112. https://onlinelibrary.wiley.com/doi/epdf/10.1002/jcad.12403

Lei, H., Wang, Z., Peng, Z., Yuan, Y., & Li, Z. (2019). Hope across socioeconomic status: Examining measurement invariance of the Children's Hope Scale across socioeconomic status groups. *Frontiers in Psychology, 10*, Article 2593. https://doi.org/10.3389/fpsyg.2019.02593

Lepkowski, J. M., Mosher, W. D., Davis, K. E., Groves, R. M., & Van Hoewyk, J. (2010). *The 2006–2010 National Survey of Family Growth: Sample design and analysis of a continuous survey.* Centers for Disease Control and Prevention. https://stacks.cdc.gov/view/cdc/5673

Levinson, M., Parvez, B., Aboudi, D., & Shah, S. (2022). Impact of maternal stressors and neonatal clinical factors on post-partum depression screening scores. *The Journal of Maternal-Fetal & Neonatal Medicine, 35*(7), 1328–1136. https://doi.org/10.1080/14767058.2020.1754394

Lindh Jorgensen, M., Prinds, C., Mork, S., & Hvidtjorn, D. (2021). Stillbirth—transitions and rituals when birth brings death: Data from a Danish national cohort seen through an anthropological lens. *Scandinavian Journal of Caring Sciences, 36*, 100–108. https://doi.org/10.1111/scs.12967

Loudon, I. (1992). The transformation of maternal mortality. *British Medical Journal, 305*, 1557–1560. https://doi.org/10.1136/bmj.305.6868.1557

Marcin, J., Shaikh, U., & Steinhorn, R. (2016). Addressing health disparities in rural communities using telehealth. *Pediatric Research, 79*, 169–176. https://doi.org/10.1038/pr.2015.192

Marshall, A. (2013, March 11). *Using the EPDS to screen for anxiety disorders: Conceptual and methodological considerations.* MGH Center for Women's Mental Health. https://womensmentalhealth.org/posts/using-the-epds-to-screen-for-anxiety-disorders-conceptual-and-methodological-considerations/

Masters, G. A., Brenckle, L., Sankaran, P., Person, S. D., Allison, J., Moore Simas, T. A., Ko, J. Y., Robbins, C. L., Marsh, W., & Byatt, N. (2019). Positive screening rates for bipolar disorder in pregnant and postpartum women and associated risk factors. *General Hospital Psychiatry, 61*, 53–59. https://doi.org/10.1016/j.genhosppsych.2019.09.002

McCabe-Beane, J.E., Segre, L.S., Perkhounkova, Y., Stuart, S., & O'Hara, M.W. (2016). The identification of severity ranges for the Edinburgh Postnatal Depression Scale. *Journal of Reproductive and Infant Psychology, 34*(3), 293–303. https://doi.org/10.1080/02646838.2016.1141346

McDonald, K. (2018). Social support and mental health in LGBTQ adolescents: A review of the literature. *Issues in Mental Health Nursing, 39*(1), 16–29. https://doi.org/10.1080/01612840.2017.1398283

Meinhofer, A., Witman, A., Maclean, J. C., & Bao, Y. (2022). Prenatal substance use policies and newborn health. *Health Economics, 31*(7), 1452–1467. https://doi.org/10.1002/hec.4518

Miranda, L., Dixon, V., & Reyes, C. (2015, September 30). *How states handle drug use during pregnancy.* ProPublica. https://projects.propublica.org/graphics/maternity-drug-policies-by-state

Misri, S., Abizadeh, J., Sanders, S., & Swift, E. (2015). Perinatal generalized anxiety disorder: Assessment and treatment. *Journal of Women's Health, 24*(9), 762–770. https://doi.org/10.1089/jwh.2014.5150

Moyo, G. P. K., & Djoda, N. (2020). Relationship between the baby blues and postpartum depression: A study among Cameroonian women. *American Journal of Psychiatry and Neuroscience, 8*(1), 22–25. https://doi.org/10.11648/j.ajpn.20200801.16

Mule, V., Reilly, N. M., Schmied, V., Kingston, D., & Austin, M. V. (2022). Why do some pregnant women not fully disclose at comprehensive psychosocial assessment with their midwife? *Women and Birth, 35*(1), 80–86. https://doi.org/10.1016/j.wombi.2021.03.001

Muzik, M., McGinnis, E. W., Bocknek, E., Morelen, D., Rosenblum, K. L., Liberzon, I., Seng, J., & Abelson, J. L. (2016). PTSD symptoms across pregnant and early postpartum among women with lifetime PTSD diagnosis. *Depression and Anxiety, 33*(7), 584–591. https://doi.org/10.1002/da.22465

Nagoski, E., & Nagoski, A. (2019). *Burnout: The secret to unlocking the stress cycle.* Ballantine Books.

Neff, K. (2015). *Self-compassion: The proven power of being kind to yourself.* William Morrow Paperbacks.

Neff, K. (2022). *Exercise 2: Self-compassion break.* Self-Compassion. https://self-compassion.org/exercise-2-self-compassion-break/

Nidey, N., Tabb, K. M., Carter, K. D., Bao, W., Strathearn, L., Rohlman, D. S., Wehby, G., & Ryckman, K. (2020). Rurality and risk of perinatal depression among women in the United States. *The Journal of Rural Health, 36*(1), 9–16. https://doi.org/10.1111/jrh.12401

Niehues, L. J., & Klovenski, V. (2021). Vagal maneuver. In *StatPearls*. StatPearls Publishing. https://www.ncbi.nlm.nih.gov/books/NBK551575/

Nynas, J., Narang, P., Kolikonda, M. K., & Lippmann, S. (2015). Depression and anxiety following early pregnancy loss: Recommendations for primary care providers. *The Primary Care Companion for CNS Disorders, 17*(1). https://doi.org/10.4088/PCC.14r01721

O'Brien, A. P., McNeil, K. A., Fletcher, R., Conrad, A., Wilson, A. J., Jones, D., & Chan, S. W. (2017). New fathers' perinatal depression and anxiety—treatment options: An integrative review. *American Journal of Men's Health, 11*(4), 863–876. https://doi.org/10.1177/1557988316669047

O'Hara, M. W., & Wisner, K. L. (2014). Perinatal mental illness: Definition, description and aetiology. *Best Practice & Research Clinical Obstetrics & Gynaecology, 28*(1), 3–12. https://doi.org/10.1016/j.bpobgyn.2013.09.002

Odendaal, H., Wright, C., Brink, L., Schubert, P., Geldenhuys, E., & Groenewald, C. (2019). Association of late second trimester miscarriages with placental histology and autopsy findings. *European Journal of Obstetrics, Gynecology, and Reproductive Biology, 243,* 32–35. https://doi.org/10.1016/j.ejogrb.2019.10.024

Oliver, E. A., Rood, K. M., Ma'ayeh, M., Berghella, V., & Silver, R. R. (2020). Stillbirth and fetal autopsy rates in the United States: Analysis of fetal death certificates. *Obstetrics & Gynecology, 135,* 1665. https://doi.org/10.1097/01.AOG.0000664004.95365.1c

Patterson, E. J., Becker, A., & Baluran, D. A. (2022). Gendered racism on the body: An intersectional approach to maternal mortality in the United States. *Population Research and Policy Review, 41,* 1261–1294. https://doi.org/10.1007/s11113-021-09691-2

Phipps, M. G., Son, S., Zahn, C., O'Reilly, N., Cantor, A., Frost, J., Gregory, K. D., Jones, M., Kendig, S. M., Nelson, H. D., Pappas, M., Qaseem, A., Ramos, D., Salganicoff, A., Taylor, G., & Conry, J., for the Women's Preventive Services Initiative. (2019). Women's preventive services initiative's well-woman chart: A summary of preventive health recommendations for women. *Obstetrics & Gynecology, 134*(3), 465–469. https://doi.org/10.1097/AOG.0000000000003368

Pluym, I. D., Tandel, M., Kwan, L., Mok, T., Holliman, K., Afshar, Y., & Rao, R. (2021). 57 randomized control trial of postpartum visits at 2 and 6 weeks. *American Journal of Obstetrics and Gynecology, 3*(4), 100363. https://doi.org/10.1016/j.ajogmf.2021.100363

Polk, S., Edwardson, J., Lawson, S., Valenzuela, E., Hobbins, E., Prichett, L., & Bennett, W. L. (2021). Bridging the postpartum gap: A randomized controlled trial to improved postpartum visit attendance among low-income women with limited English proficiency. *Women's Health Reports, 2*(1), 381–388. https://doi.org/10.1089/whr.2020.0123

Posmontier, B., & Horowitz, J. A. (2004). Postpartum practices and depression prevalences: Technocentric and ethnokinship cultural perspectives. *Journal of Transcultural Nursing, 15*(1), 34–43. https://doi.org/10.1177/1043659603260032

Postpartum Support Virginia. (2023). *About depression.* https://postpartumva.org/depression/

Raguz, N., McDonald, S. W., Metcalfe, A., O'Quinn, C., & Tough, S. C. (2014). Mental health outcomes of mothers who conceived using fertility treatment. *Reproductive health, 11*(1), Article 19. https://doi.org/10.1186/1742-4755-11-19

Rai, S., Pathak, A., & Sharma, I. (2015). Postpartum psychiatric disorders: Early diagnosis and management. *Indian Journal of Psychiatry, 57*(Suppl 2), S216–S221. https://doi.org/10.4103/0019-5545.161481

Ranji, U., Long, M., Salganicoff, A., Silow-Carroll, S., Rosenzweig, C., Rodin, D., & Kellenberg, R. (2019, November 14). *Beyond the numbers: Access to reproductive health care for low-income women in five communities.* Kaiser Family

Foundation. https://www.kff.org/report-section/beyond-the-numbers-access-to-reproductive-health-care-for-low-income-women-in-five-communities-executive-summary/

Rasminsky, A. (2018, July 31). *Your guide to postpartum recovery*. Healthline. https://www.healthline.com/health/postpartum-recovery-timeline

Renbarger, K. M., Place, J. M., & Schreiner, M. (2021). The influence of four constructs of social support on pregnancy experiences in group prenatal care. *Women's Health Report, 2*(1), 154–162. https://doi.org/10.1089/whr.2020.0113

Resolve: The National Infertility Association. (2022). *Insurance coverage by state*. https://resolve.org/learn/financial-resources-for-family-building/insurance-coverage/insurance-coverage-by-state/

Sacks, A., & Birndorf, C. (2019). *What no one tells you: A guide to your emotions from pregnancy to motherhood*. Simon and Schuster.

Schaffir, J. (2014). Biological changes during pregnancy and the postpartum period. In A. Wenzel (Eds.), *The oxford handbook of perinatal psychology* (pp. 26–37). Oxford University Press.

Shaikh, U., & Ahmed, O. (2006). Islam and infant feeding. *Breastfeeding Medicine, 1*(3), 164–167. https://doi.org/10.1089/bfm.2006.1.164

Sharma, V., & Corpse, C. (2011). Is your depressed postpartum patient bipolar? *Current Psychiatry, 10*(6), 81–82.

Sharma, V., Mazmania, D., Palagini, L., & Bramante, A. (2022). Postpartum psychosis: Revisiting the phenomenology, nosology, and treatment. *Journal of Affective Disorders Reports, 10*, 100378. https://doi.org/10.1016/j.jadr.2022.100378

Shuman, C. J., Morgan, M. E., Pareddy, N., Chiangong, J., Veliz, P., Peahl, A., & Dalton, V. (2022). Associations among postpartum posttraumatic stress disorder symptoms and COVID-19 pandemic-related stressors. *Journal of Midwifery & Women's Health, 67*(5), 626–634. https://doi.org/10.1111/jmwh.13399

Sit, D. K., & Wisner, K. L. (2009). The identification of postpartum depression. *Clinical Obstetrics and Gynecology, 52*(3), 456–468. https://doi.org/10.1097/GRF.0b013e3181b5a57c

Spinelli, M. (2021). Postpartum psychosis: A diagnosis for the DSM-V. *Archives of Women's Mental Health, 24*, 817–822. https://doi.org/10.1007/s00737-021-01175-8

Stern, D. N. (1995). *The mother constellation: A unified view of parent-infant psychotherapy*. Basic Book.

Sundaram, S., Harman, J. S., & Cook, R. L. (2014). Maternal morbidities and postpartum depression: An analysis using the 2007 and 2008 pregnancy risk assessment monitoring system. *Women's Health Issues, 24*(4), 381–388. https://doi.org/10.1016/j.whi.2014.05.001

The American College of Obstetricians and Gynecology. (2020, March). *Management of stillbirth*. https://www.acog.org/clinical/clinical-guidance/obstetric-care-consensus/articles/2020/03/management-of-stillbirth

The American College of Obstetricians and Gynecology. (2022, January). *Early pregnancy loss: Frequently asked questions*. https://www.acog.org/womens-health/faqs/early-pregnancy-loss

Thomas, D. (2020, April 10). *As family structures change in the U.S., a growing share of Americans say it makes no difference*. Pew Research Center. https://www.pewresearch.org/fact-tank/2020/04/10/as-family-structures-change-in-u-s-a-growing-share-of-americans-say-it-makes-no-difference/

Torres, F. (2020, October). *What is peripartum depression (formerly postpartum)?* American Psychiatric Association. https://www.psychiatry.org/patients-families/postpartum-depression/what-is-postpartum-depression

Treyvaud, K., Inder, T. E., Lee, K. J., Northam, E. A., Doyle, L. W., & Anderson, P. J. (2012). Can the home environment promote resilience for children born very preterm in the context of social and medical risk? *Journal of Experimental Child Psychology, 112*, 326–37. https://doi.org/10.1016/j.jecp.2012.02.009

Trujillo, J., Vieira, M. C., Lepsch, J., Rebelo, F., Poston, L., Pasupathy, D., & Kac, G. (2018). A systematic review of the associations between maternal nutritional biomarkers and depression and/or anxiety during pregnancy and postpartum. *Journal of Affective Disorders, 232*, 185–203. https://doi.org/10.1016/j.jad.2018.02.004

Tsakiridis, I., Giouleka, S., Mamopoulos, A., Athanasiadis, A. & Dagklis, T. (2022). Investigation and management of stillbirth: A descriptive review of major guidelines. *Journal of Perinatal Medicine, 50*(6), 796–813. https://doi.org/10.1515/jpm-2021-0403

UNICEF. (2023, January). *Neonatal mortality*. https://data.unicef.org/topic/child-survival/neonatal-mortality/

van Daalen, K. R., Kaiser, J., Kebede, S., Kaiser, J., Kebede, S., Cipriano, G., Maimouni, H., Olumese, E., Chui, A., Kuhn, I., & Oliver-Williams, C. (2022). Racial discrimination and adverse pregnancy outcomes: A systematic review and meta-analysis. *BMJ Global Health, 7*(8), Article e009227. https://doi.org/10.1136/bmjgh-2022-009227

Viktorin, A., Meltzer-Brody, S., Kuja-Halkola, R., Sullivan, P. F., Landén, M., Lichtenstein, P., & Magnusson, P. K. (2016). Heritability of perinatal depression and genetic overlap with nonperinatal depression. *American Journal of Psychiatry, 73*(2), 58–65. https://doi.org/10.1176/appi.ajp.2015.15010085

Wadadekar, G. S., Inamdar, D. B., & Nimbargi, V. R. (2021). Assessment of impact of infertility & its treatment on quality of life of infertile couples using Fertility Quality of Life Questionnaire. *Journal of Human Reproductive Sciences, 14*(1), 3–10. https://doi.org/10.4103/jhrs.jhrs_163_20

Waugh, L. J. (2011). Beliefs associated with Mexican immigrant families' practice of La Cuarentena during postpartum recovery. *Journal of Obstetric, Gynecologic, & Neonatal Nursing, 40*(6), 732–741. https://doi.org/10.1111/j.1552-6909.2011.01298.x

Weber, A., Harrison, T. M., Steward, D., & Ludington-Hoe, S. (2018). Paid family leave to enhance the health outcomes of preterm infants. *Policy, Politics & Nursing Practice, 19*(1-2), 11–28. https://doi.org/10.1177/1527154418791821

Winnicott, D. W. (1953). Transitional objects and transitional phenomena. *International Journal of Psychoanalysis, 34*(2), 89–97.

Winnicott, D. W. (1960). The theory of the parent-child relationship. *International Journal of Psychoanalysis, 41*, 585–595.

Winnicott, D. W. (1965). *The maturational processes and the facilitating environment: Studies in the theory of emotional development.* Hogarth Press and the Institute of Psychoanalysis.

Winnicott, D. W. (2002). *Winnicott on the child.* Perseus Books Group.

Woods-Giscombé, C. L. (2010). Superwoman schema: African American women's views on stress, strength, and health. *Qualitative Health Research, 20*(5), 668–683. https://doi.org/10.1177/1049732310361892

Yale Medicine. (2023). *Recurrent pregnancy loss.* https://www.yalemedicine.org/conditions/recurrent-pregnancy-loss

Yang, R., Vigod, S. N., & Hensel, J.M. (2019). Optional web-based videoconferencing added to office-based care for women receiving psychotherapy during the postpartum period: Pilot randomized controlled trial. *Journal of Medical Internet Research, 21*(6), Article e13172. https://doi.org/10.2196/13172

Yildiz, P. D., Ayers, S., & Phillips, L. (2017). The prevalence of posttraumatic stress disorder in pregnancy and after birth: A systematic review and meta-analysis. *Journal of Affective Disorders, 208*, 634–645. https://doi.org/10.1016/j.jad.2016.10.009

Zarzycka, B., Jankowski, T., & Krasiczynska, B. (2021). Therapeutic relationship and professional burnout in psychotherapists: A structural equation model approach. *Clinical Psychology and Psychotherapy, 29*(1), 250–259. https://doi.org/10.1002/cpp.2629

Zhang, H., Watkins, C. E., Hook, J. N., Hodge, A. S., Davis, C. W., Norton, J., Wilcox, M. M., Davis, D. E., DeBlaere, C., & Owen, J. (2021). Cultural humility in psychotherapy and clinical supervision: A research review. *Counseling and Psychotherapy Research, 22*(3), 548–557. https://doi.org/10.1002/capr.12481

About the Authors

Hilary Waller, LPC, is the Director of Education and Programming and a psychotherapist at The Postpartum Stress Center. After earning dual bachelor's degrees at Columbia University and The Jewish Theological Seminary, Hilary worked with adolescents in both formal and informal educational settings. This experience piqued her interest in parent-child relationships and led her to pursue a master's degree in counseling psychology with a specialty in marriage and family therapy. Hilary currently provides individual and group therapy services at The Postpartum Stress Center, as well as specialized trainings for both mental health care providers and non-mental health care providers seeking expertise in the treatment of perinatal mood and anxiety disorders.

Karen Kleiman, MSW, LCSW, is a well-known international maternal mental-health expert with over thirty-five years of experience. As an advocate and author of several groundbreaking books on postpartum depression and anxiety, her work has been featured worldwide within the mental health community and beyond for decades. In 1988, Karen founded The Postpartum Stress Center, the premier treatment and training facility for prenatal and postpartum depression and anxiety. In 2022, she founded The Karen Kleiman Training Center, LLC, dedicated to the advancement of clinical expertise and therapeutic strategies for the treatment of perinatal mood and anxiety disorders. All advanced trainings are heavily influenced by The Art of Holding Perinatal Women in Distress™ model of intervention she developed in 2017.

Parents can find support from The Postpartum Stress Center on Facebook (/postpartumstresscenter2), Twitter (@ppstresscenter), and Instagram (@postpartumstress), which includes their #speakthesecret campaign to bust the stigma of perinatal intrusive thoughts.